MANGILALUK

A graphic memoir about friendship, perseverance, and resiliency

WRITTEN BY
Bernard Andreason

ILLUSTRATED BY
Alan Gallo

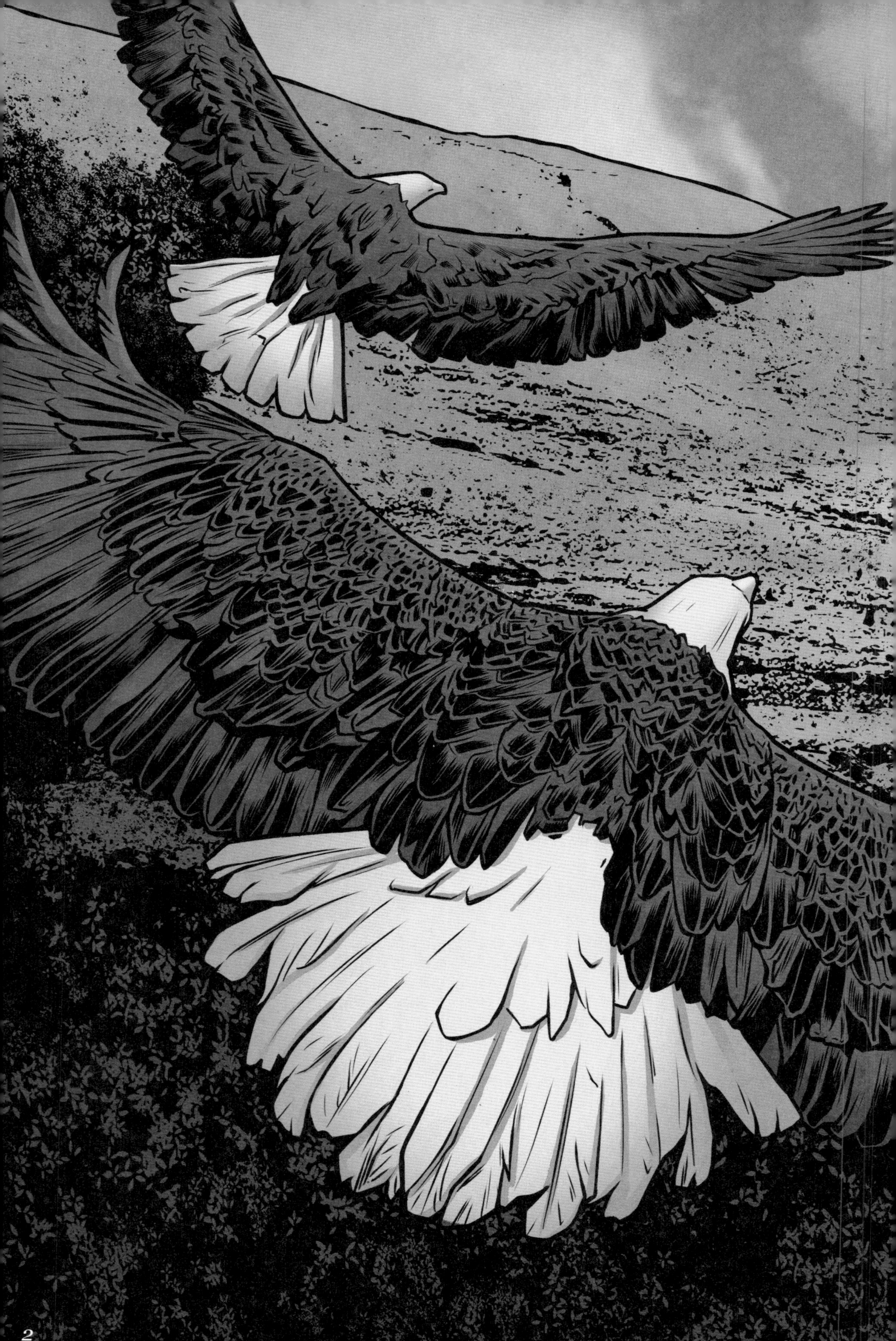

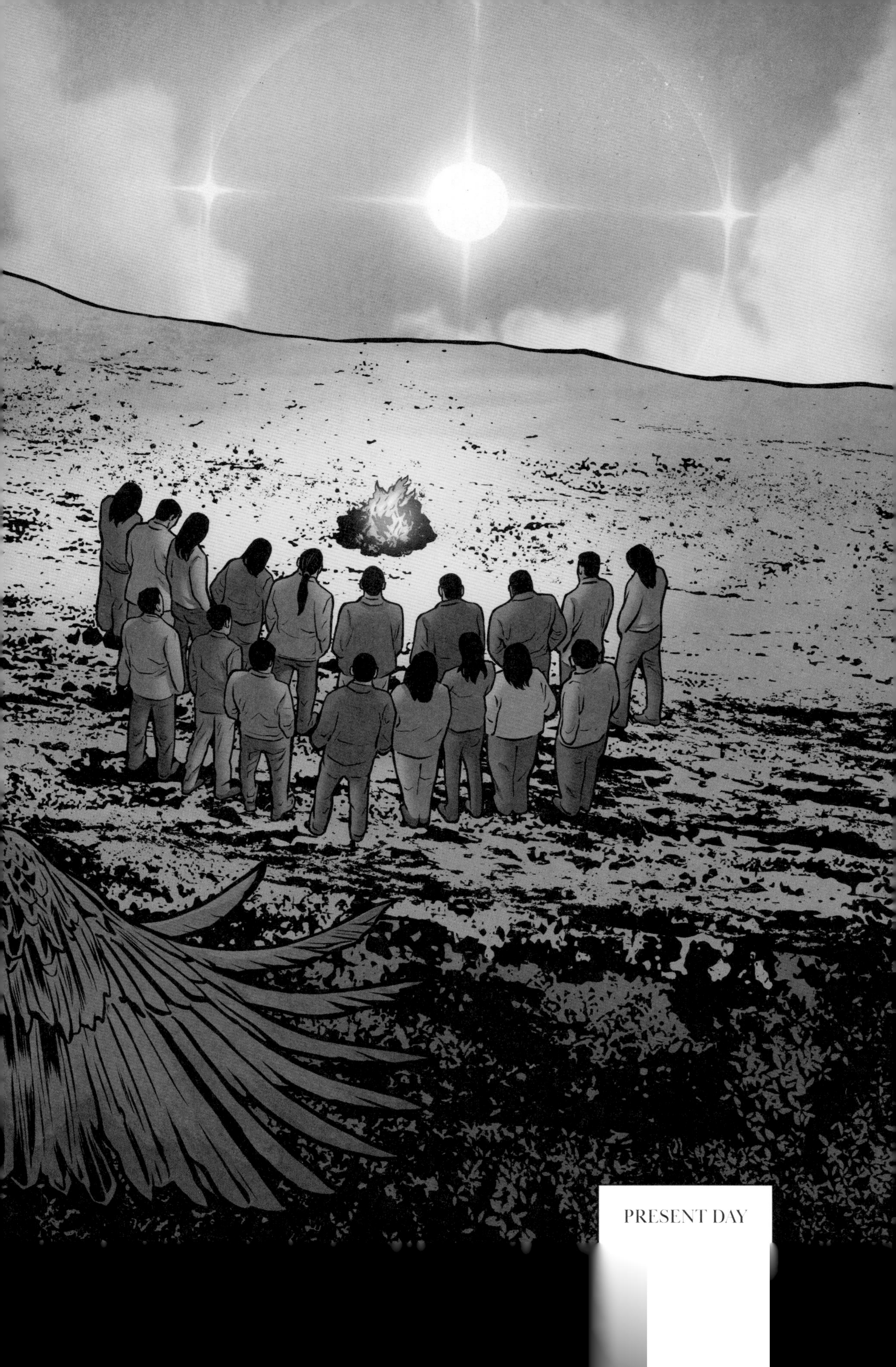
PRESENT DAY

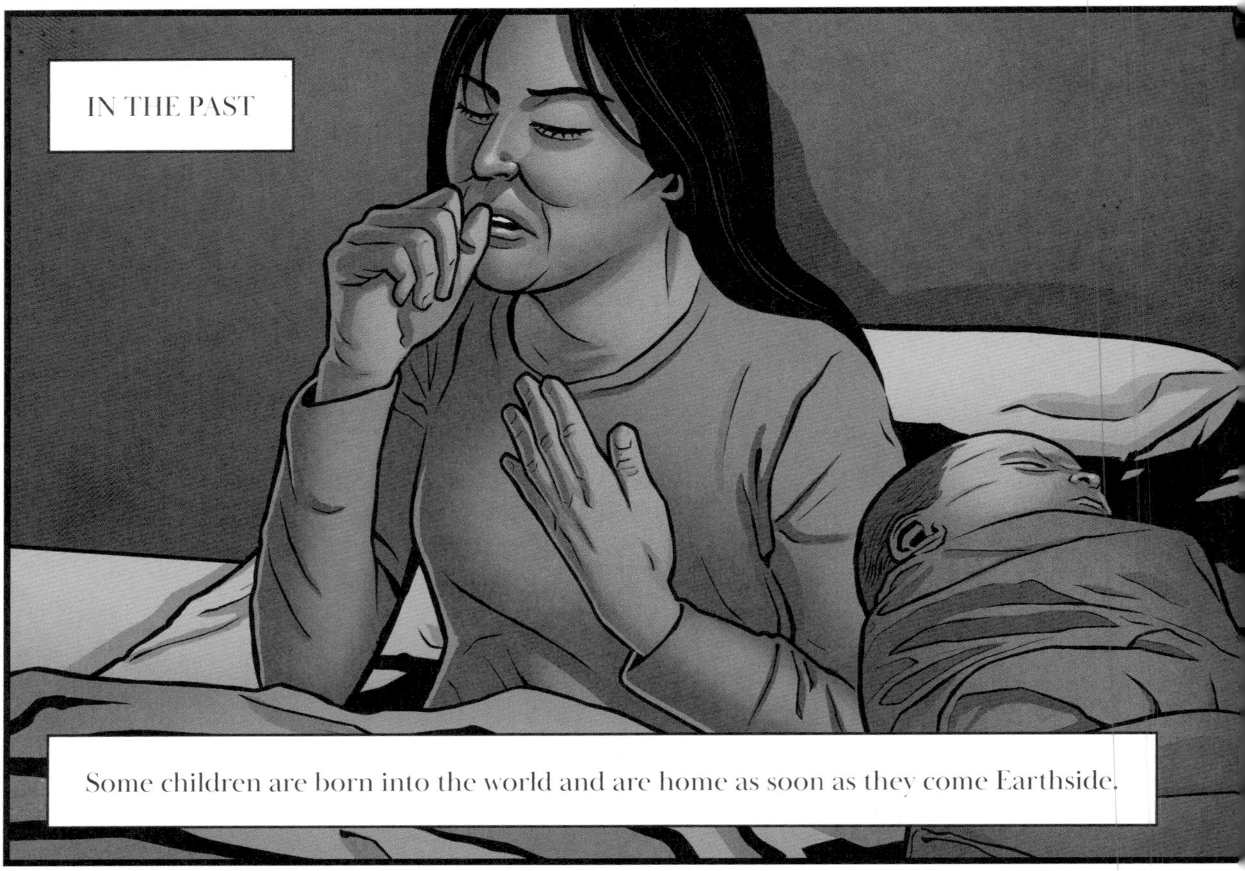
IN THE PAST
Some children are born into the world and are home as soon as they come Earthside.

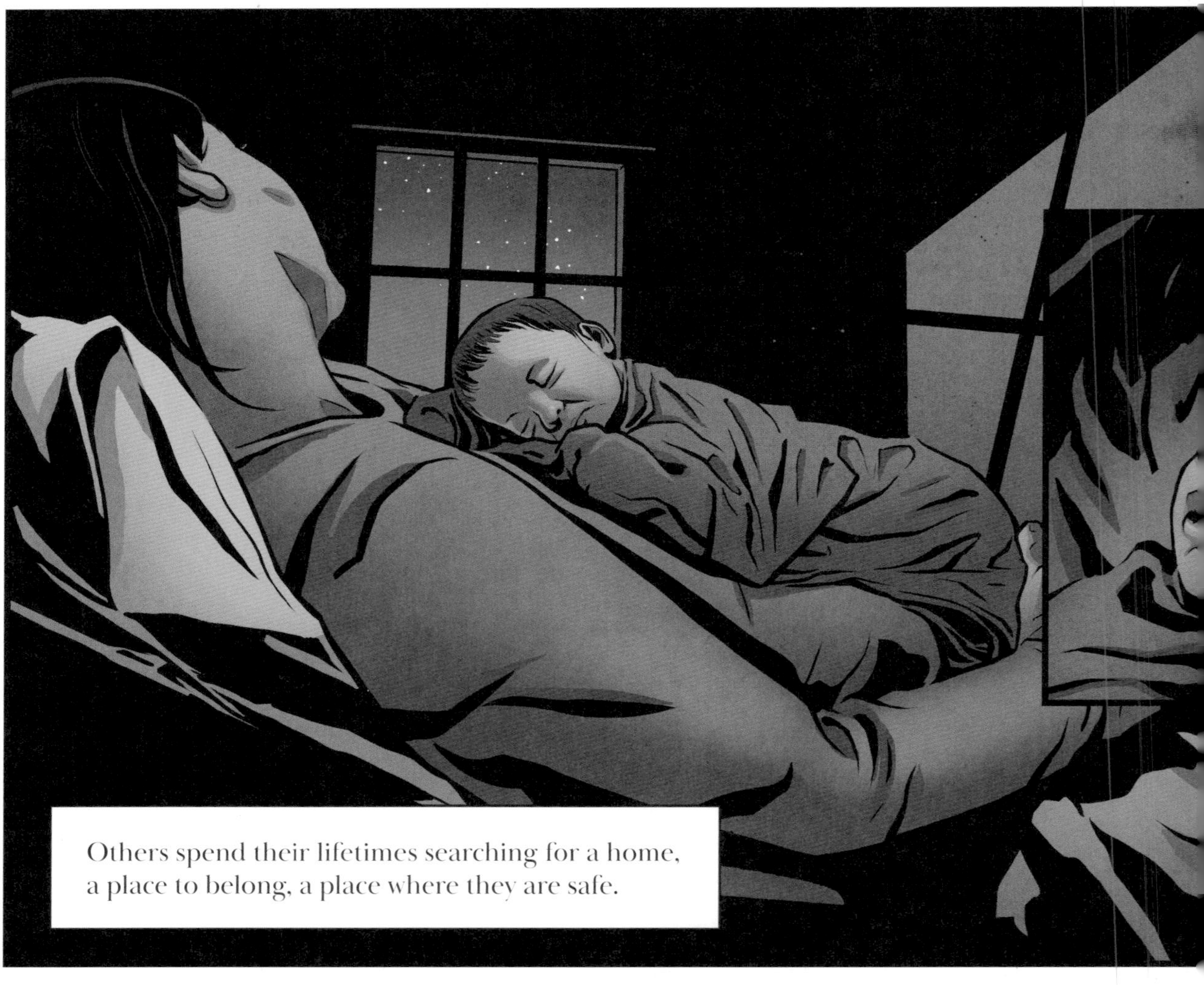
Others spend their lifetimes searching for a home, a place to belong, a place where they are safe.

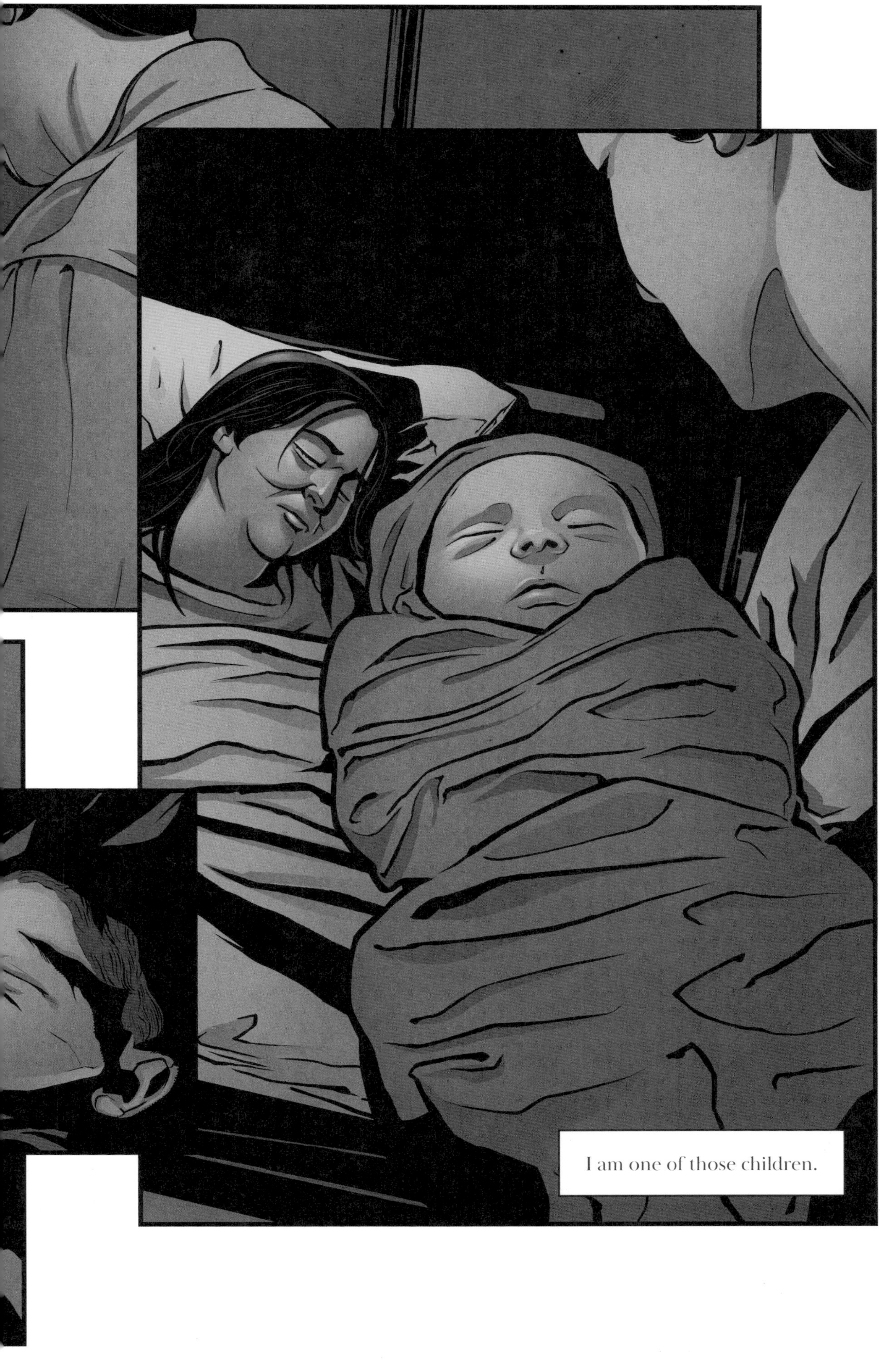
I am one of those children.

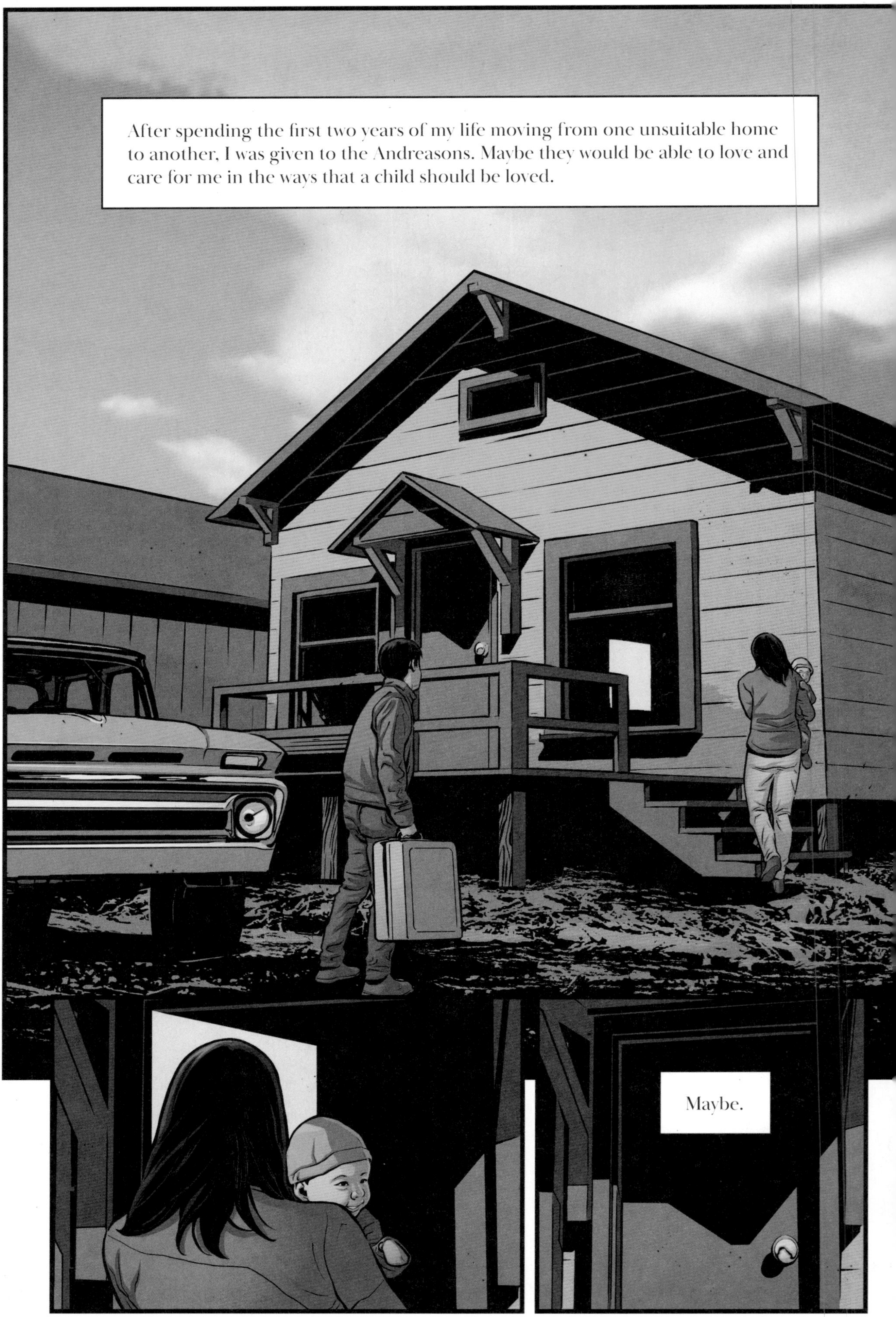
After spending the first two years of my life moving from one unsuitable home to another, I was given to the Andreasons. Maybe they would be able to love and care for me in the ways that a child should be loved.
Maybe.

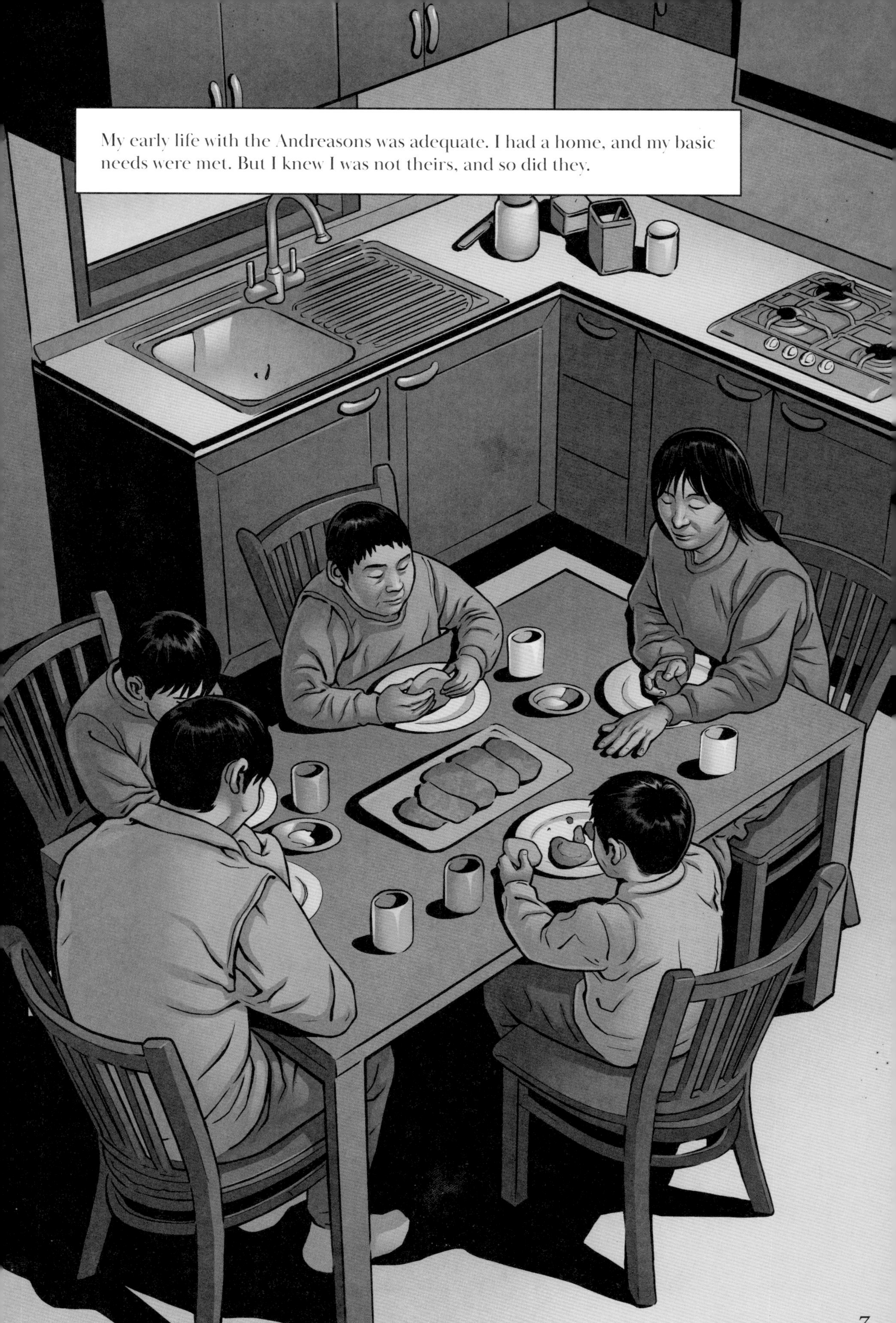
My early life with the Andreasons was adequate. I had a home, and my basic needs were met. But I knew I was not theirs, and so did they.

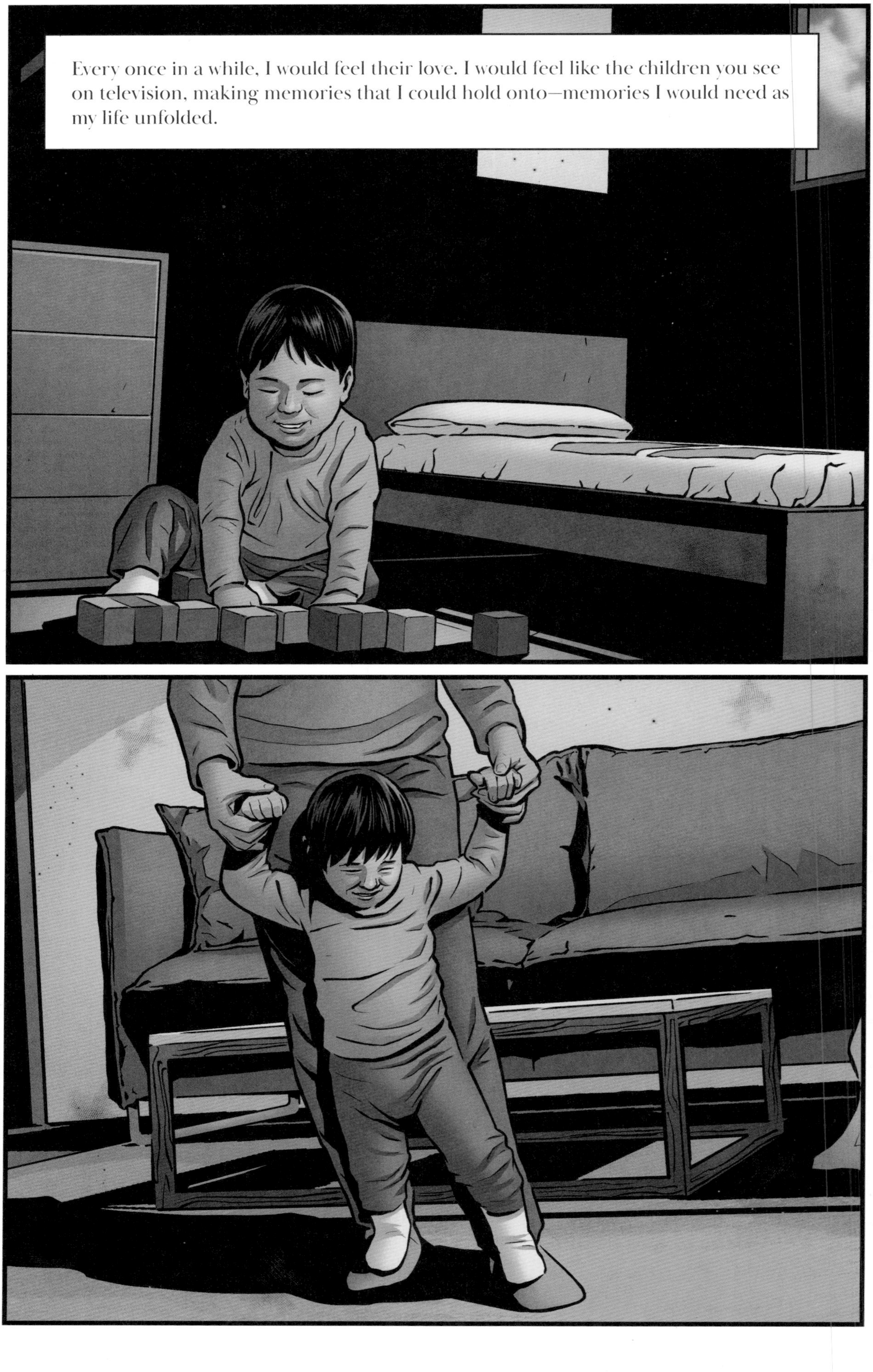
Every once in a while, I would feel their love. I would feel like the children you see on television, making memories that I could hold onto—memories I would need as my life unfolded.

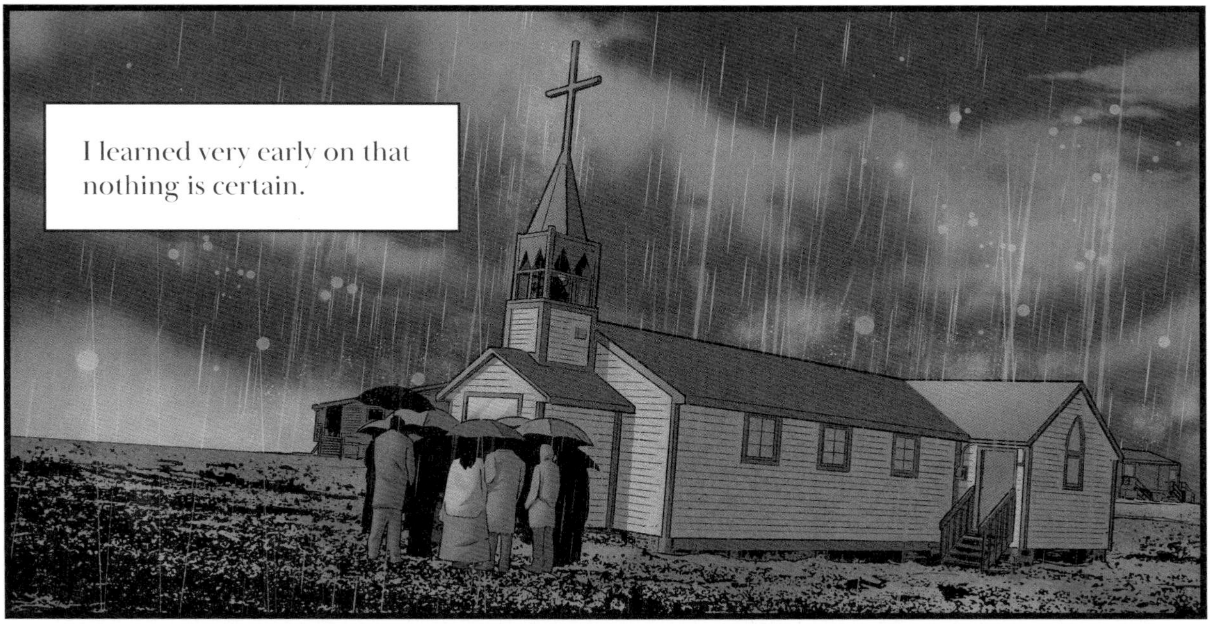
I learned very early on that nothing is certain.

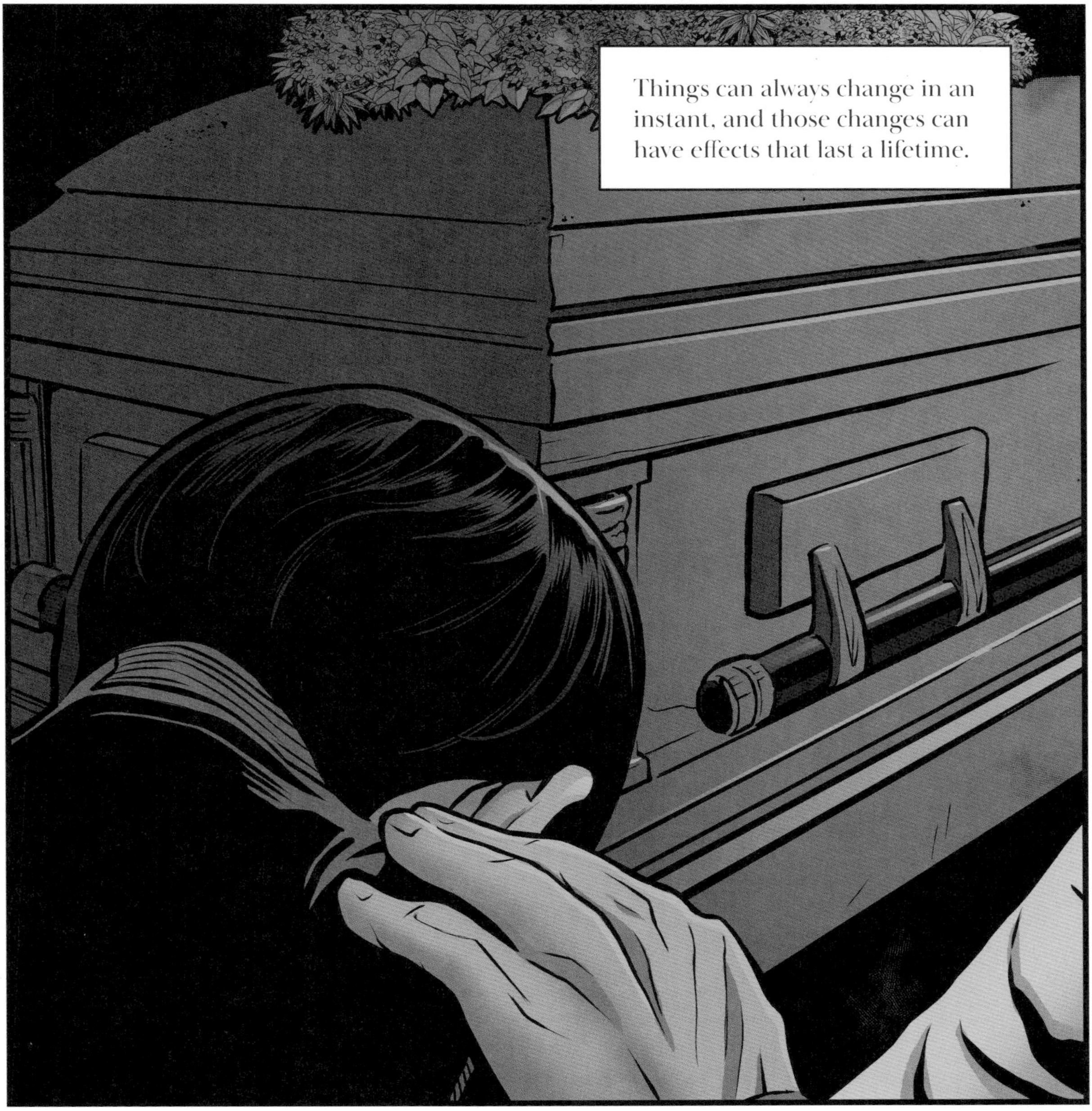
Things can always change in an instant, and those changes can have effects that last a lifetime.

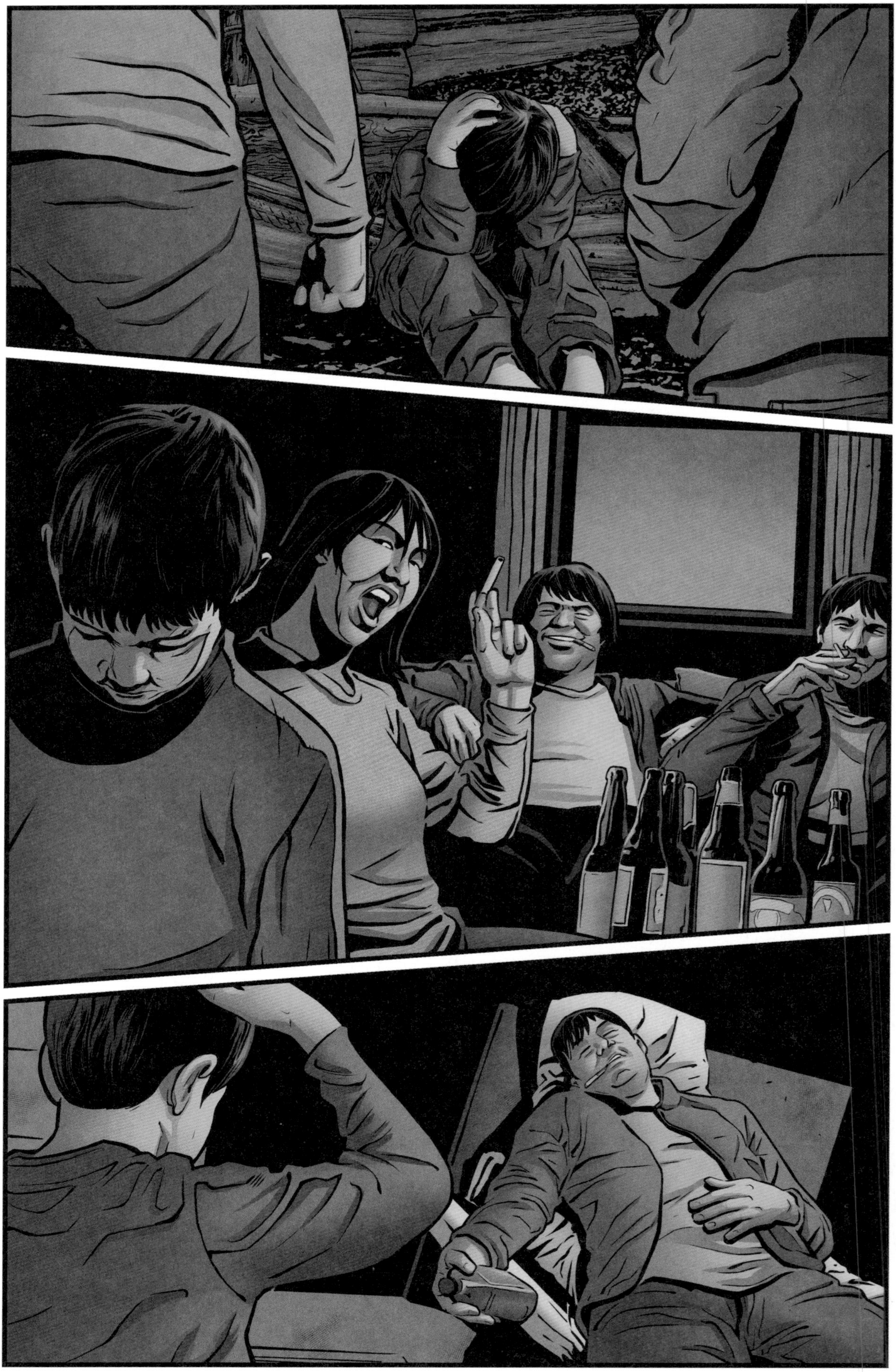

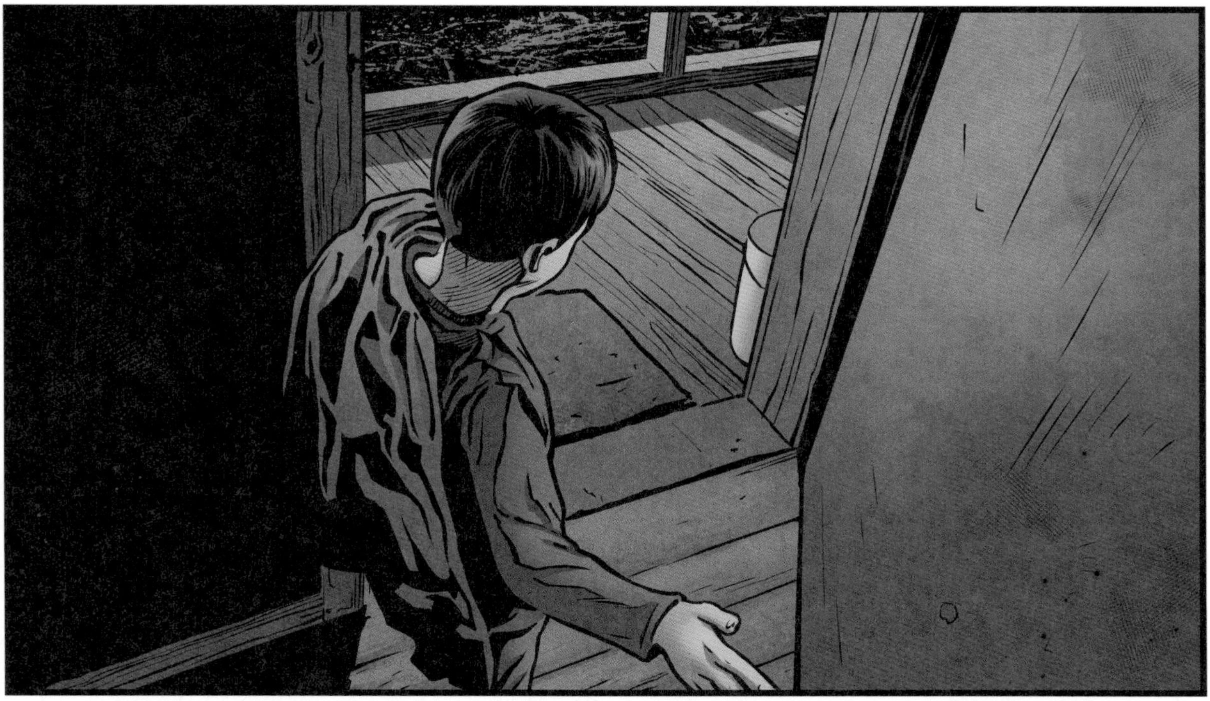

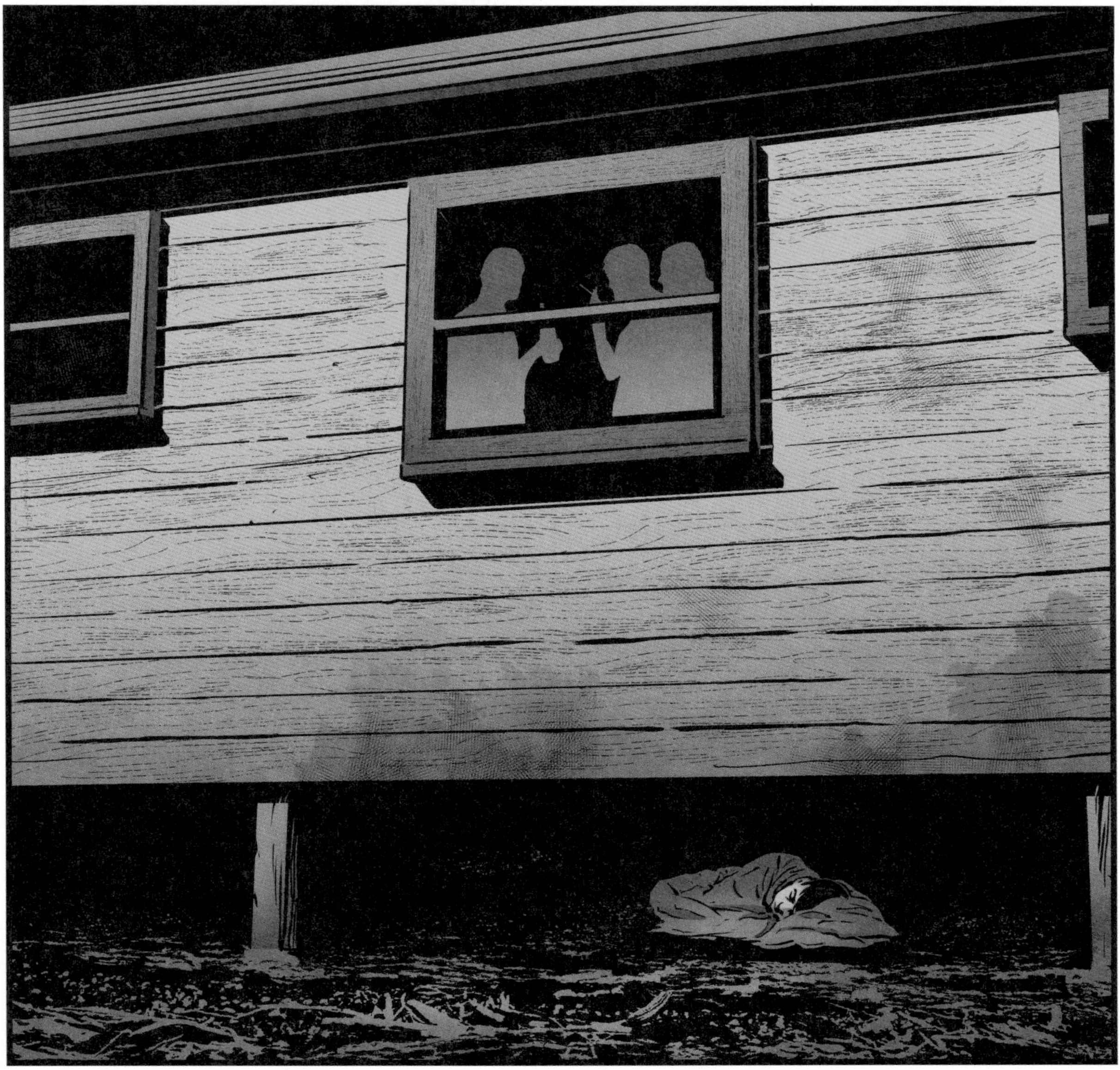

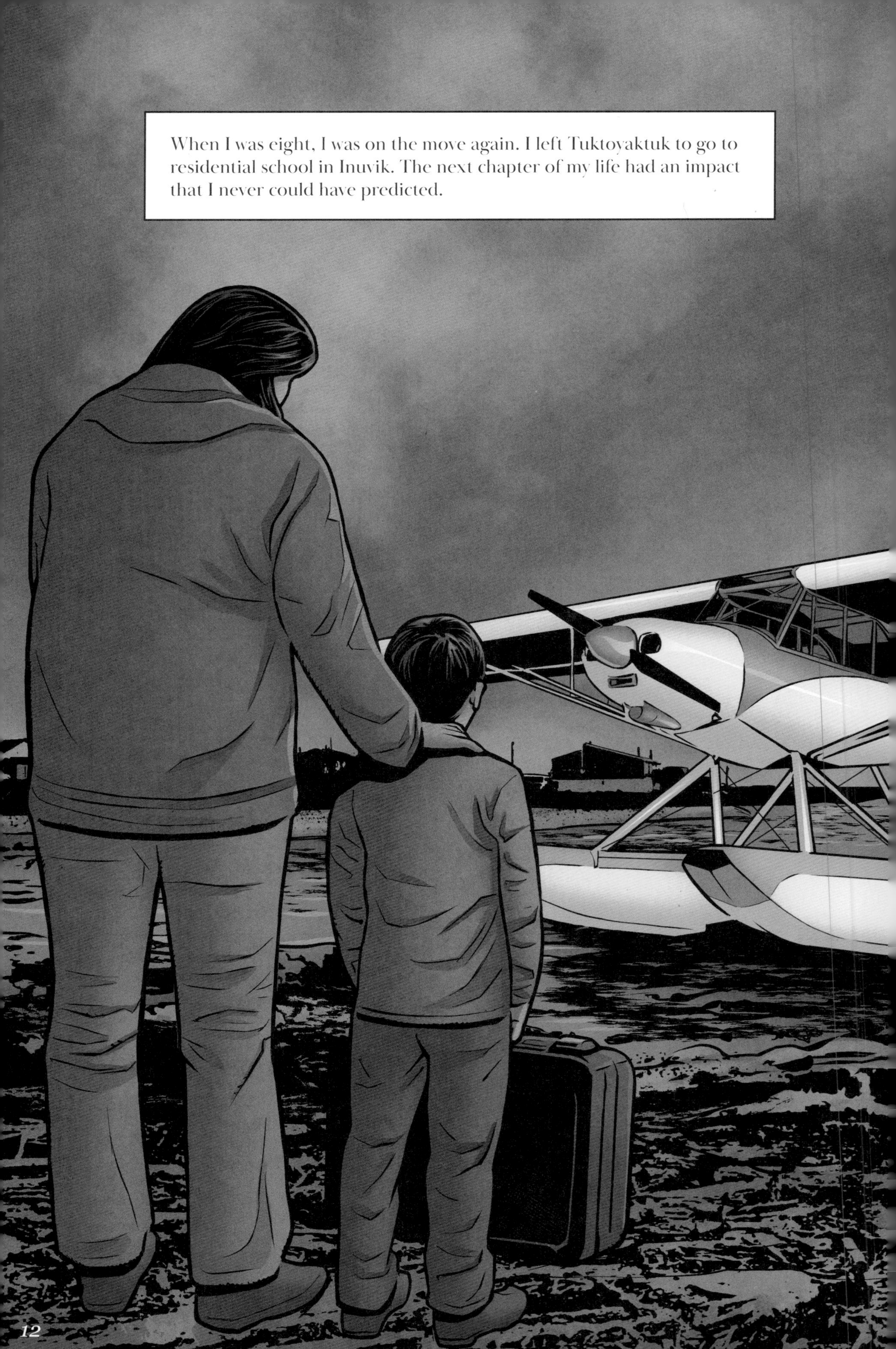
When I was eight, I was on the move again. I left Tuktoyaktuk to go to residential school in Inuvik. The next chapter of my life had an impact that I never could have predicted.

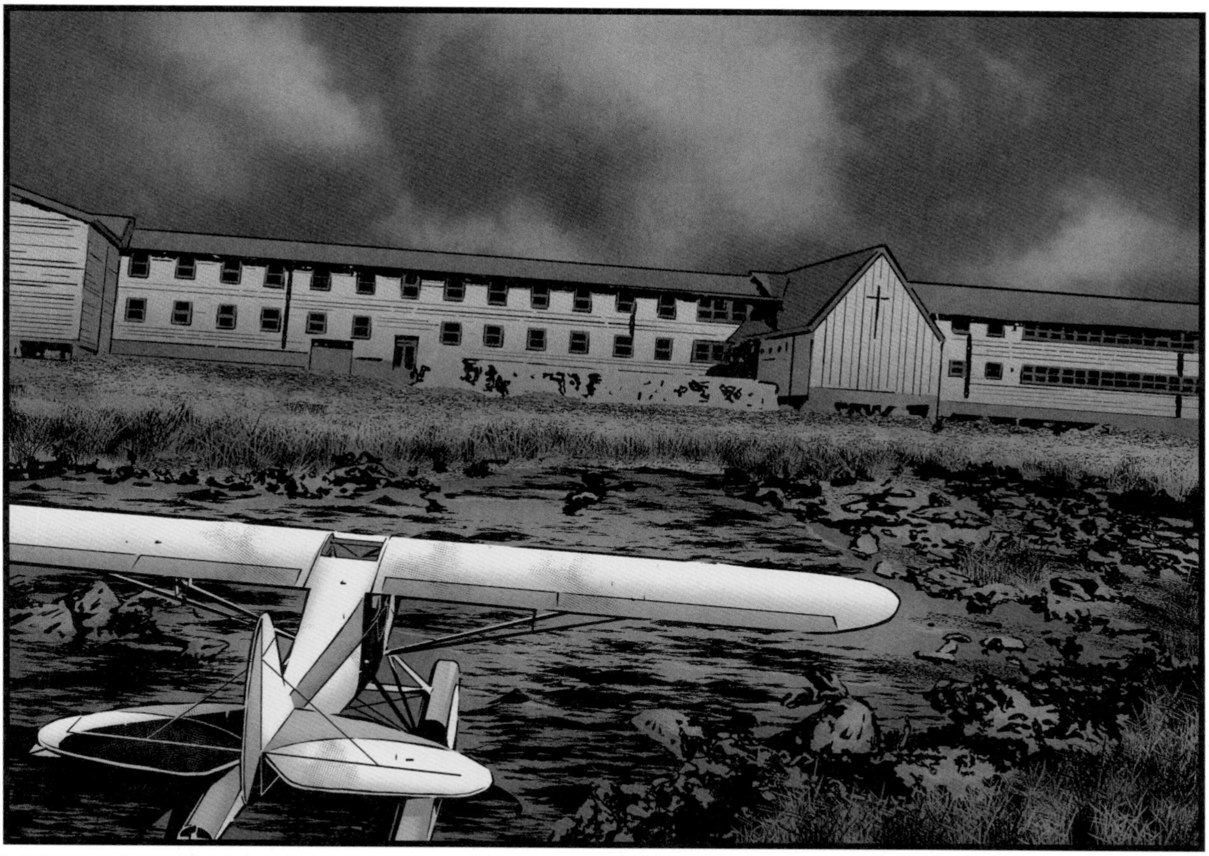

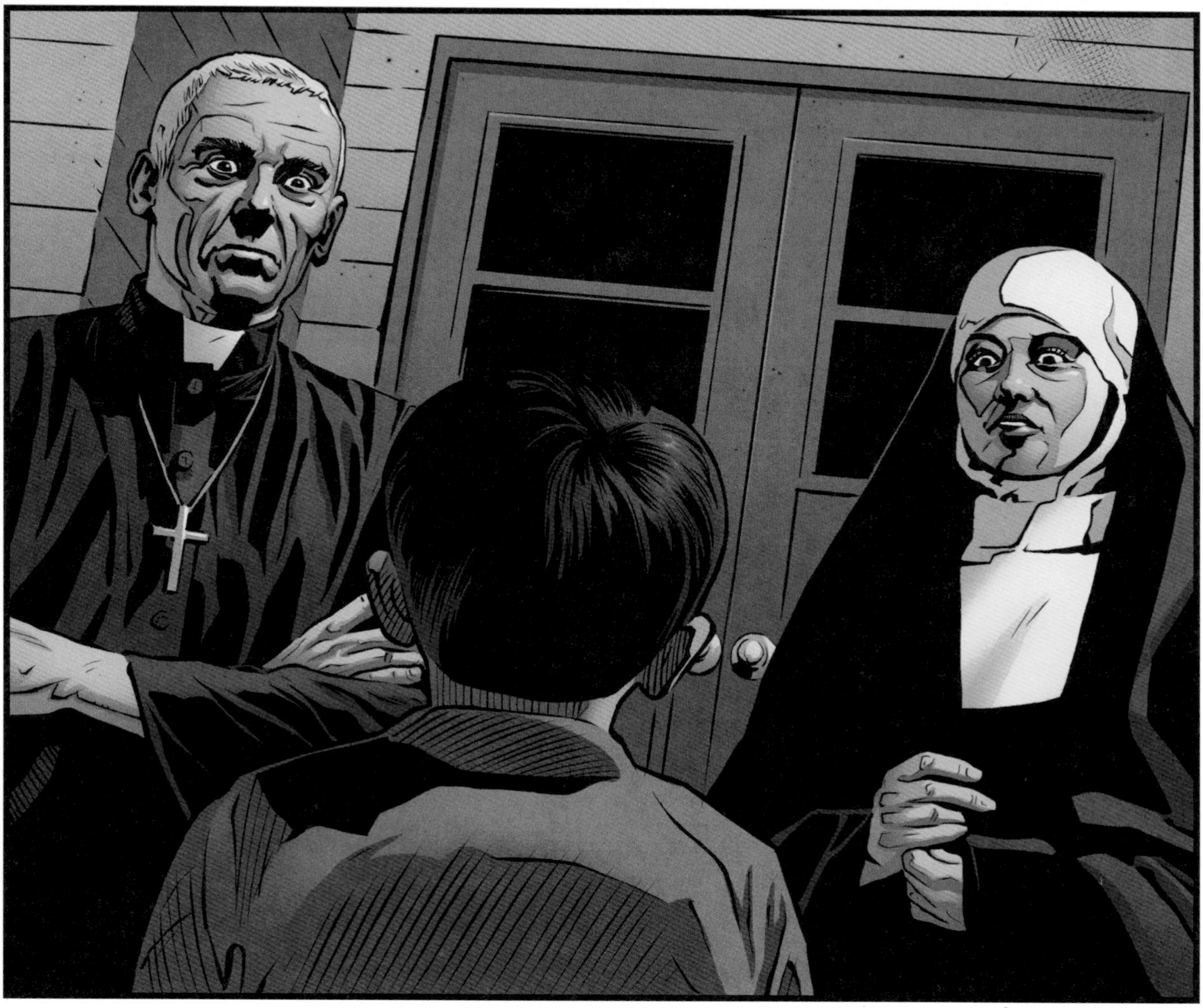

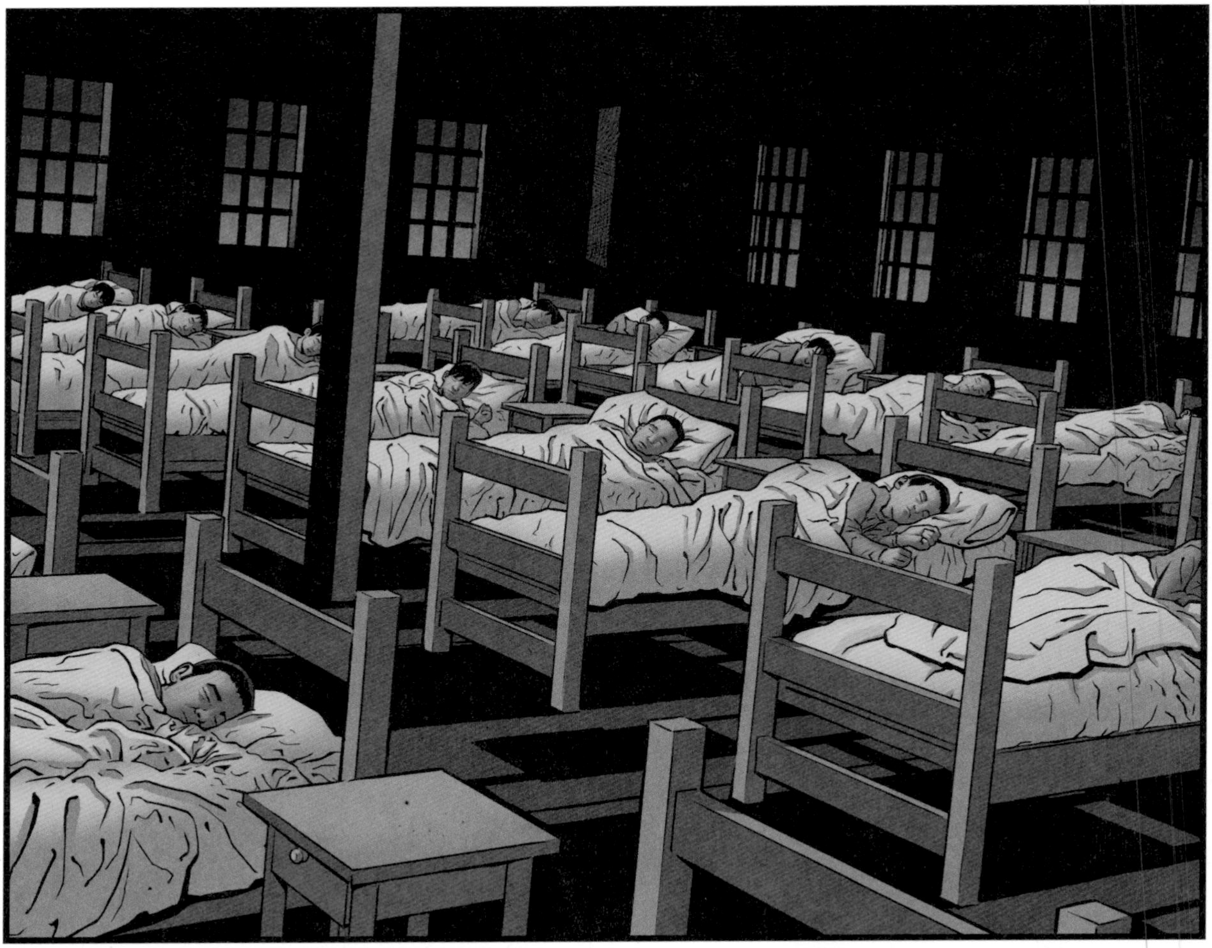

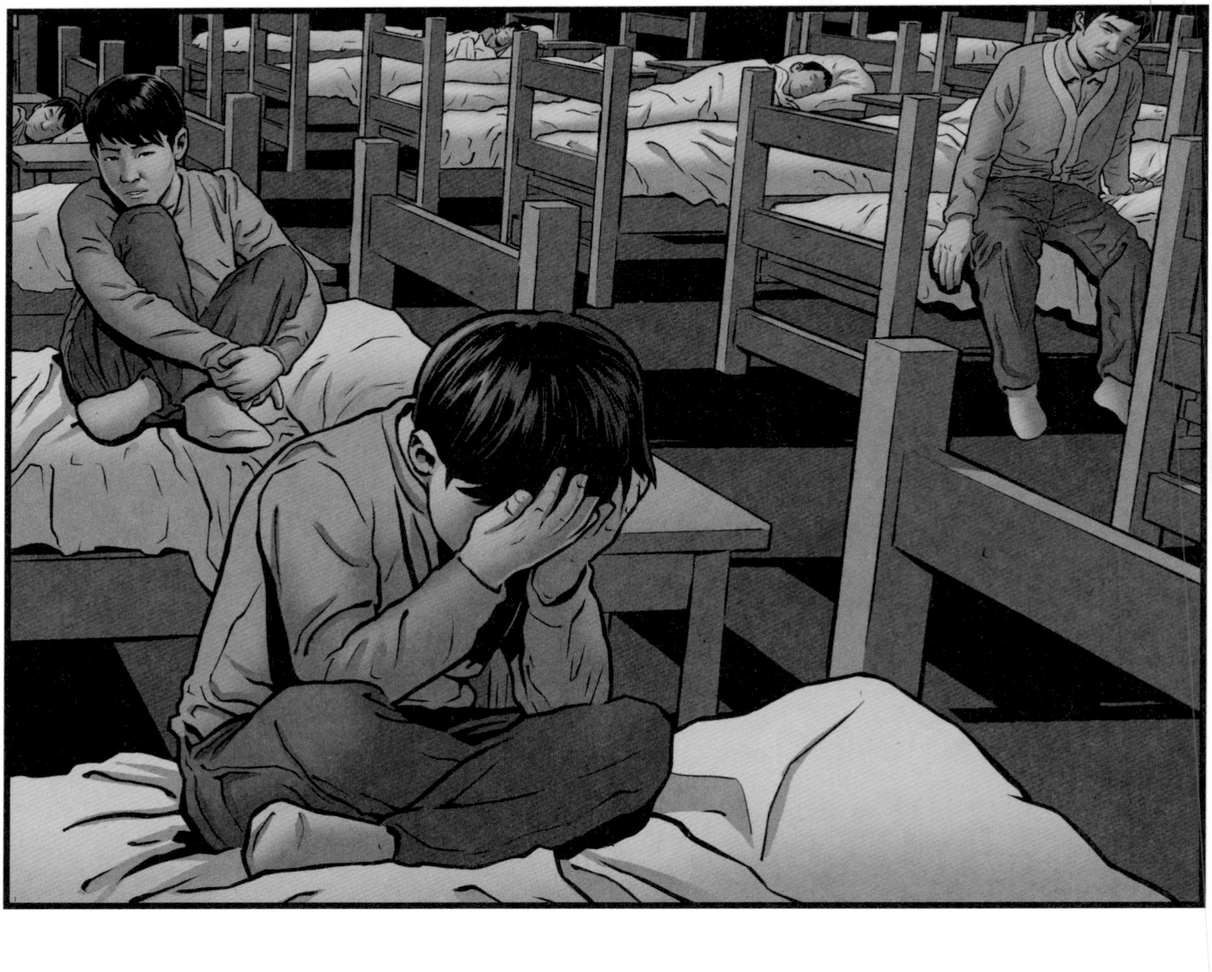

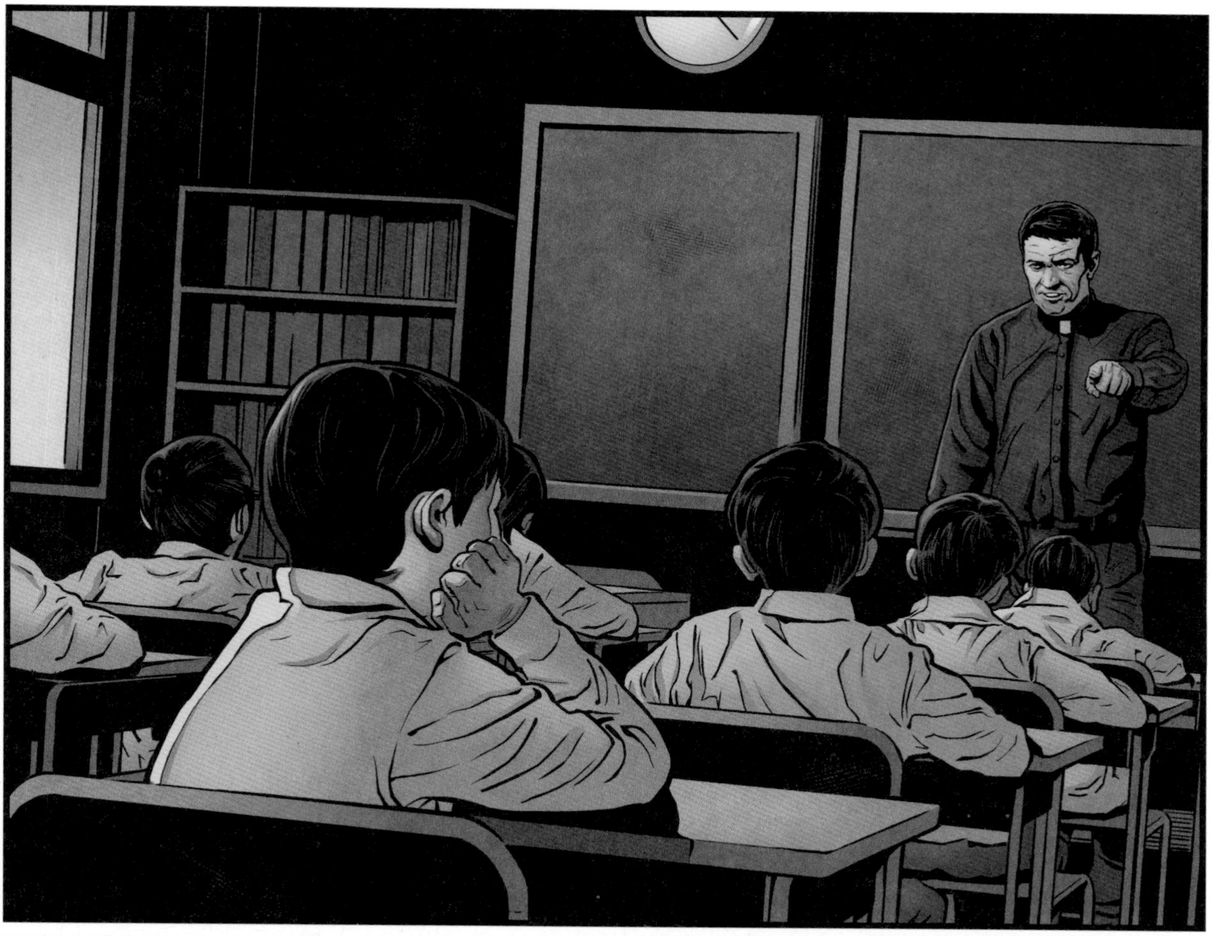

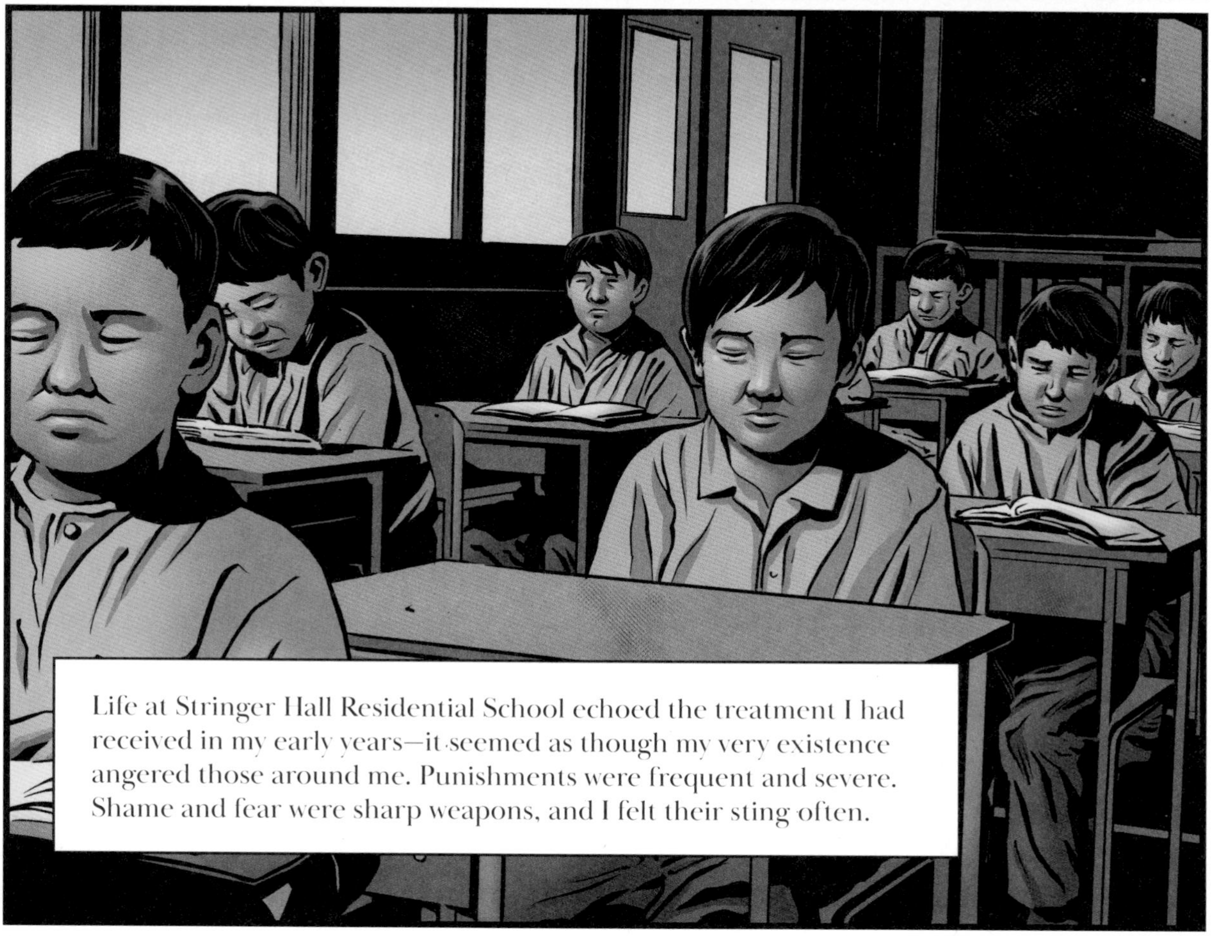
Life at Stringer Hall Residential School echoed the treatment I had received in my early years—it seemed as though my very existence angered those around me. Punishments were frequent and severe. Shame and fear were sharp weapons, and I felt their sting often.

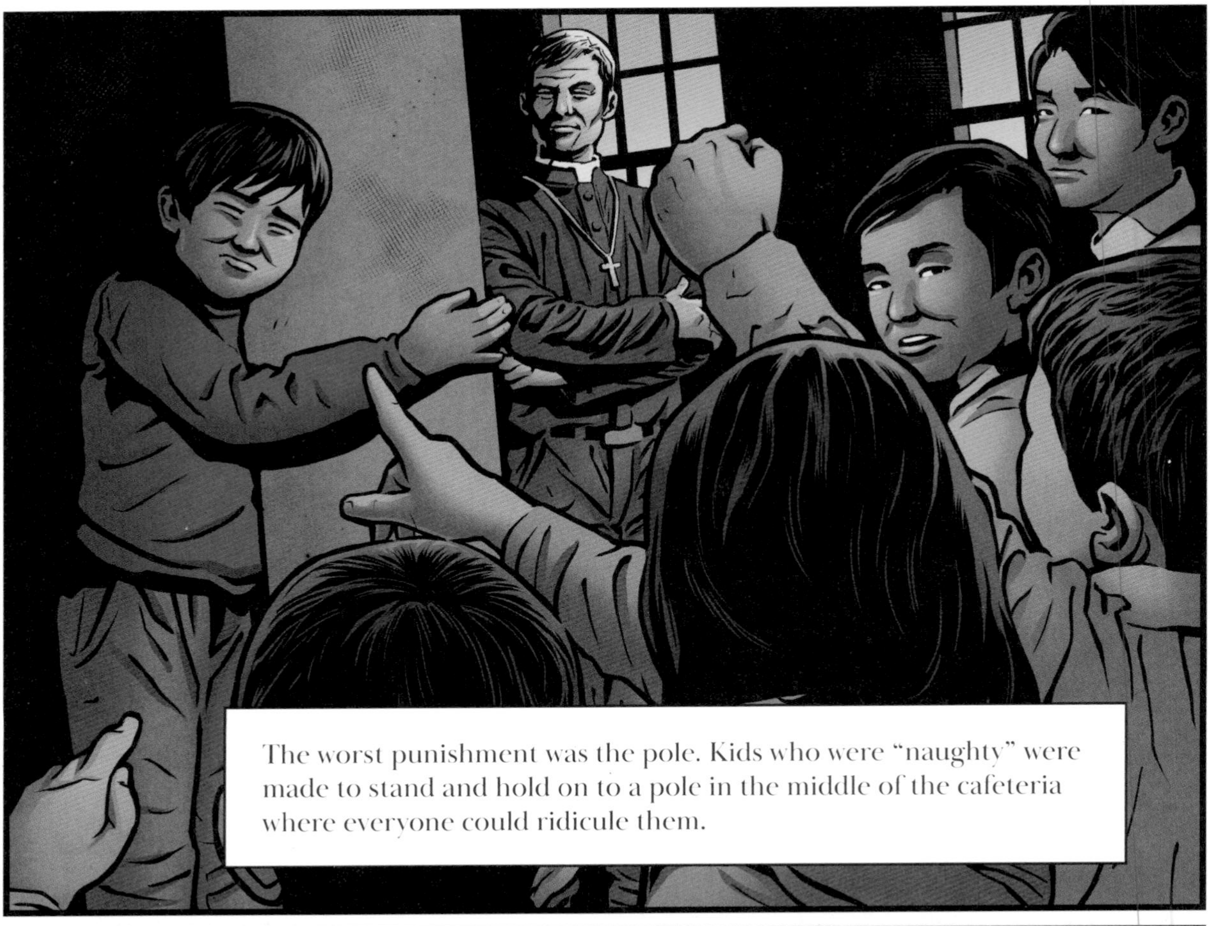
The worst punishment was the pole. Kids who were “naughty” were made to stand and hold on to a pole in the middle of the cafeteria where everyone could ridicule them.

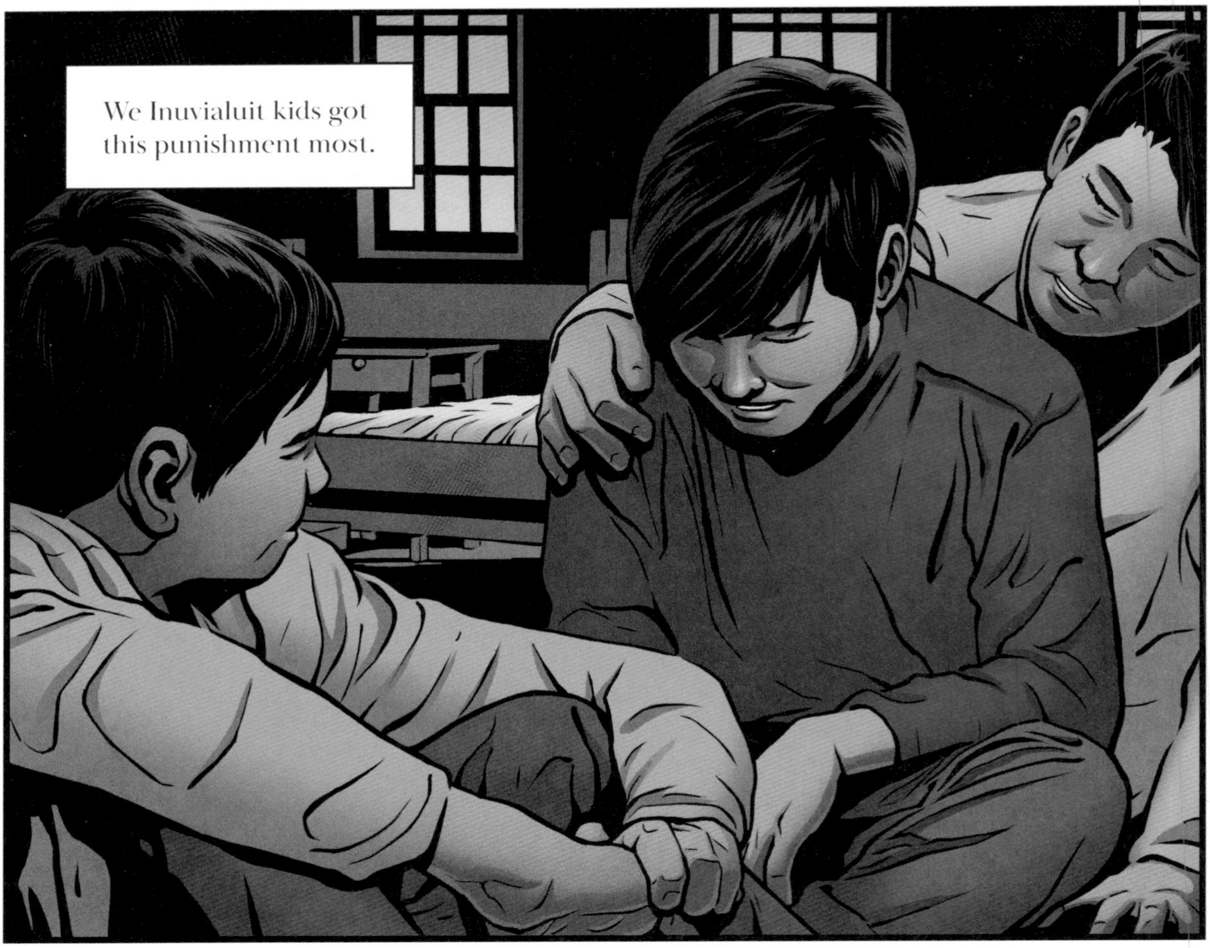
We Inuvialuit kids got this punishment most.

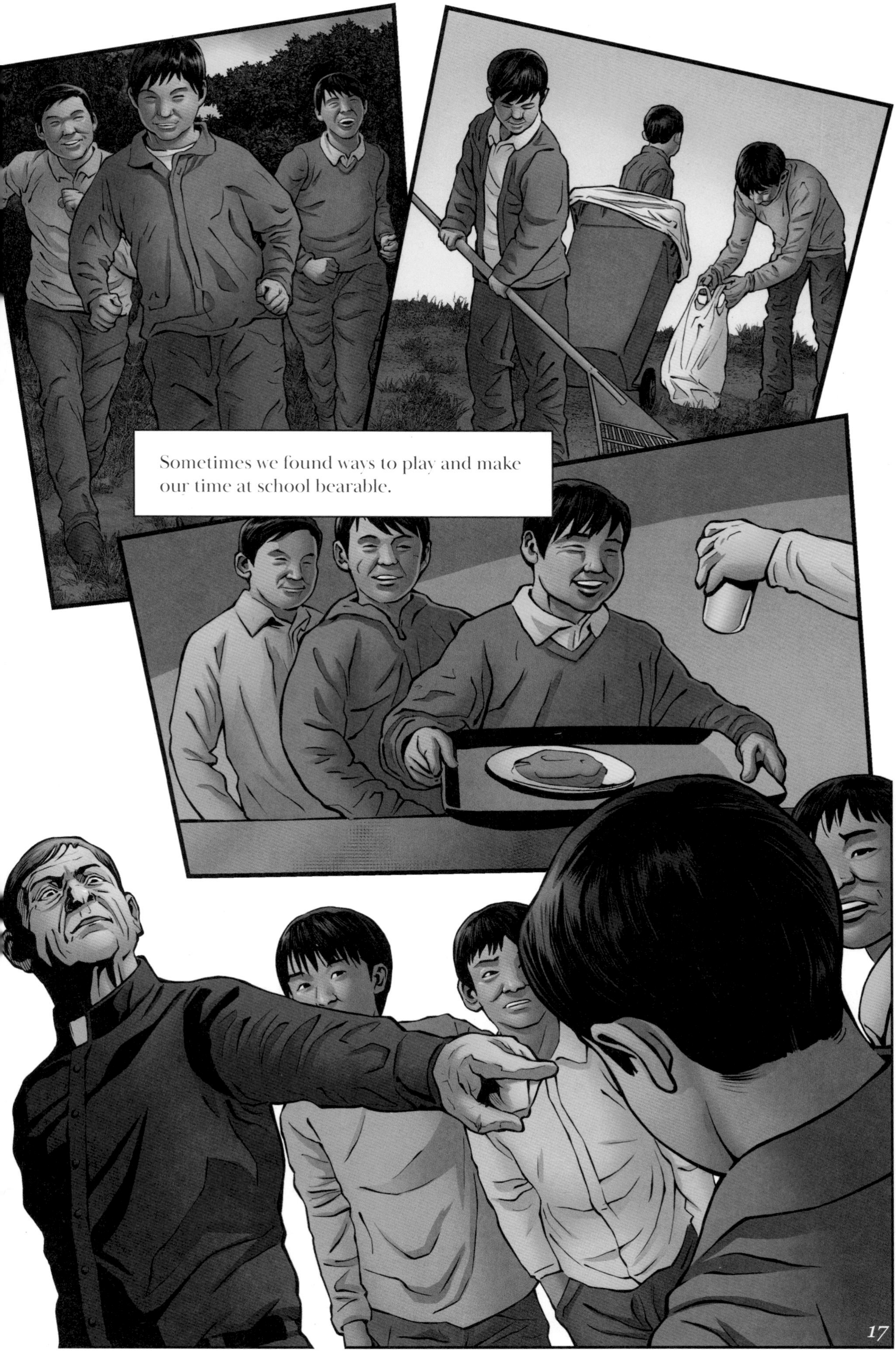
Sometimes we found ways to play and make our time at school bearable.

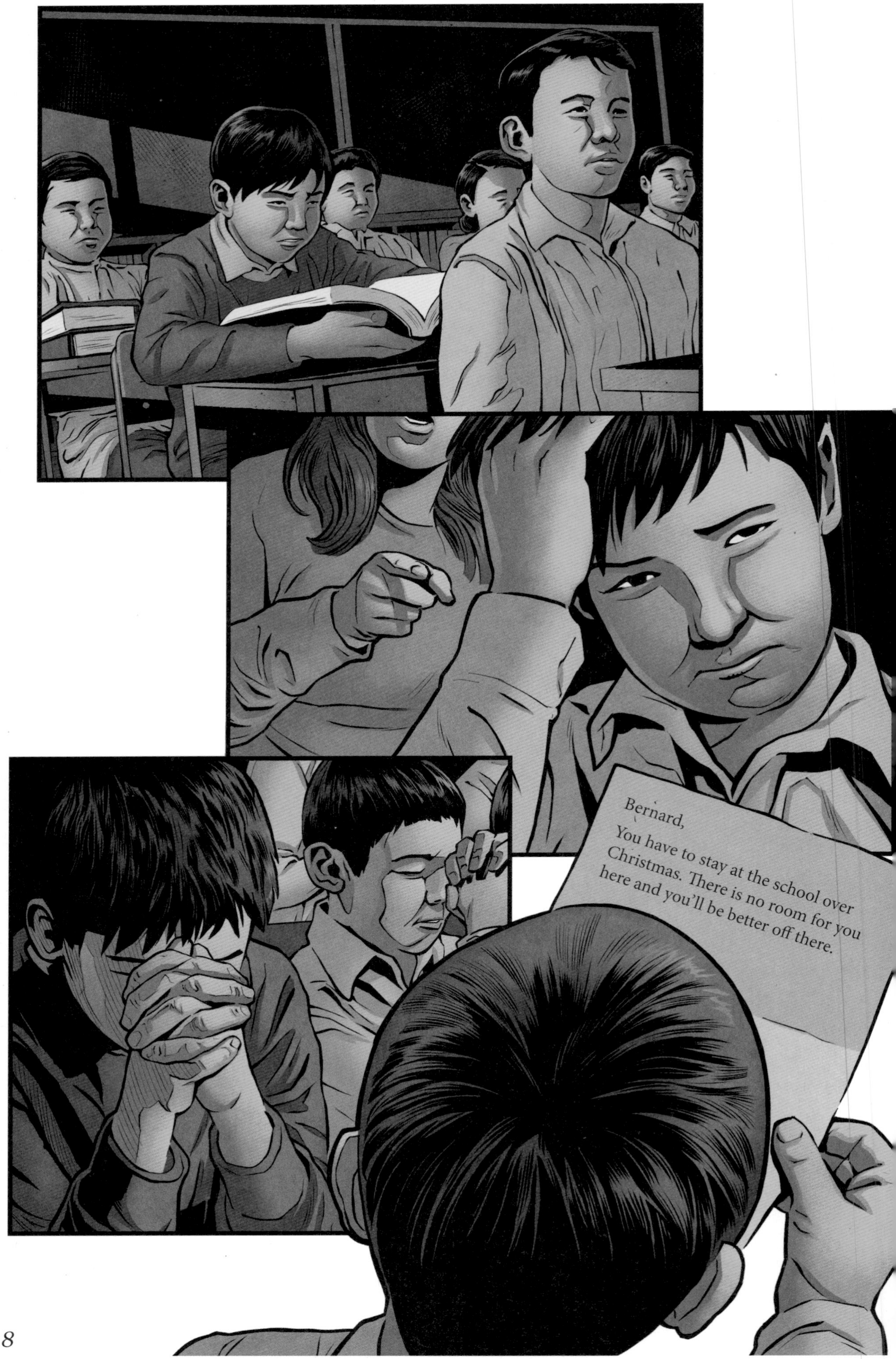
Bernard,
You have to stay at the school over Christmas. There is no room for you here and you'll be better off there.

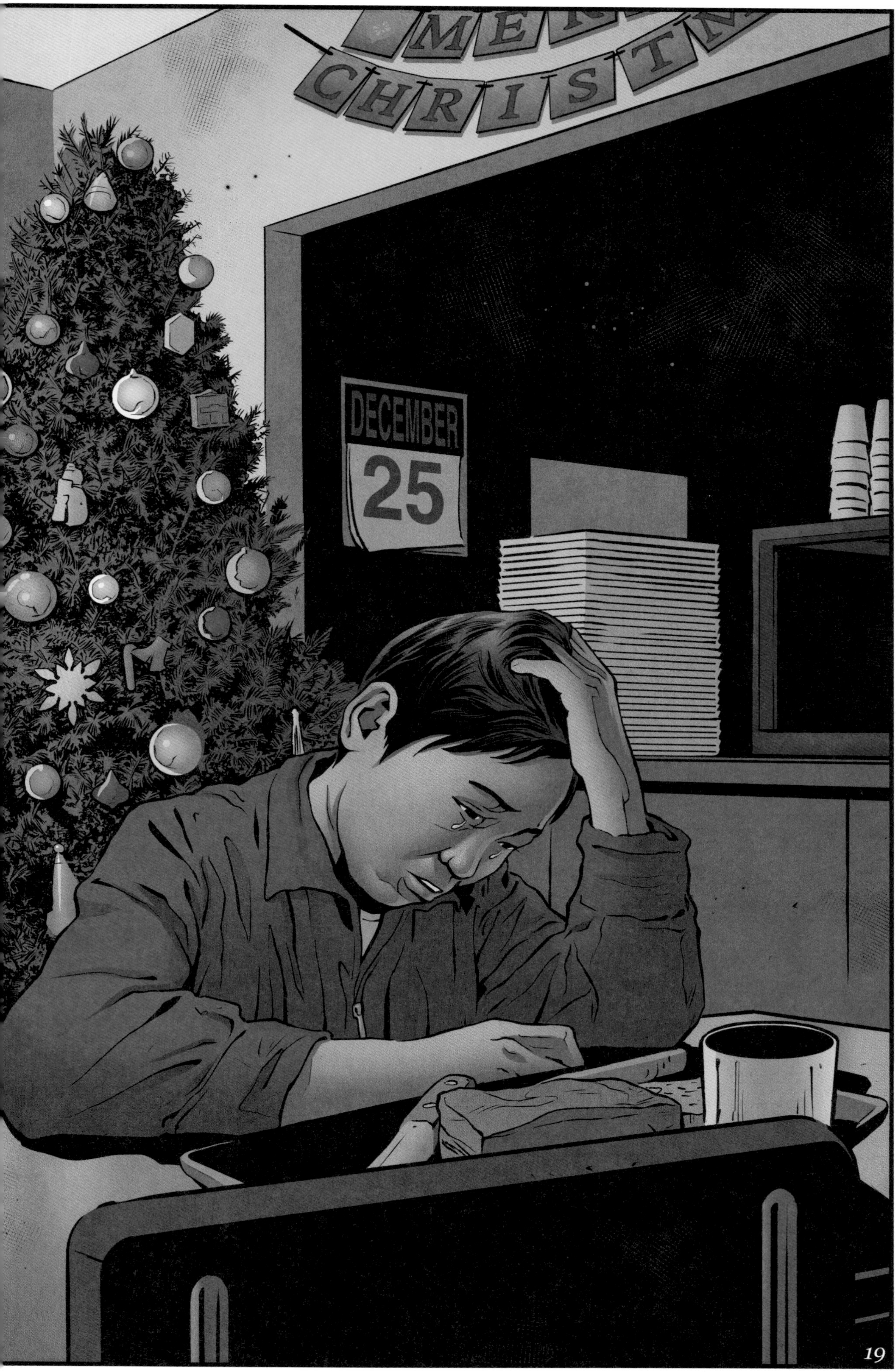
CHRIST
DECEMBER
25

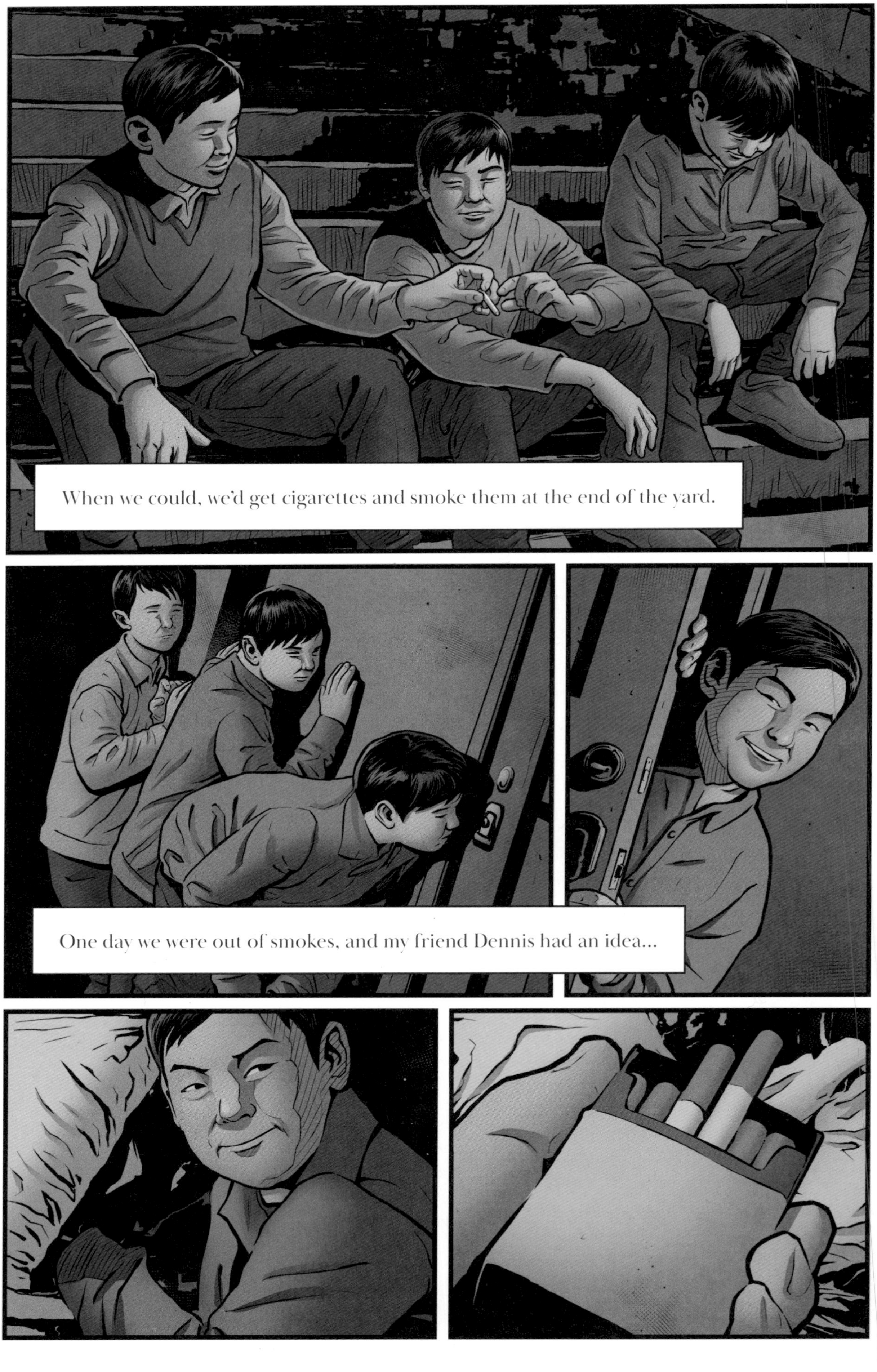
When we could, we'd get cigarettes and smoke them at the end of the yard.
One day we were out of smokes, and my friend Dennis had an idea...

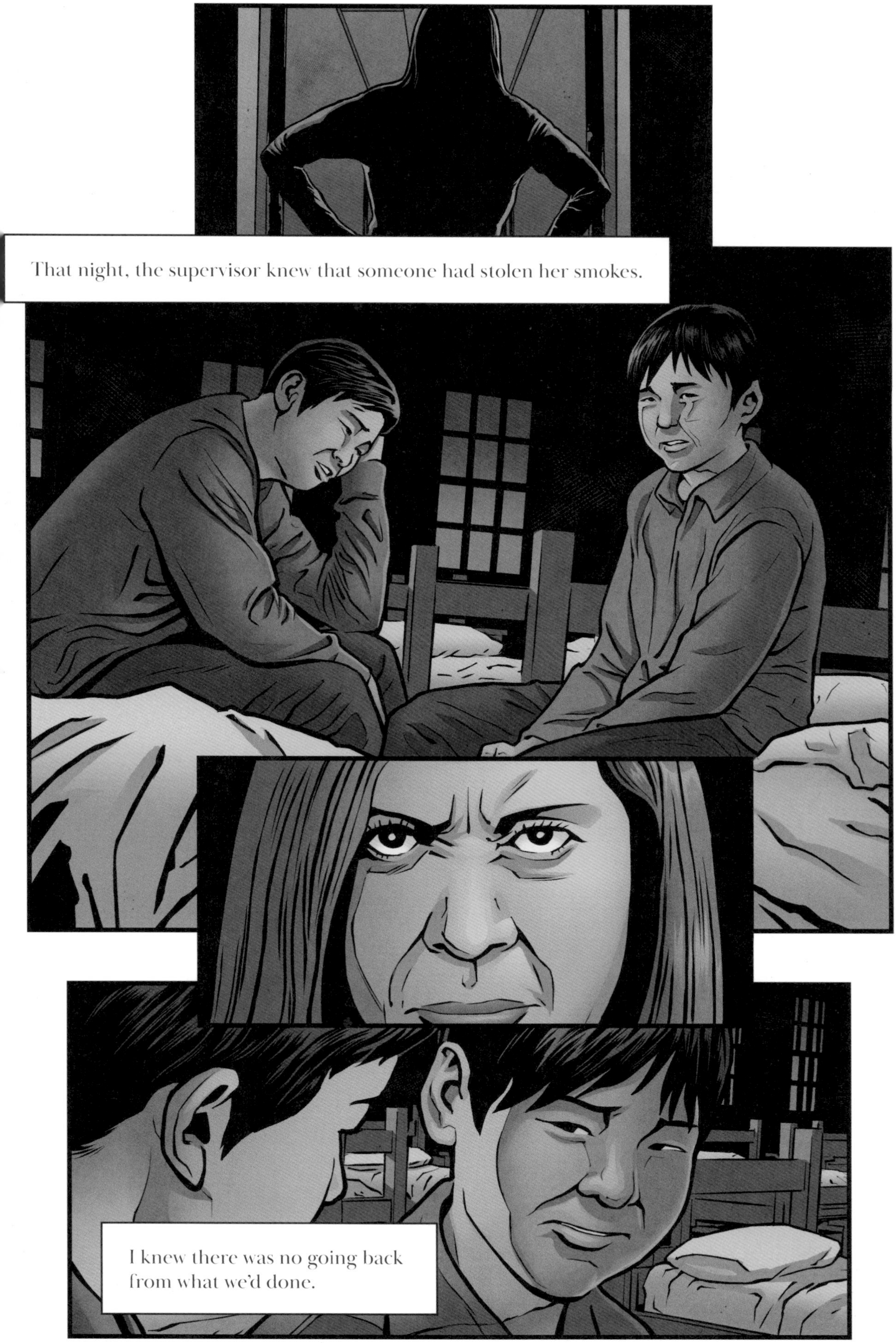
That night, the supervisor knew that someone had stolen her smokes.
I knew there was no going back from what we'd done.

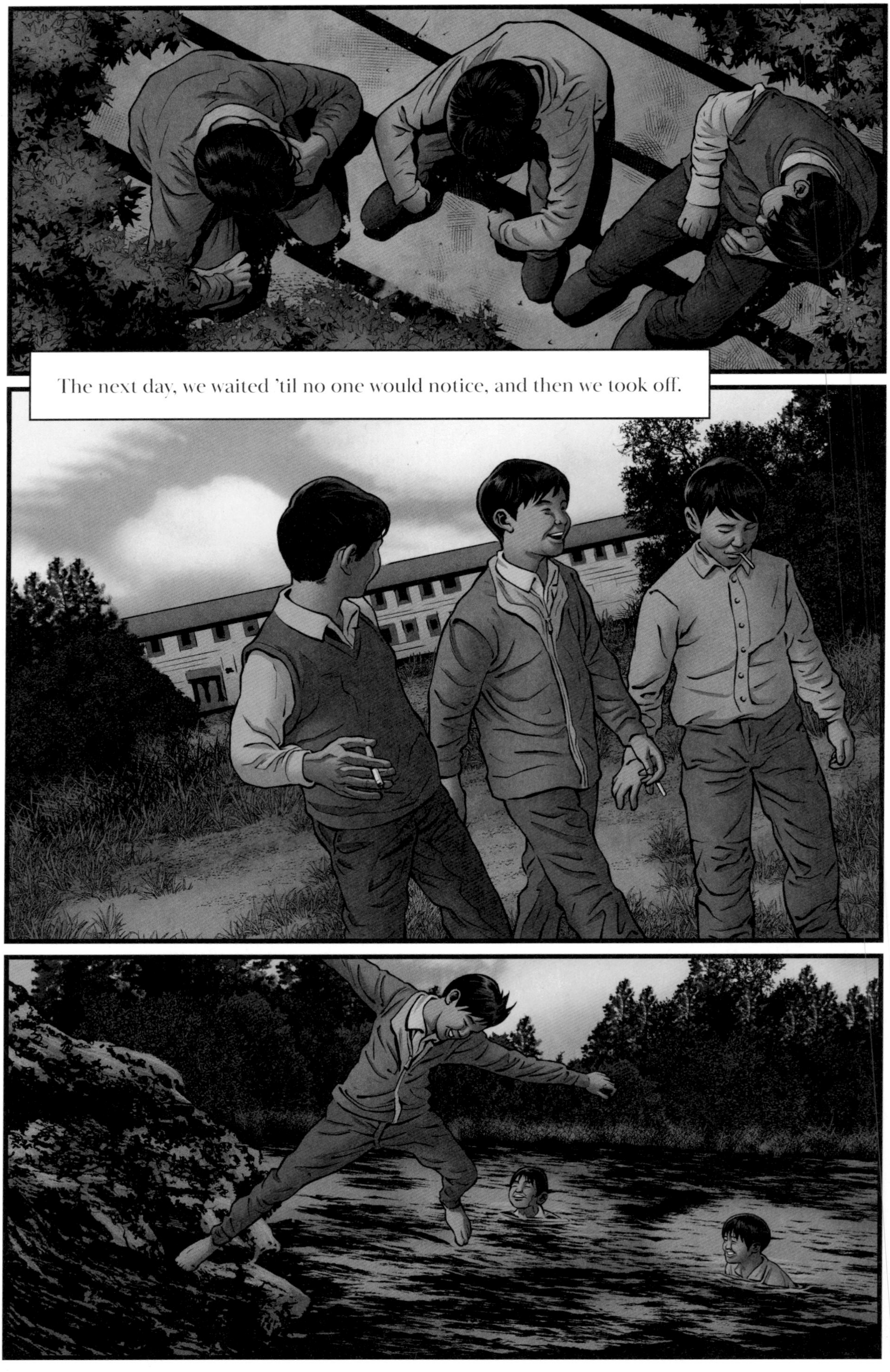
The next day, we waited 'til no one would notice, and then we took off.

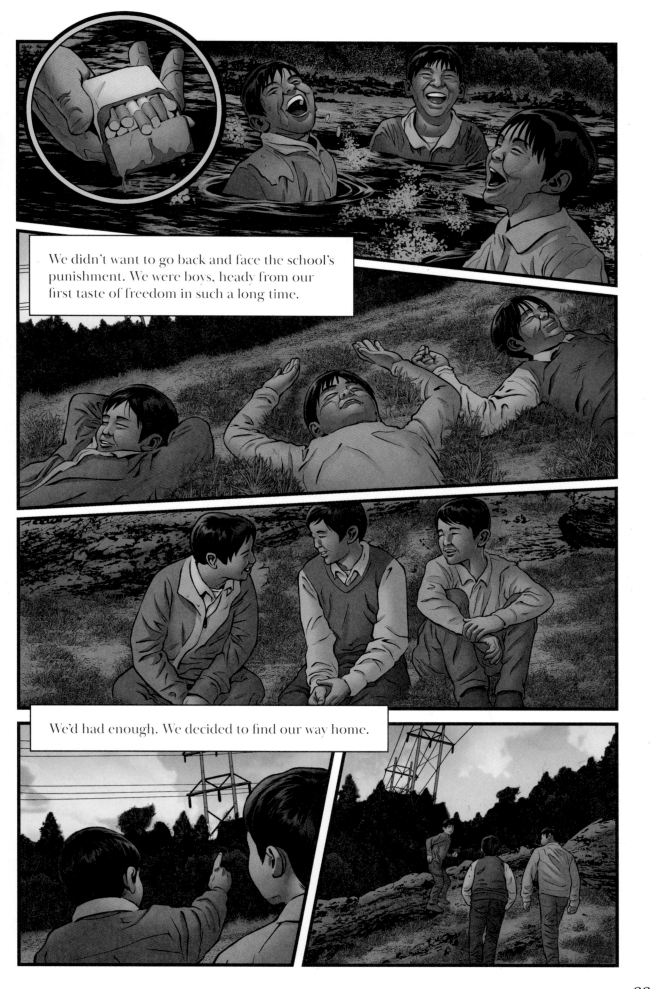

We didn't want to go back and face the school's punishment. We were boys, heady from our first taste of freedom in such a long time.

We'd had enough. We decided to find our way home.

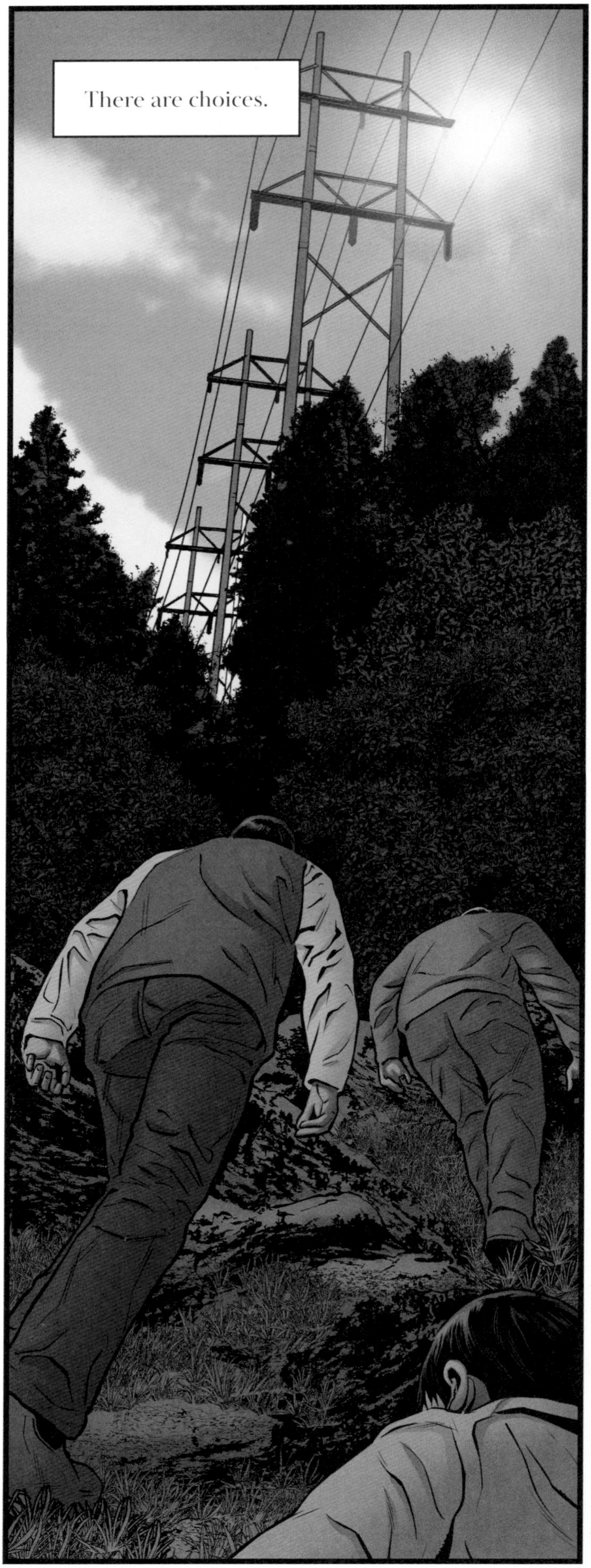
There are choices.

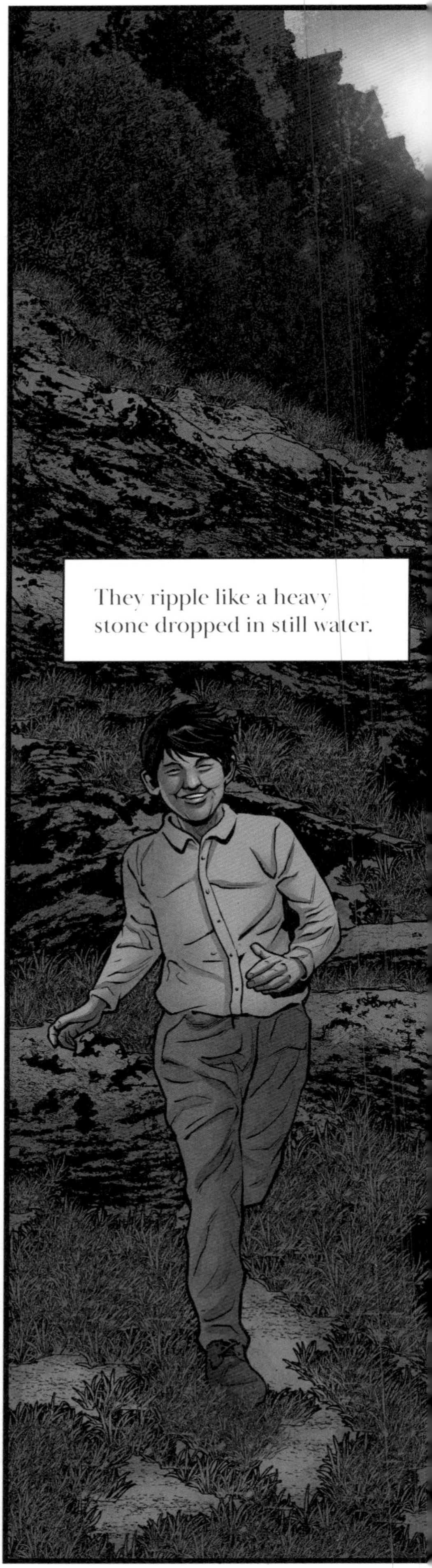
They ripple like a heavy stone dropped in still water.

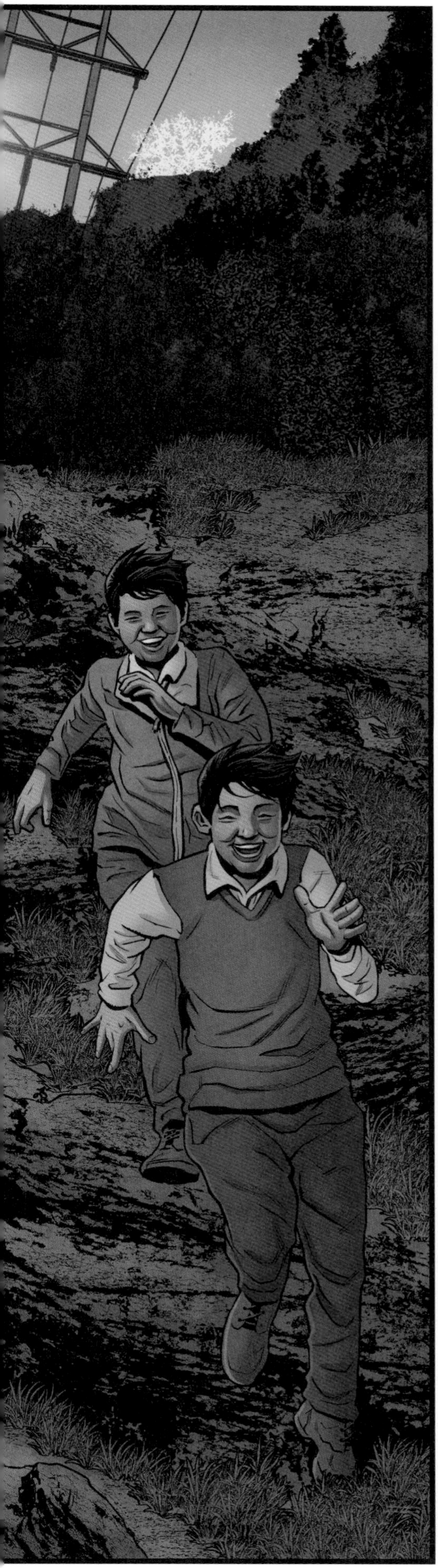

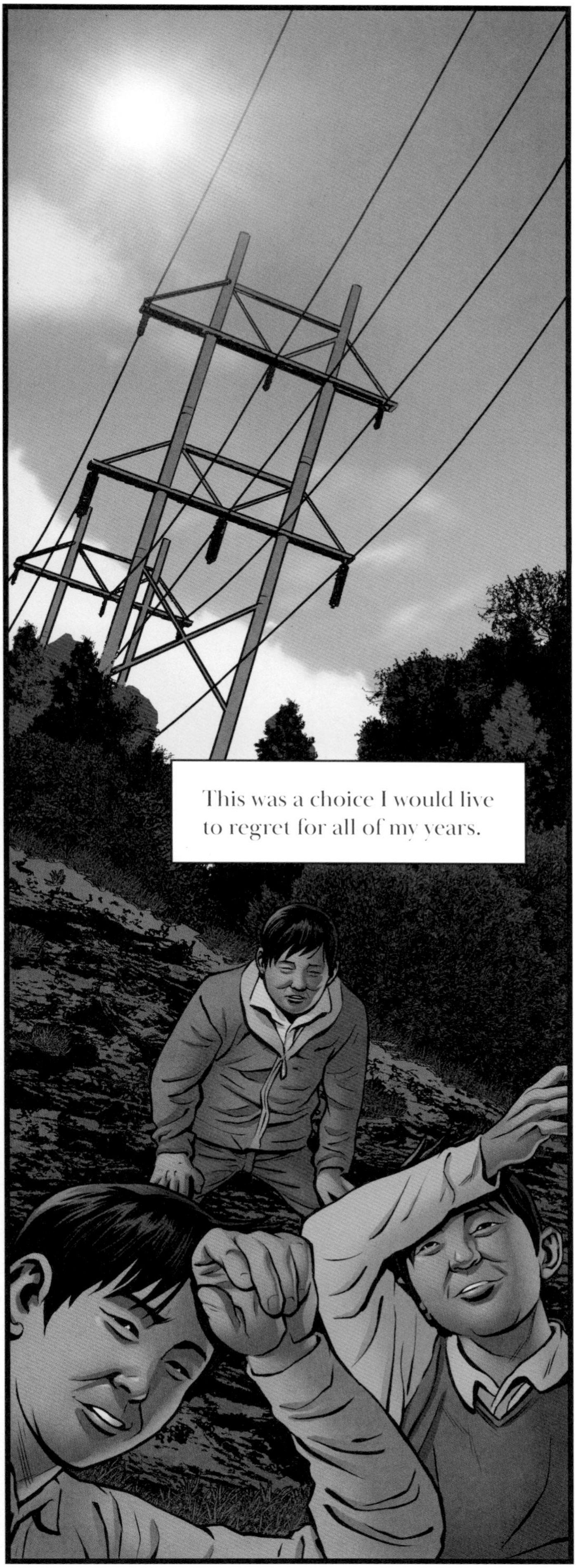
This was a choice I would live to regret for all of my years.

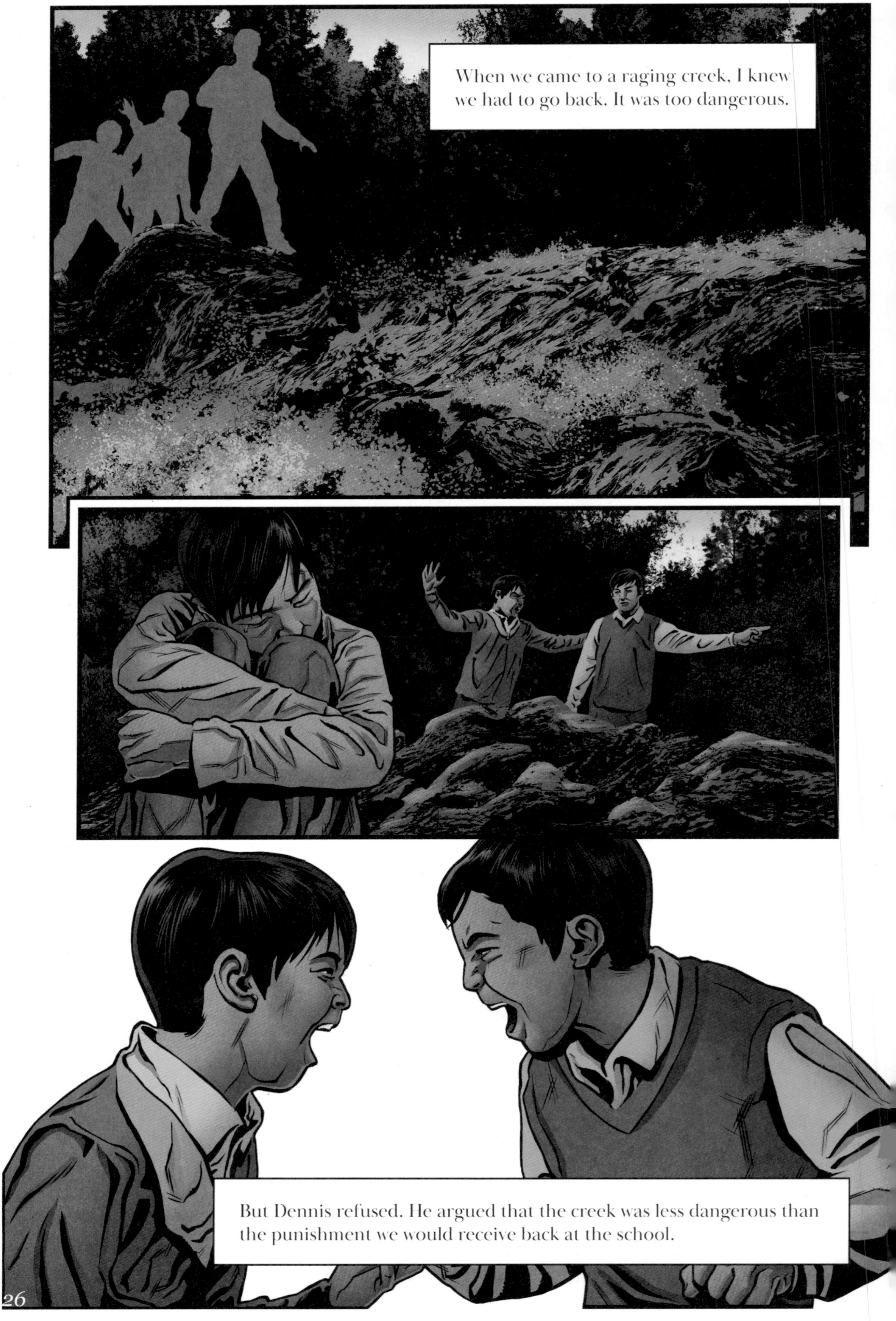
When we came to a raging creek, I knew we had to go back. It was too dangerous.
But Dennis refused. He argued that the creek was less dangerous than the punishment we would receive back at the school.

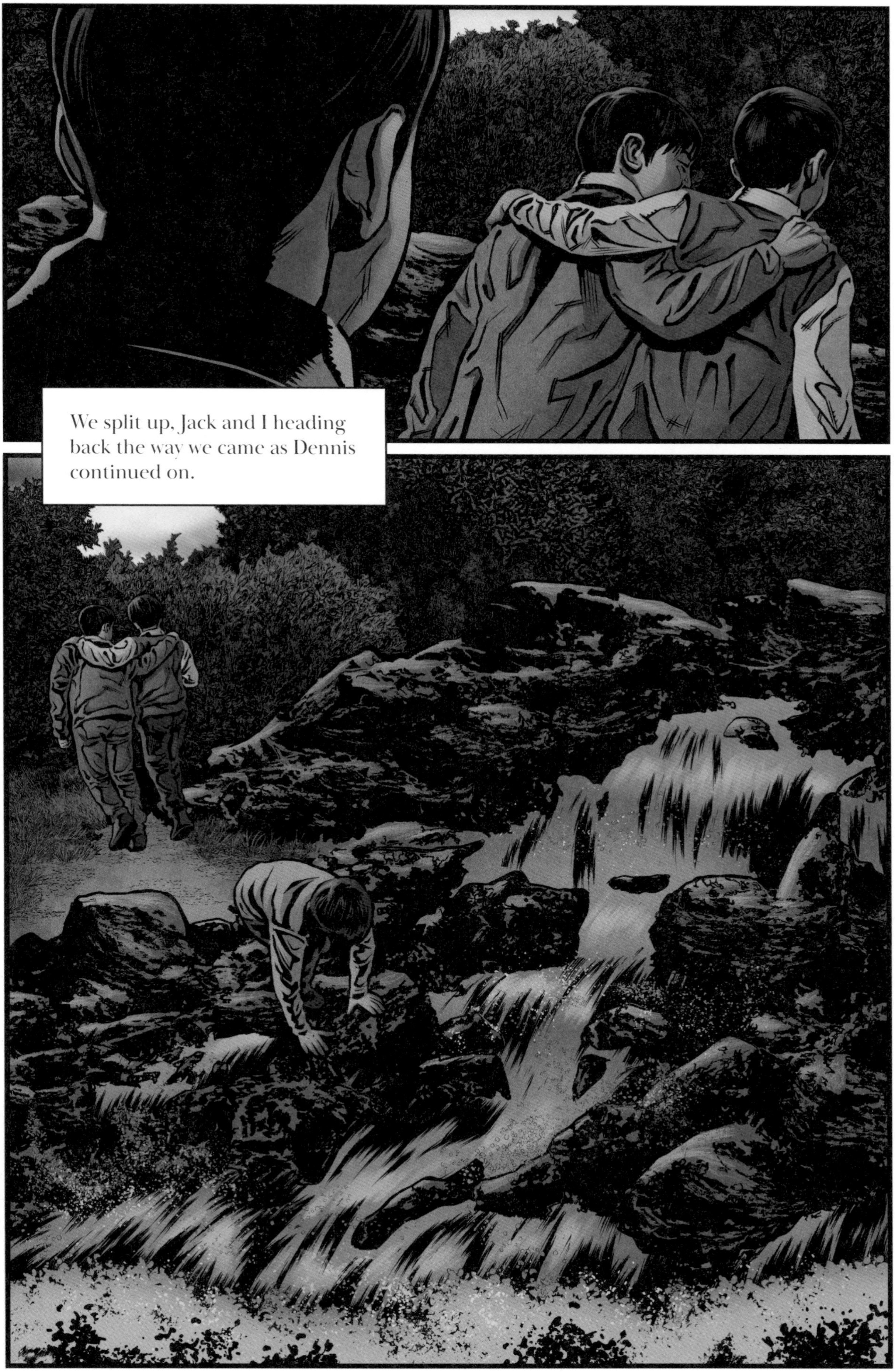
We split up, Jack and I heading back the way we came as Dennis continued on.

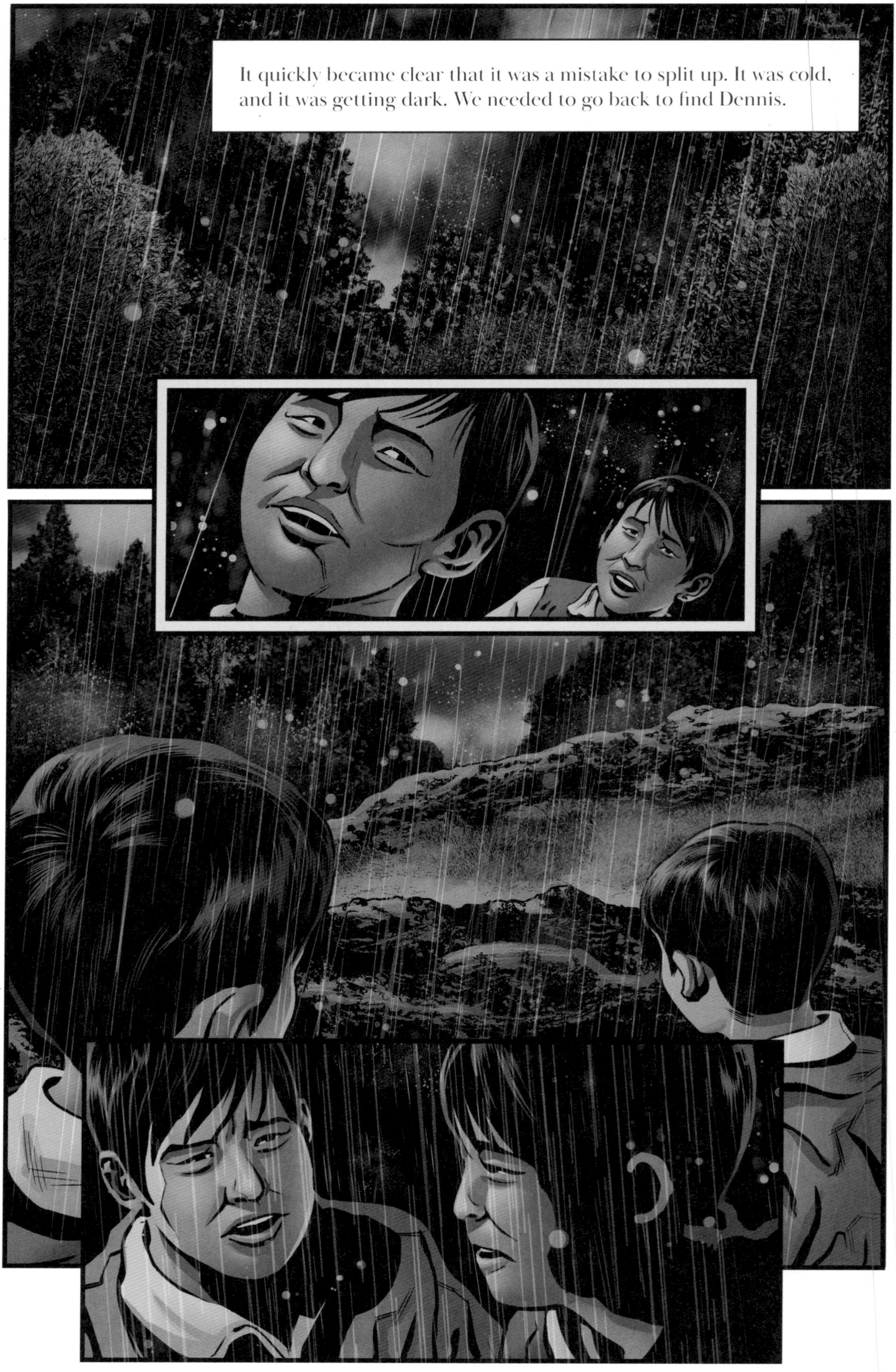
It quickly became clear that it was a mistake to split up. It was cold, and it was getting dark. We needed to go back to find Dennis.

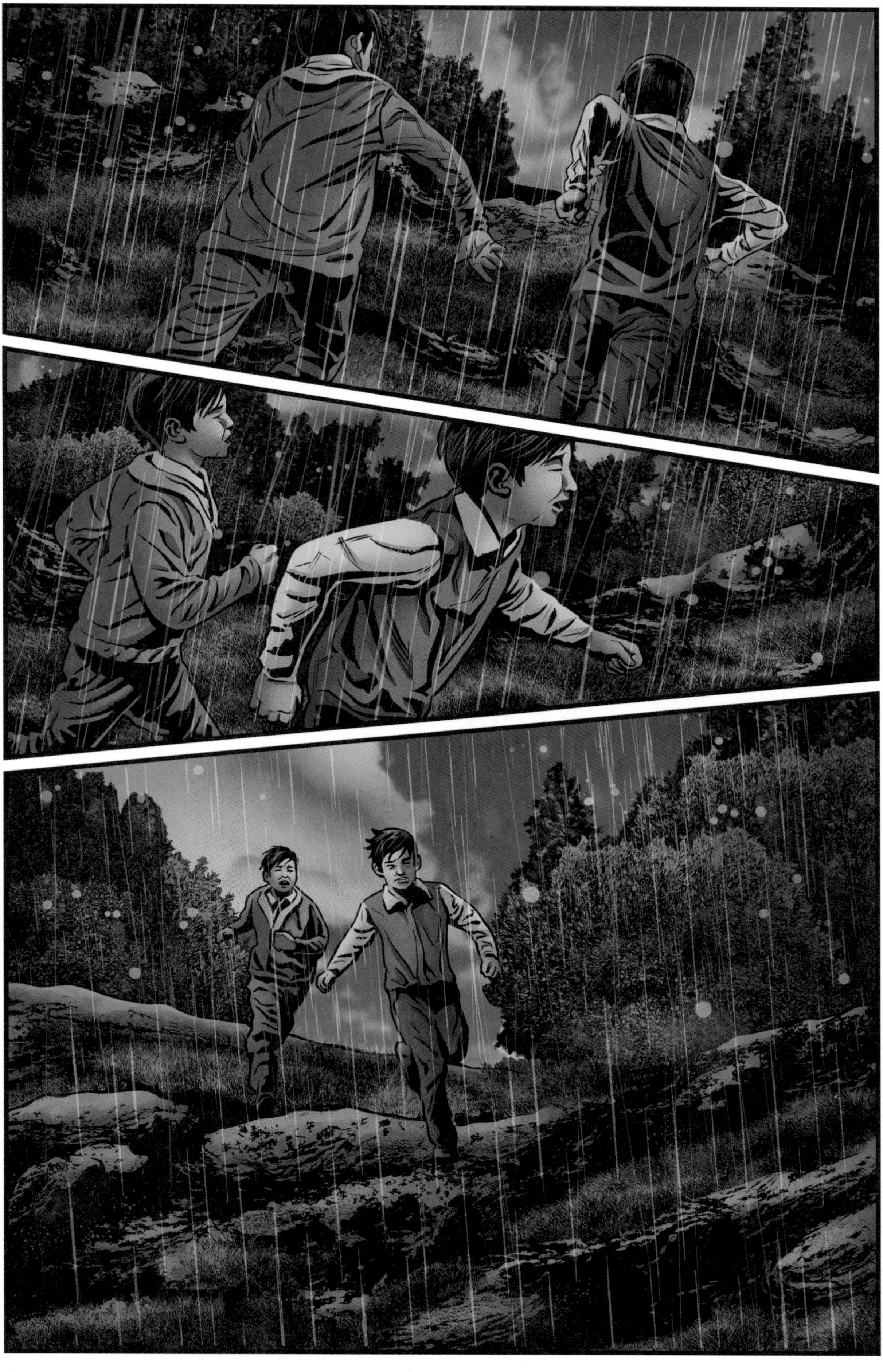

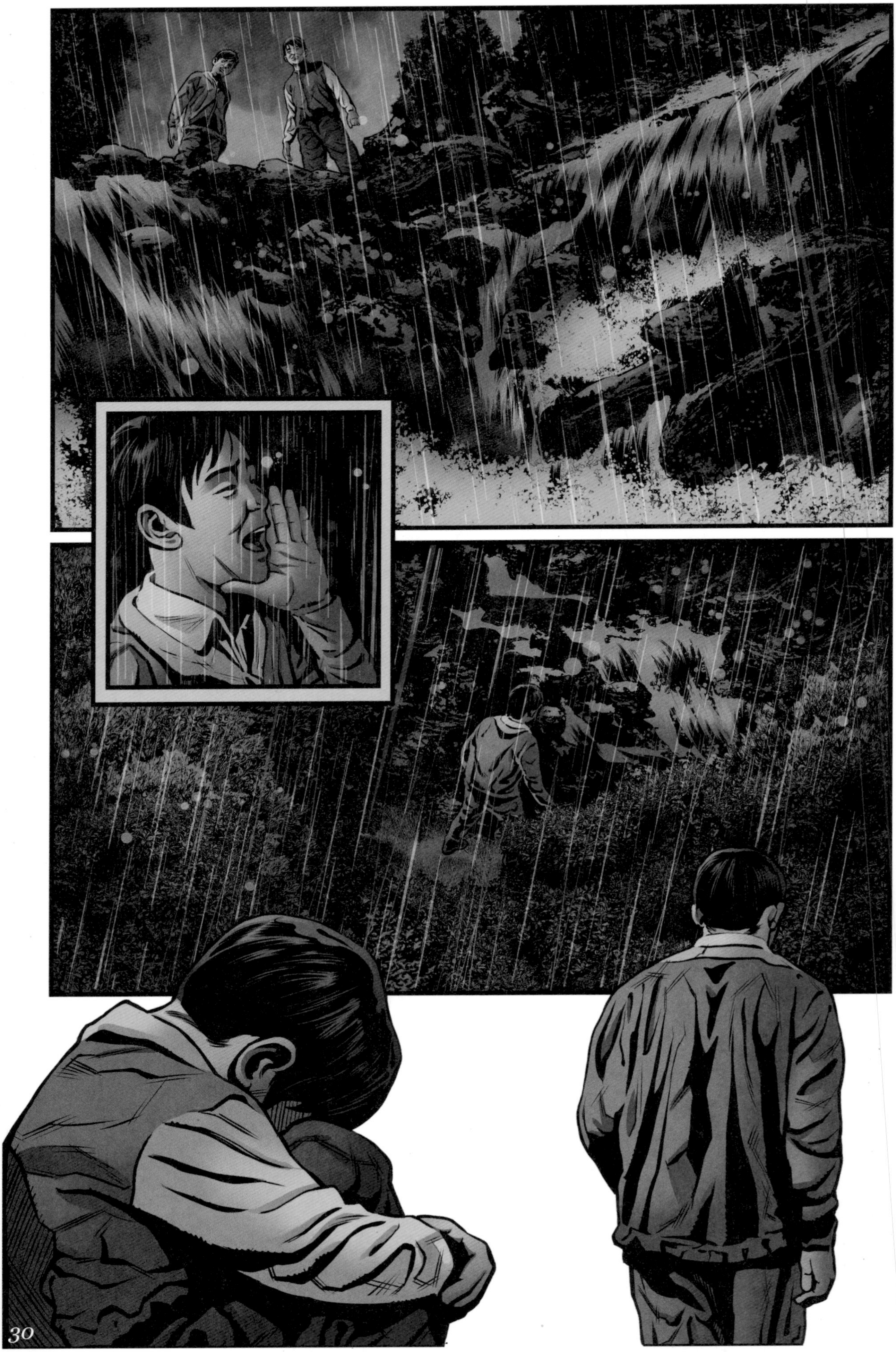

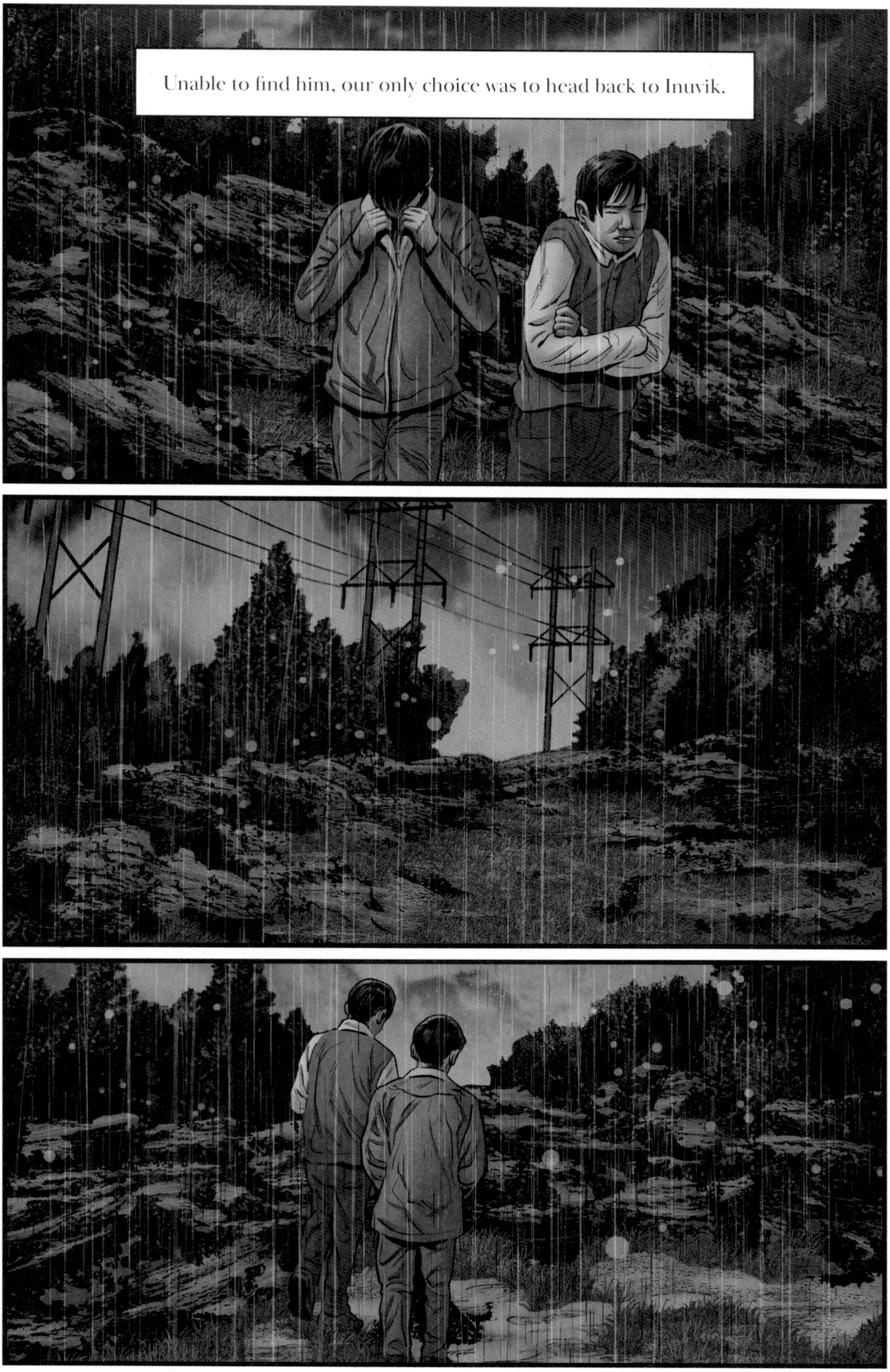
Unable to find him, our only choice was to head back to Inuvik.

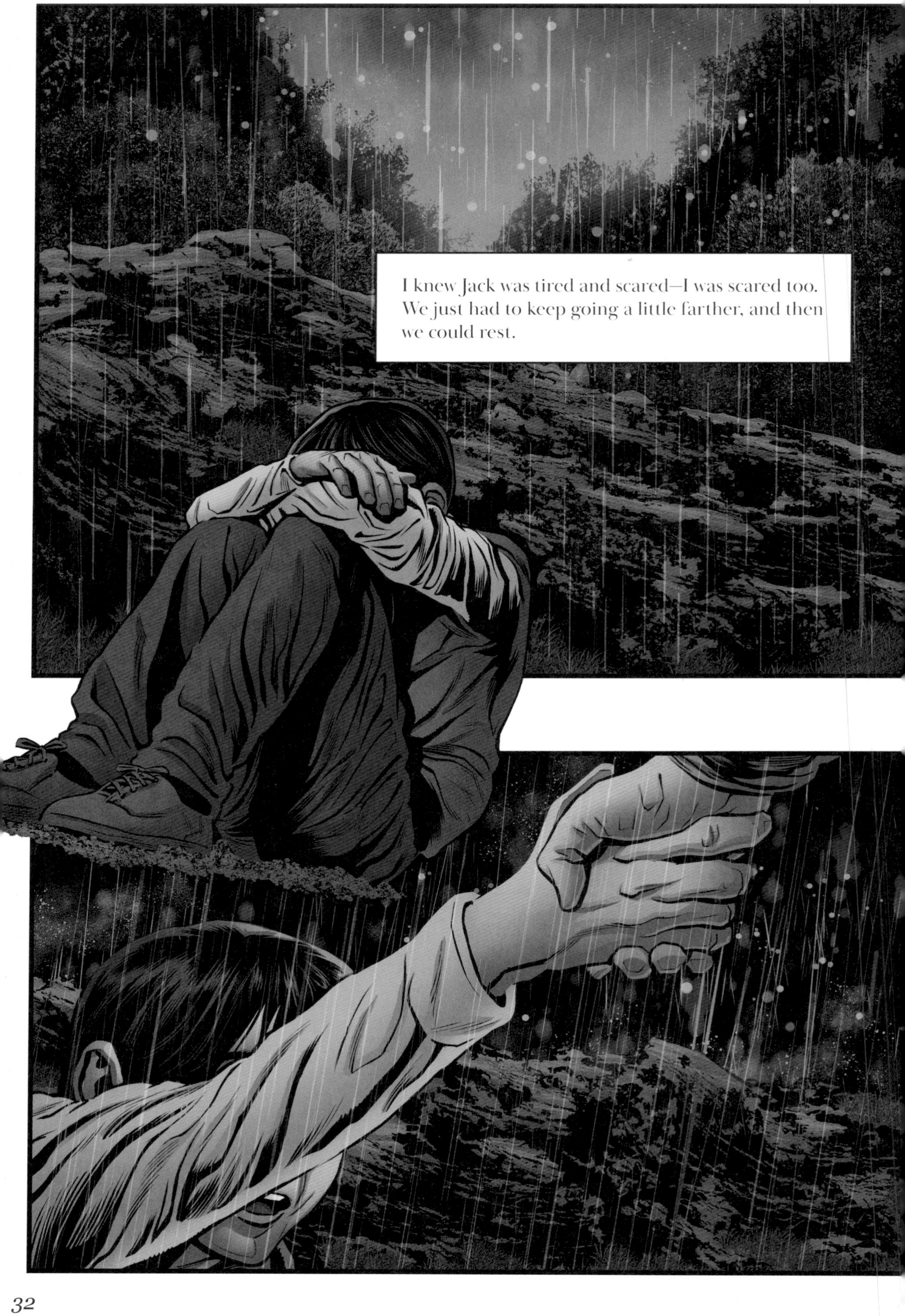
I knew Jack was tired and scared—I was scared too. We just had to keep going a little farther, and then we could rest.

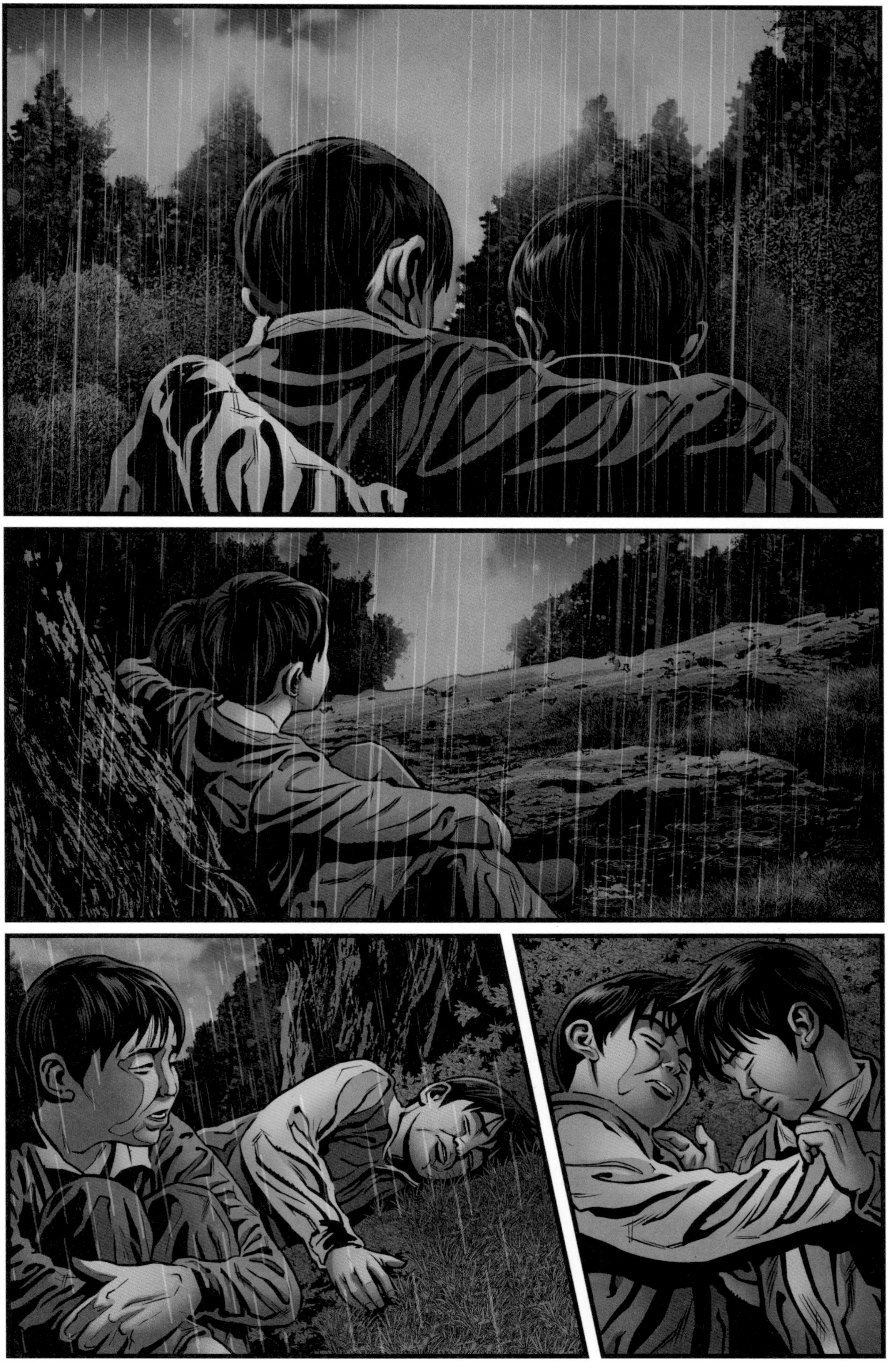

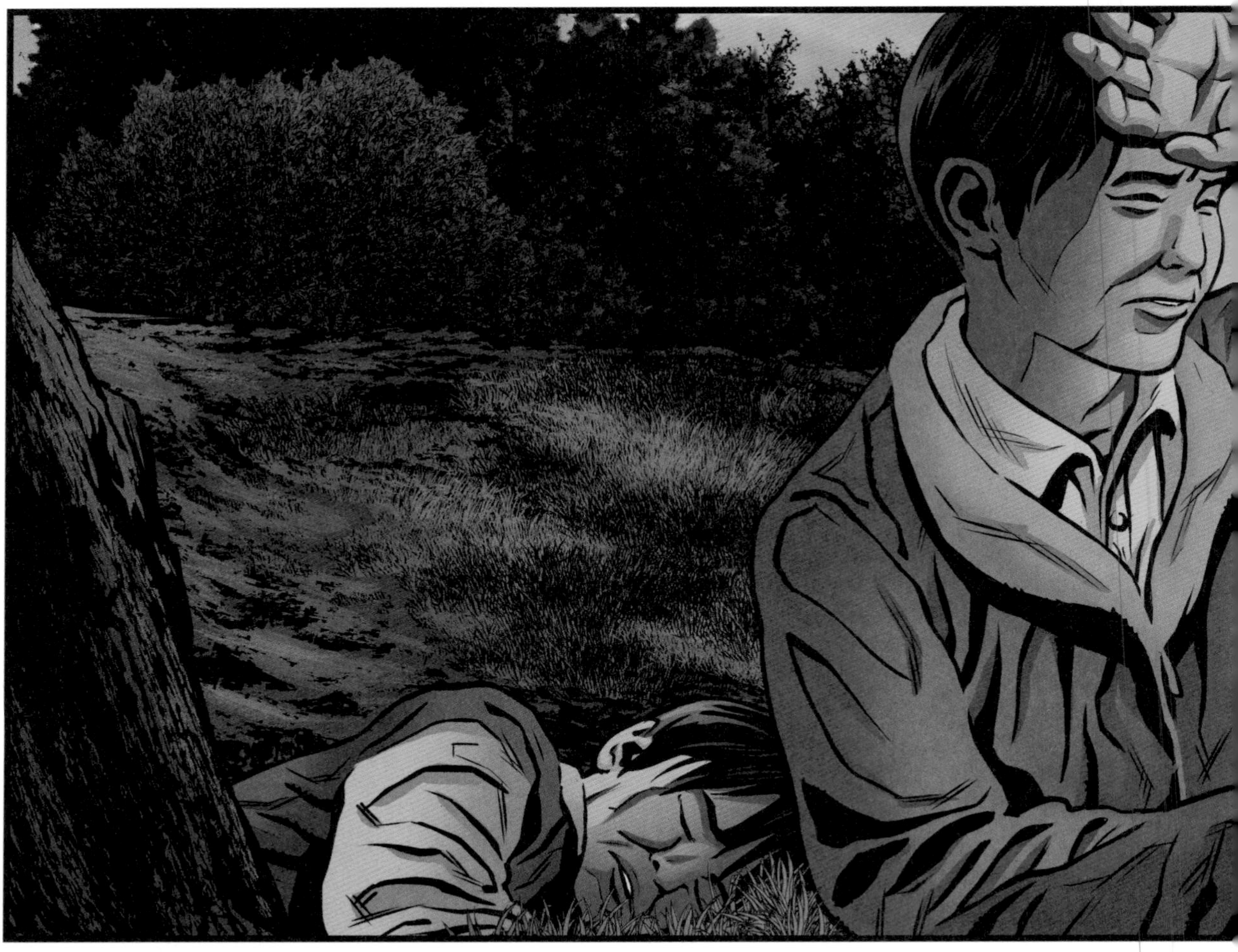

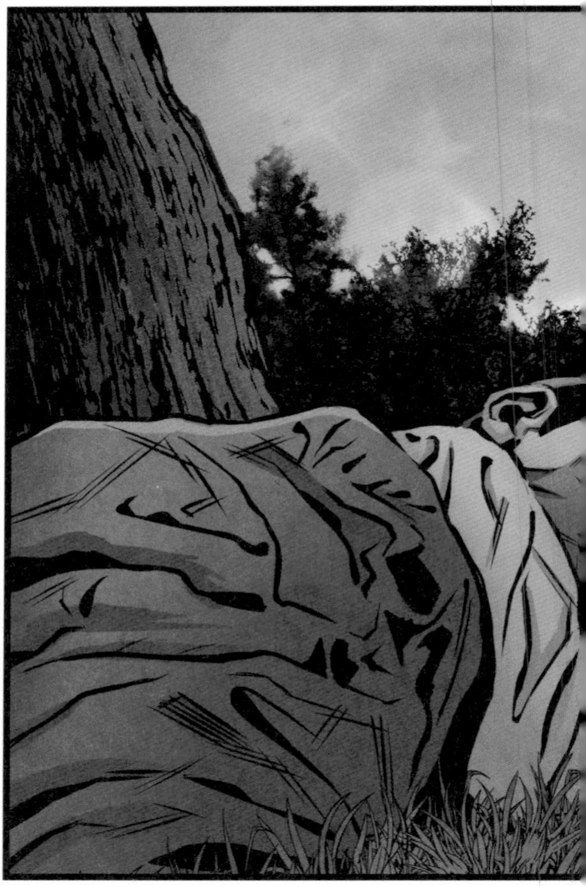

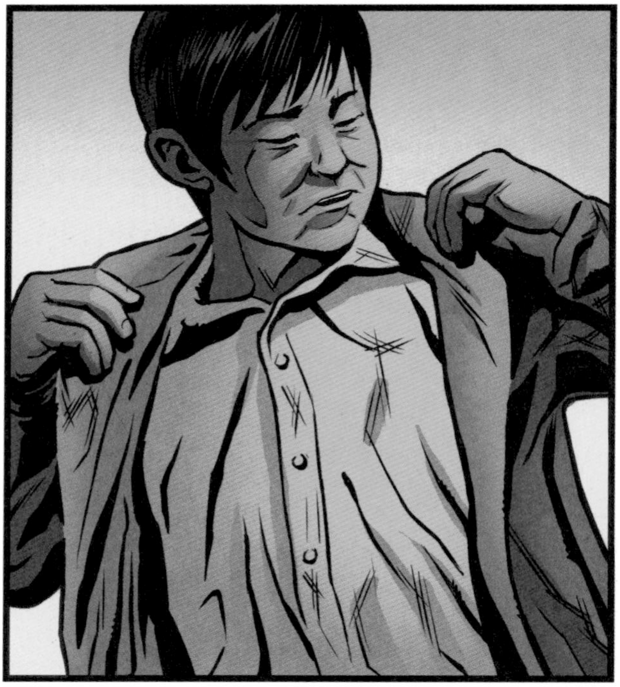

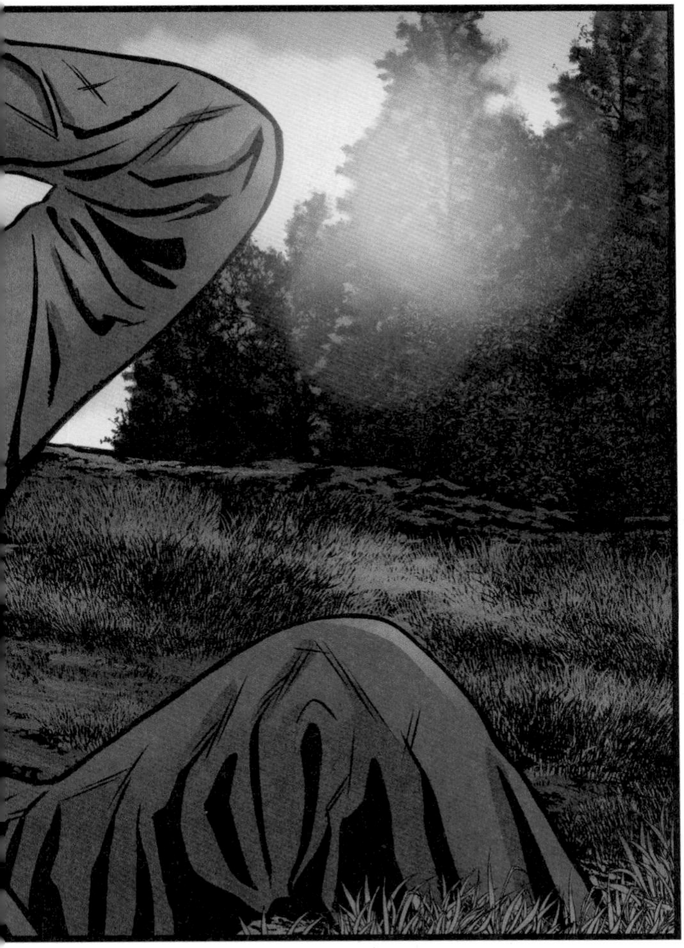

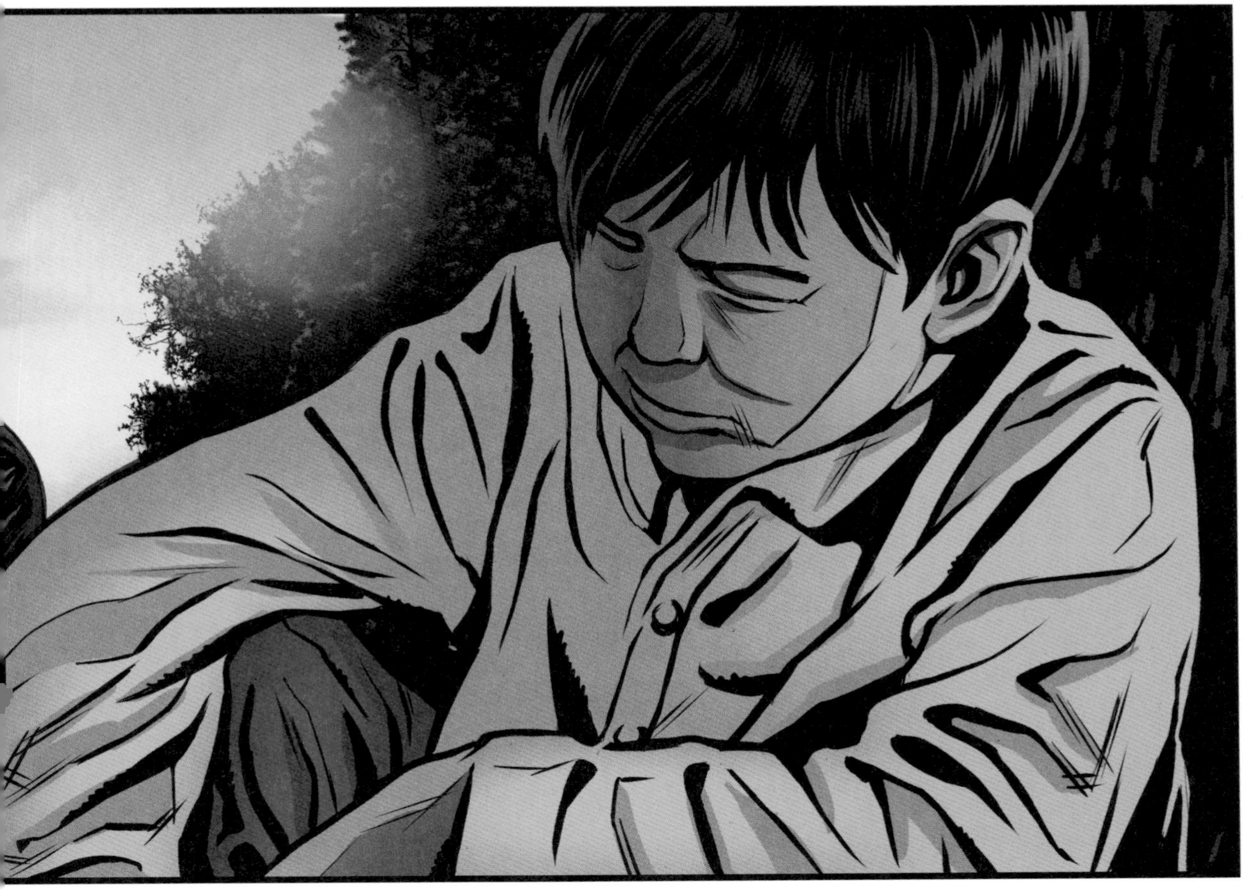

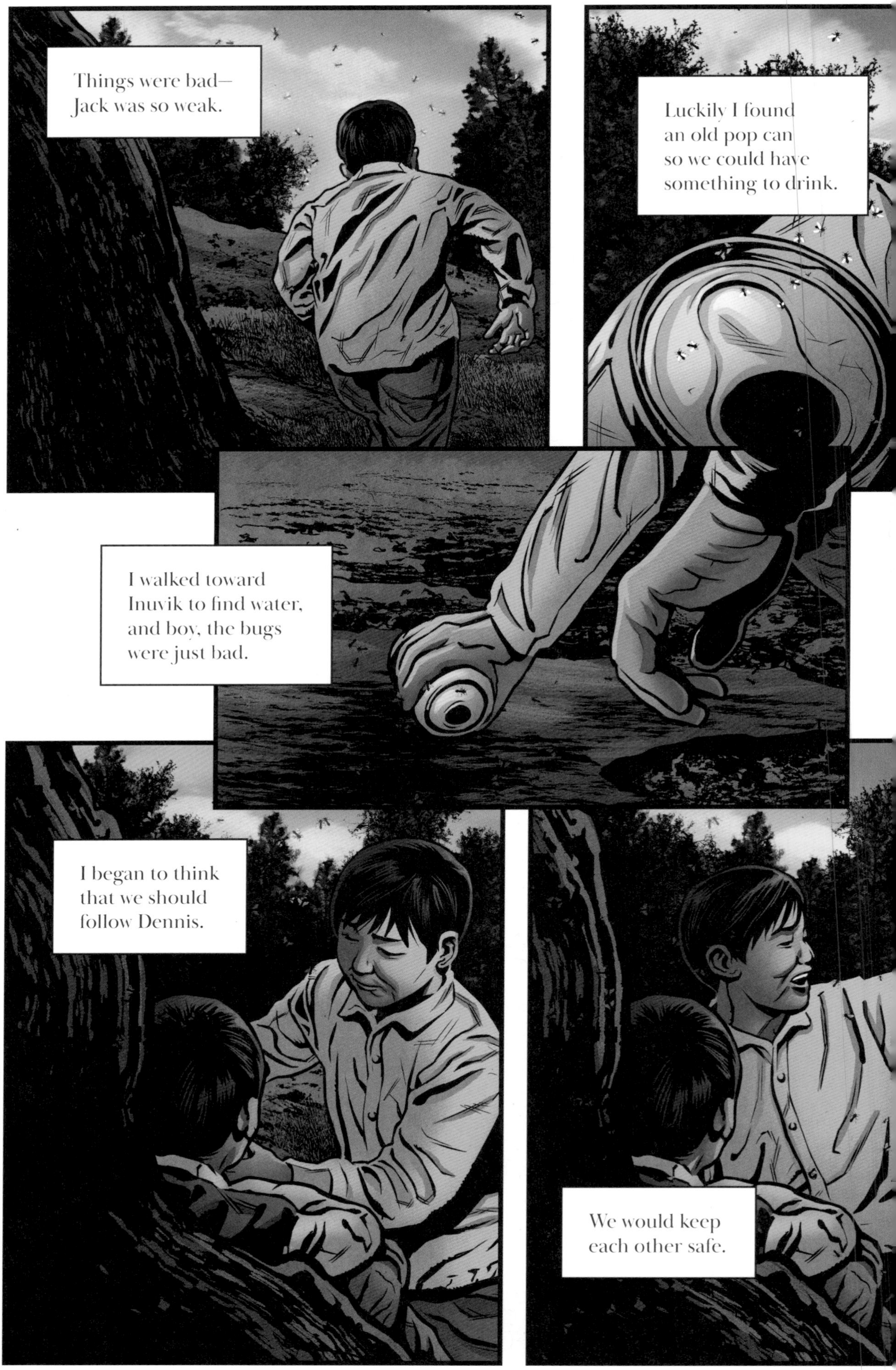
Things were bad—
Jack was so weak.
Luckily I found
an old pop can
so we could have
something to drink.
I walked toward
Inuvik to find water,
and boy, the bugs
were just bad.
I began to think
that we should
follow Dennis.
We would keep
each other safe.

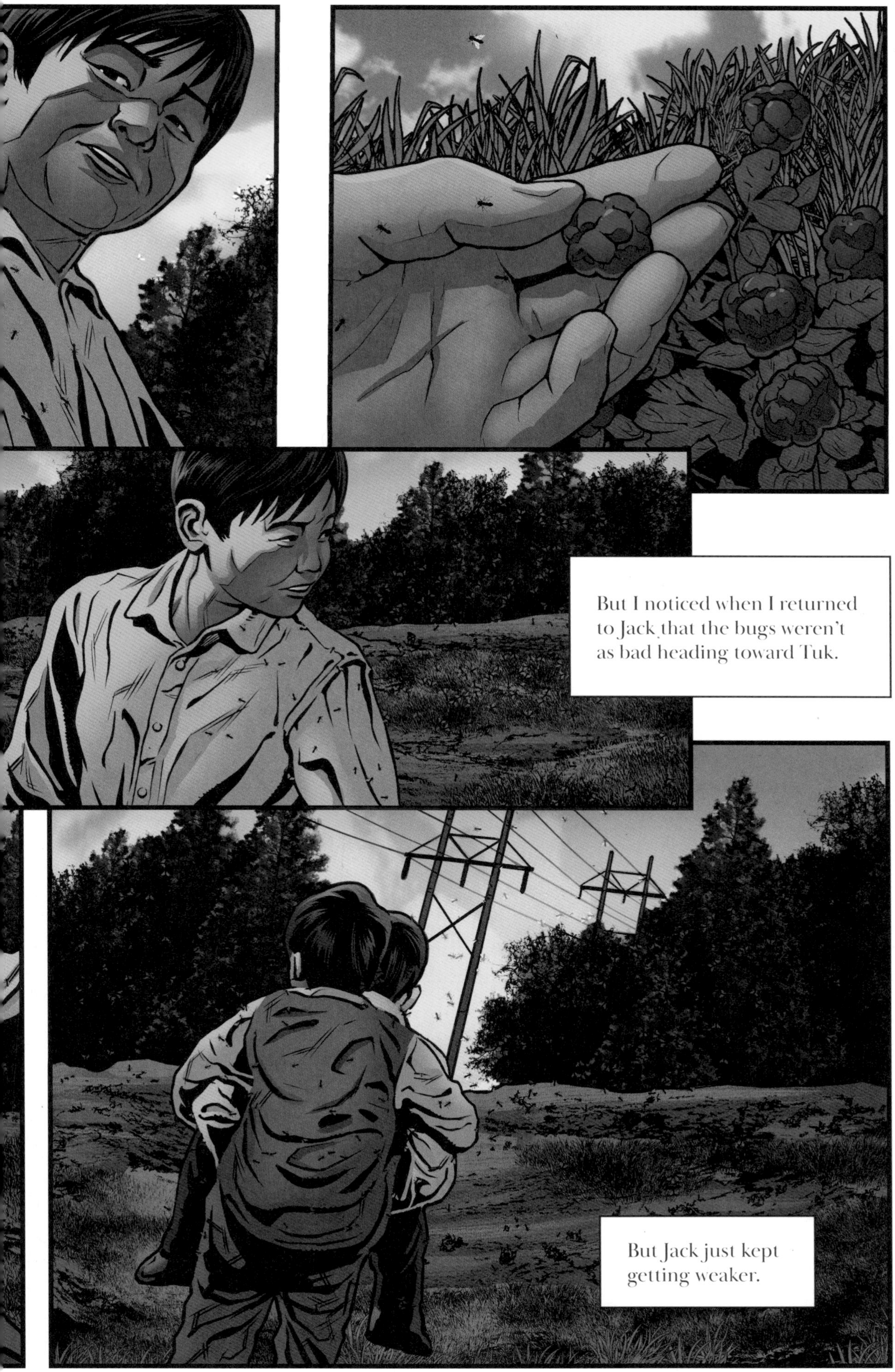
But I noticed when I returned to Jack that the bugs weren't as bad heading toward Tuk.
But Jack just kept getting weaker.

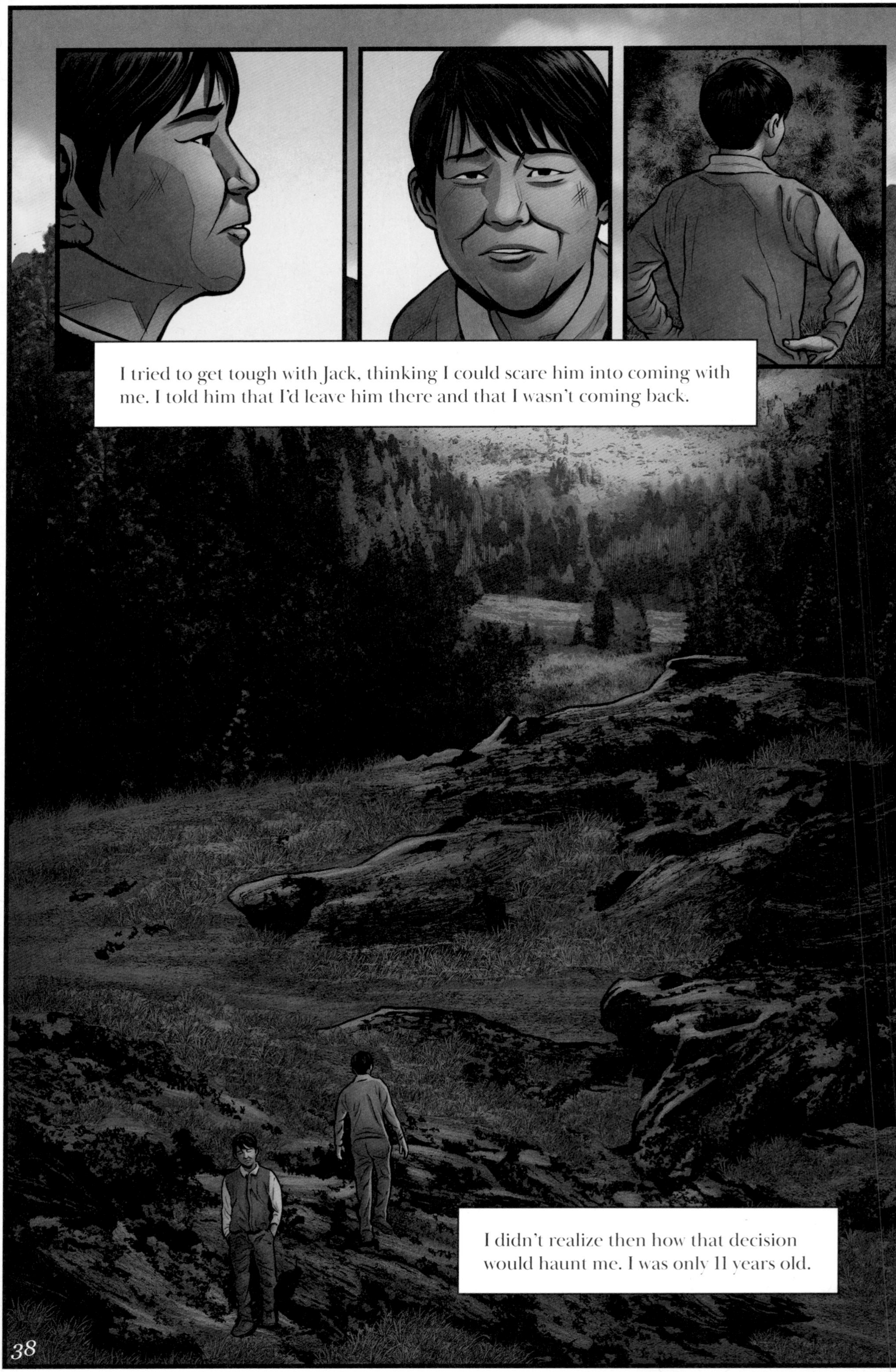
I tried to get tough with Jack, thinking I could scare him into coming with me. I told him that I'd leave him there and that I wasn't coming back.
I didn't realize then how that decision would haunt me. I was only 11 years old.

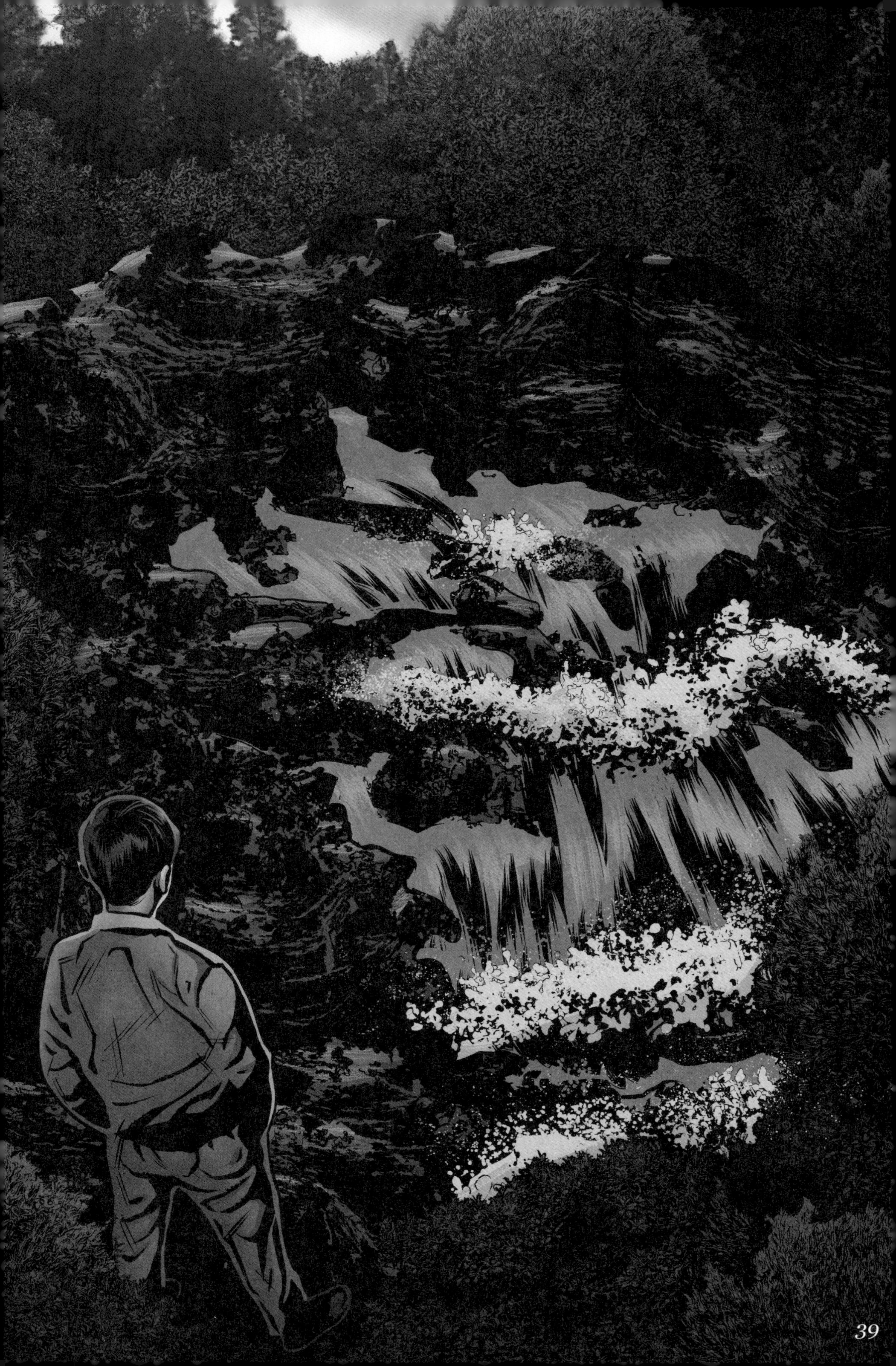

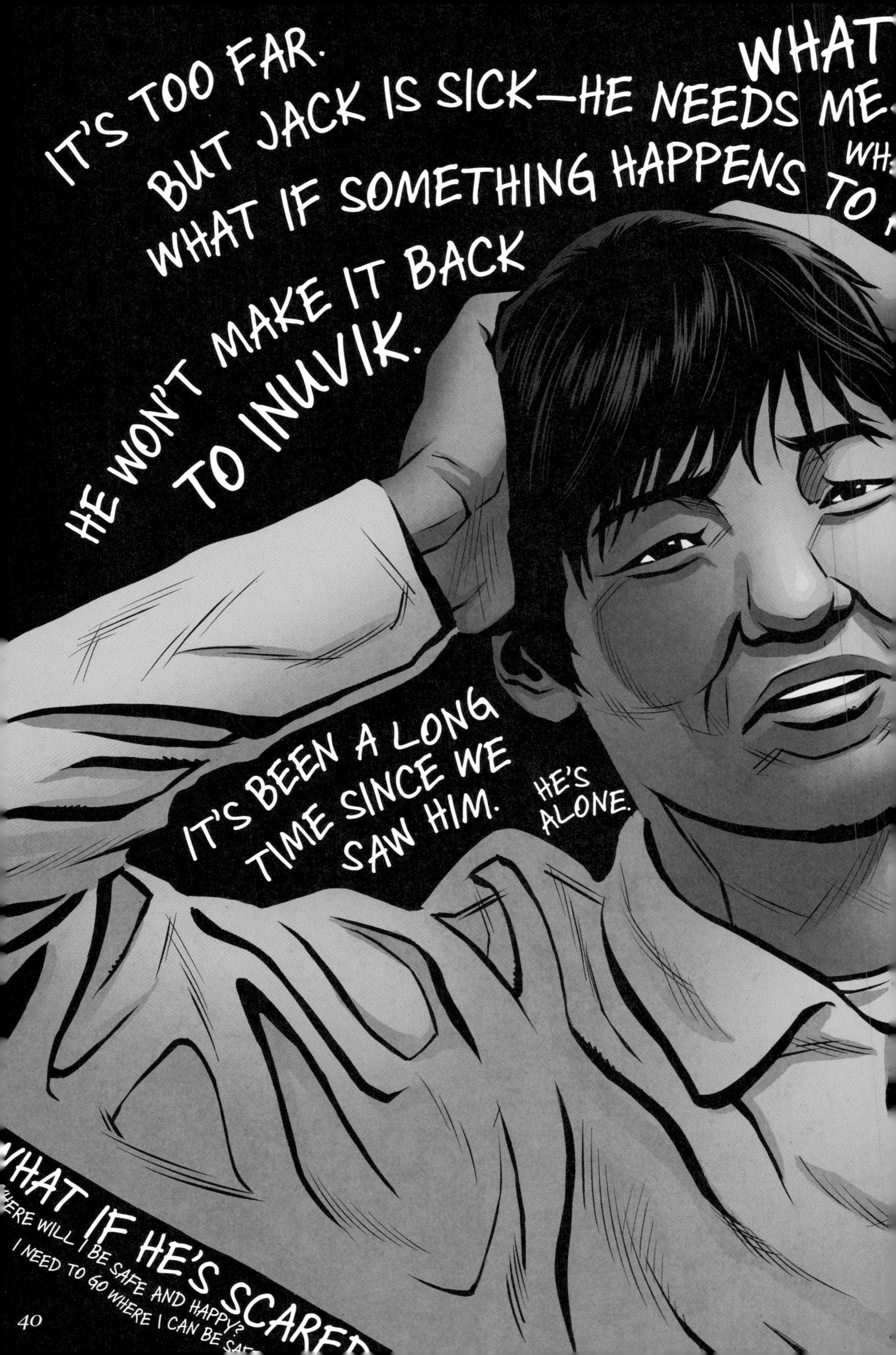
IT'S TOO FAR.
BUT JACK IS SICK—HE NEEDS ME.
WHAT
WHAT IF SOMETHING HAPPENS TO
WHA
HE WON'T MAKE IT BACK TO INUVIK.
IT'S BEEN A LONG TIME SINCE WE SAW HIM.
HE'S ALONE.
HAT IF HE'S SCARED
ERE WILL I BE SAFE AND HAPPY?
I NEED TO GO WHERE I CAN BE

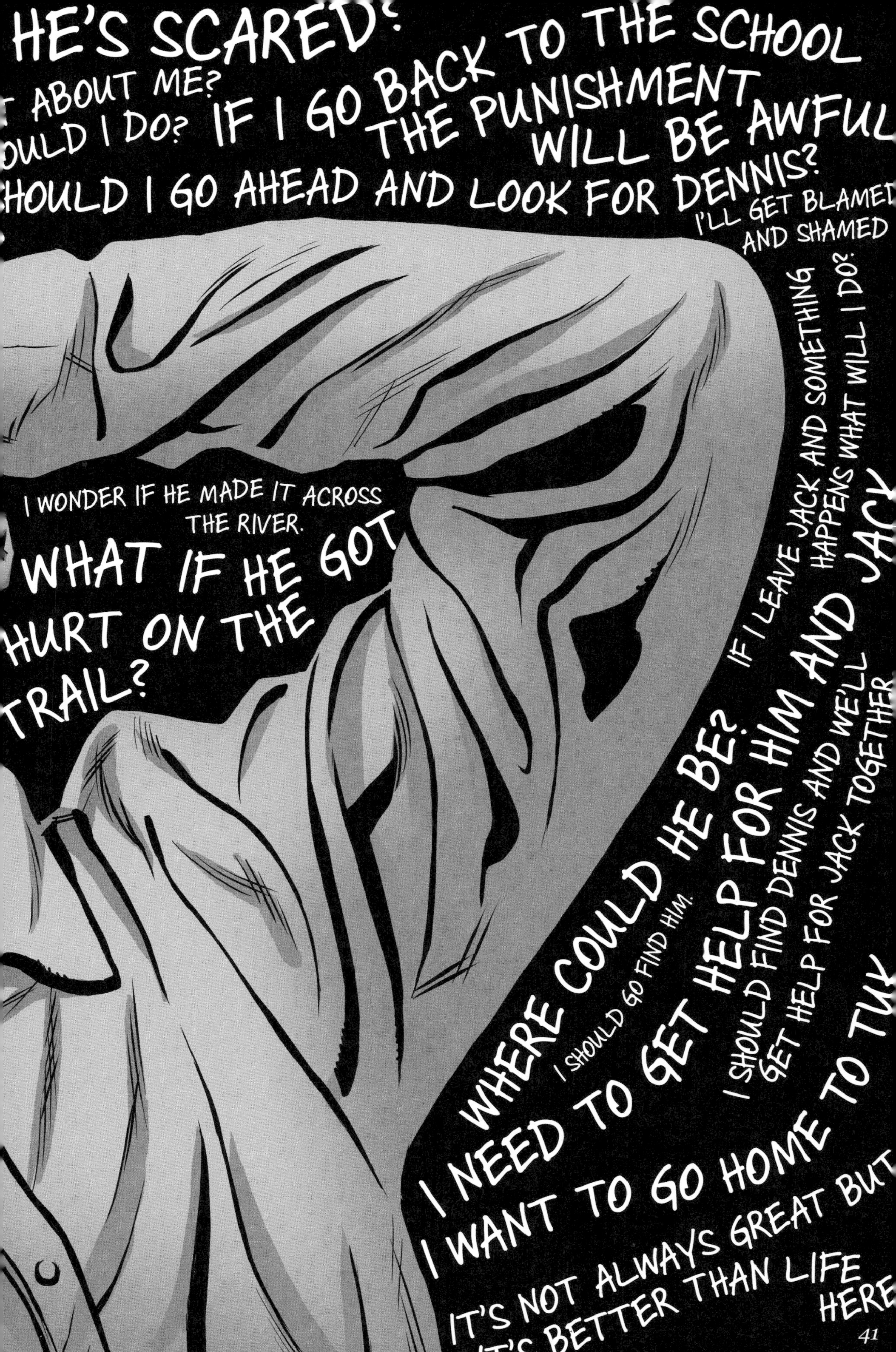

HE'S SCARED?
ABOUT ME?
OULD I DO?
IF I GO BACK TO THE SCHOOL
THE PUNISHMENT
WILL BE AWFUL
HOULD I GO AHEAD AND LOOK FOR DENNIS?
I'LL GET BLAMED
AND SHAMED
IF I LEAVE JACK AND SOMETHING
HAPPENS WHAT WILL I DO?
I WONDER IF HE MADE IT ACROSS
THE RIVER.
WHAT IF HE GOT
HURT ON THE
TRAIL?
WHERE COULD HE BE?
I SHOULD GO FIND HIM.
I NEED TO GET HELP FOR HIM AND JACK
I SHOULD FIND DENNIS AND WE'LL
GET HELP FOR JACK TOGETHER
I WANT TO GO HOME TO TUK
IT'S NOT ALWAYS GREAT BUT
IT'S BETTER THAN LIFE
HERE

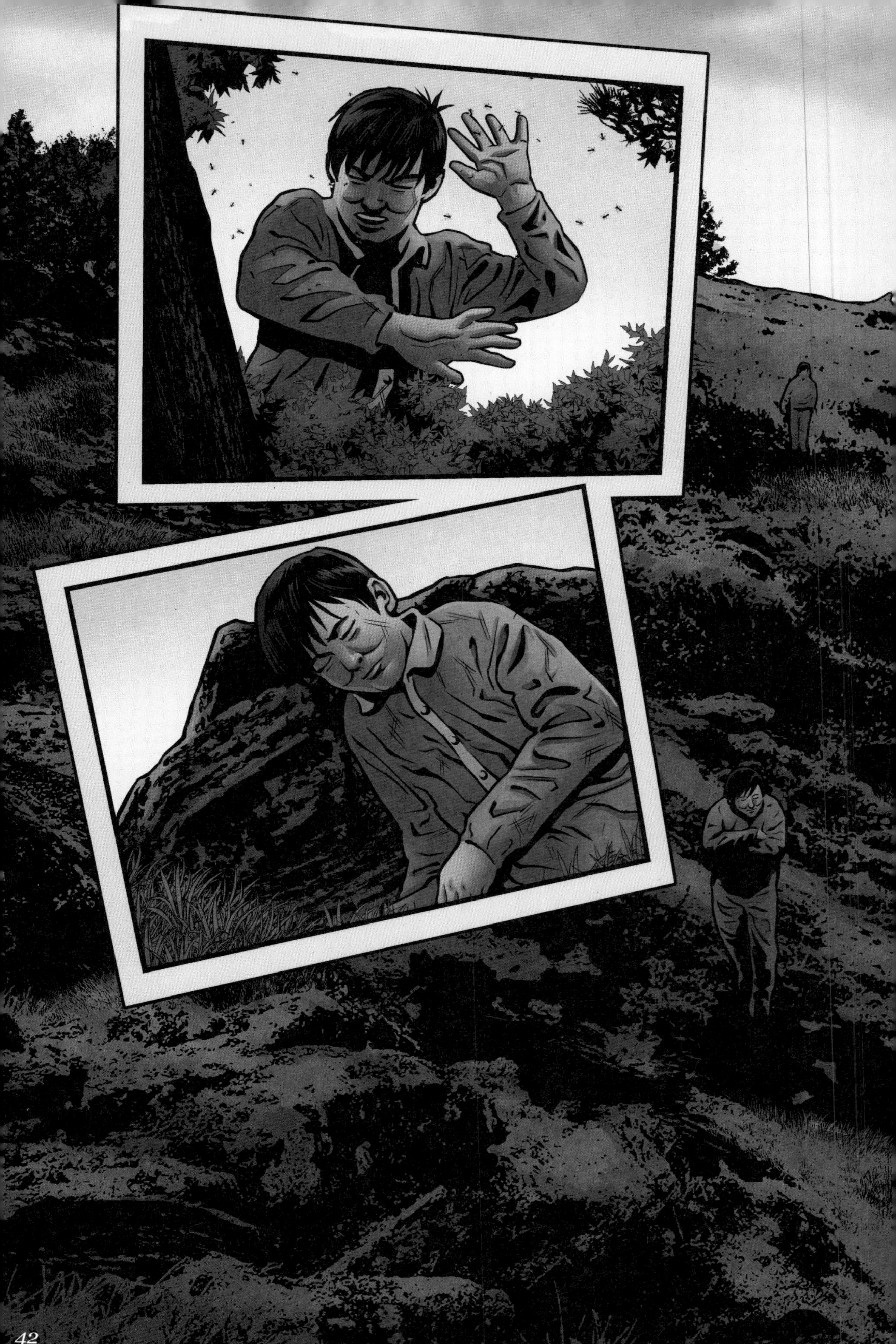

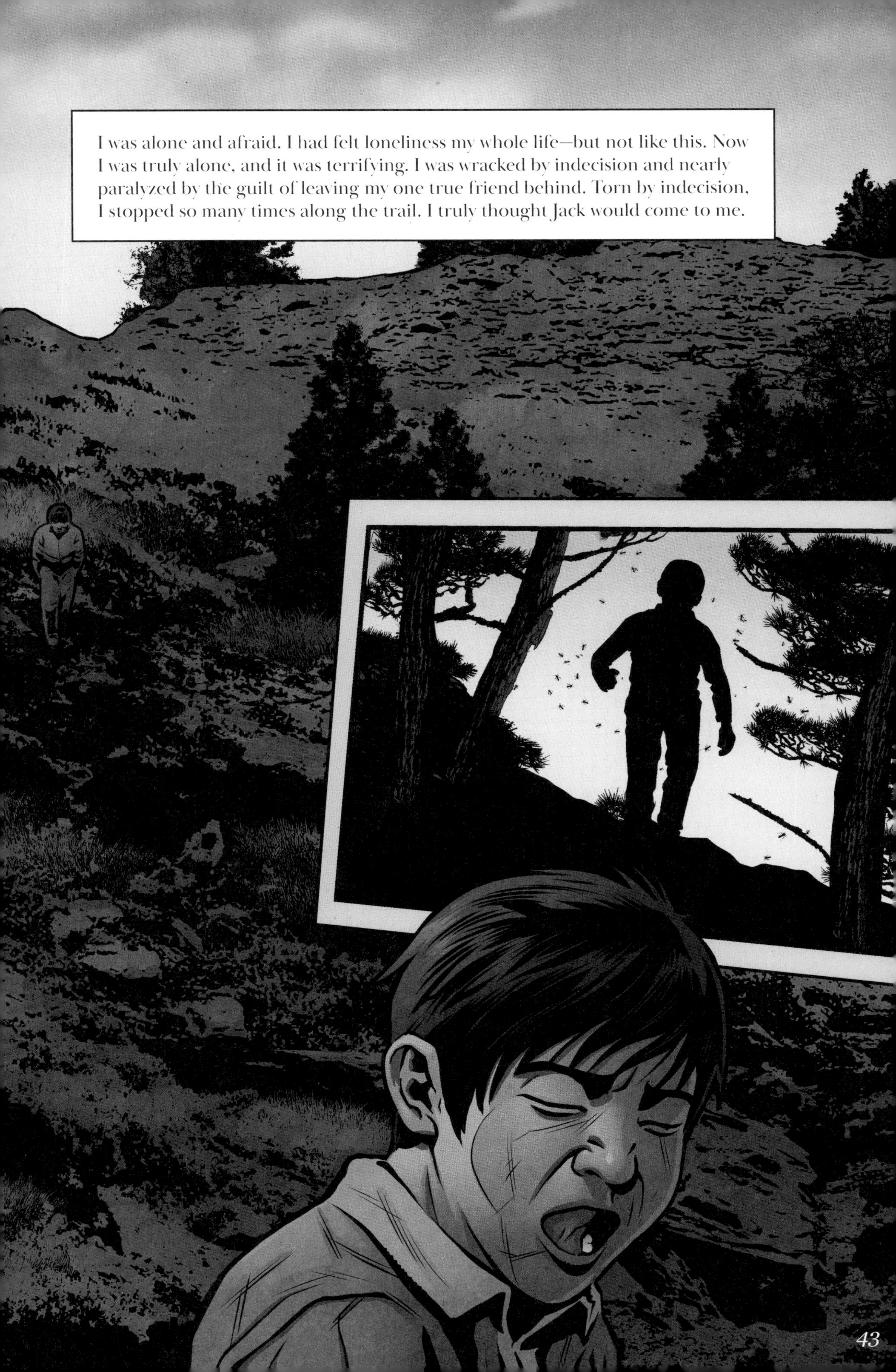
I was alone and afraid. I had felt loneliness my whole life—but not like this. Now I was truly alone, and it was terrifying. I was wracked by indecision and nearly paralyzed by the guilt of leaving my one true friend behind. Torn by indecision, I stopped so many times along the trail. I truly thought Jack would come to me.

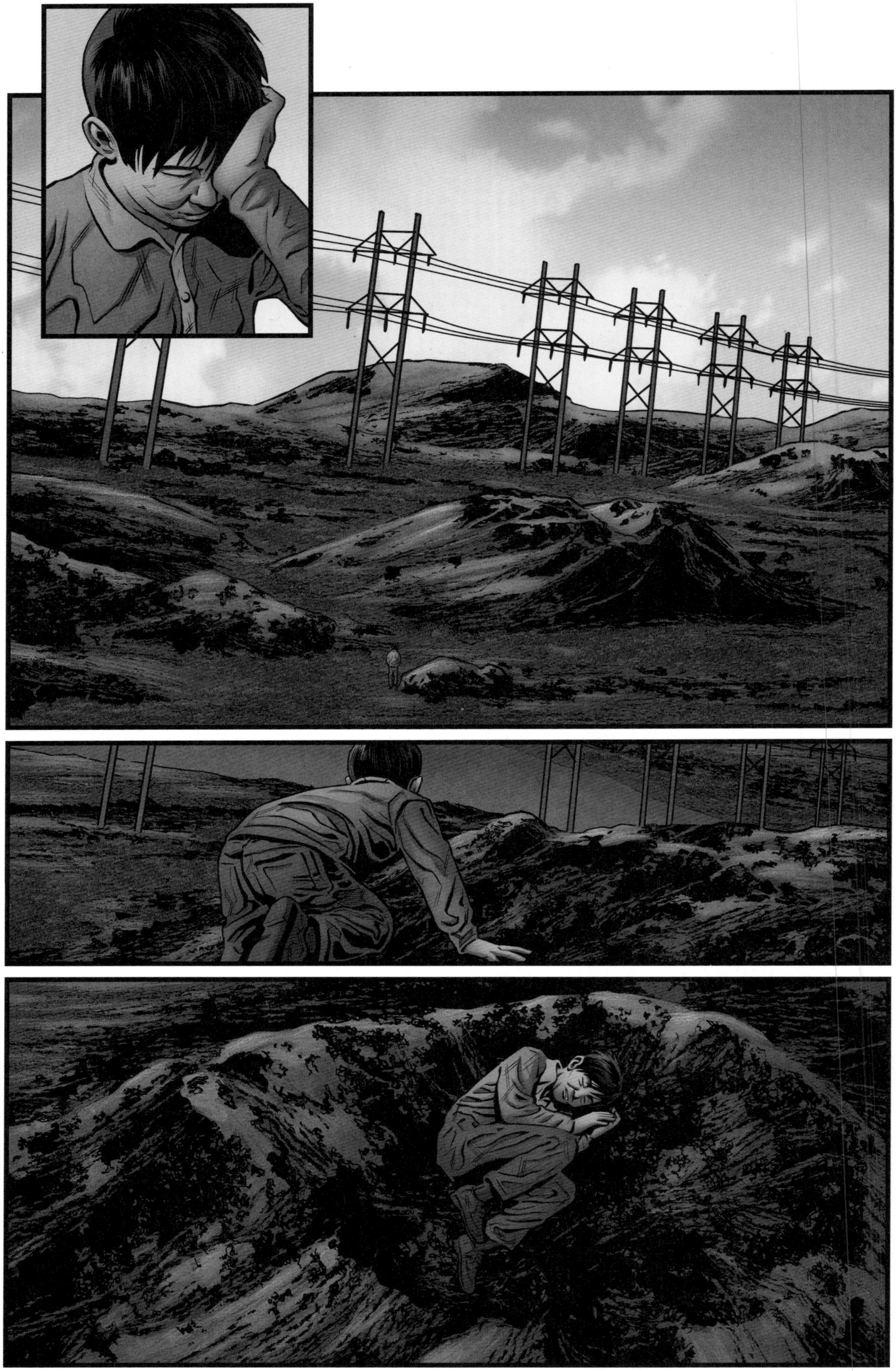

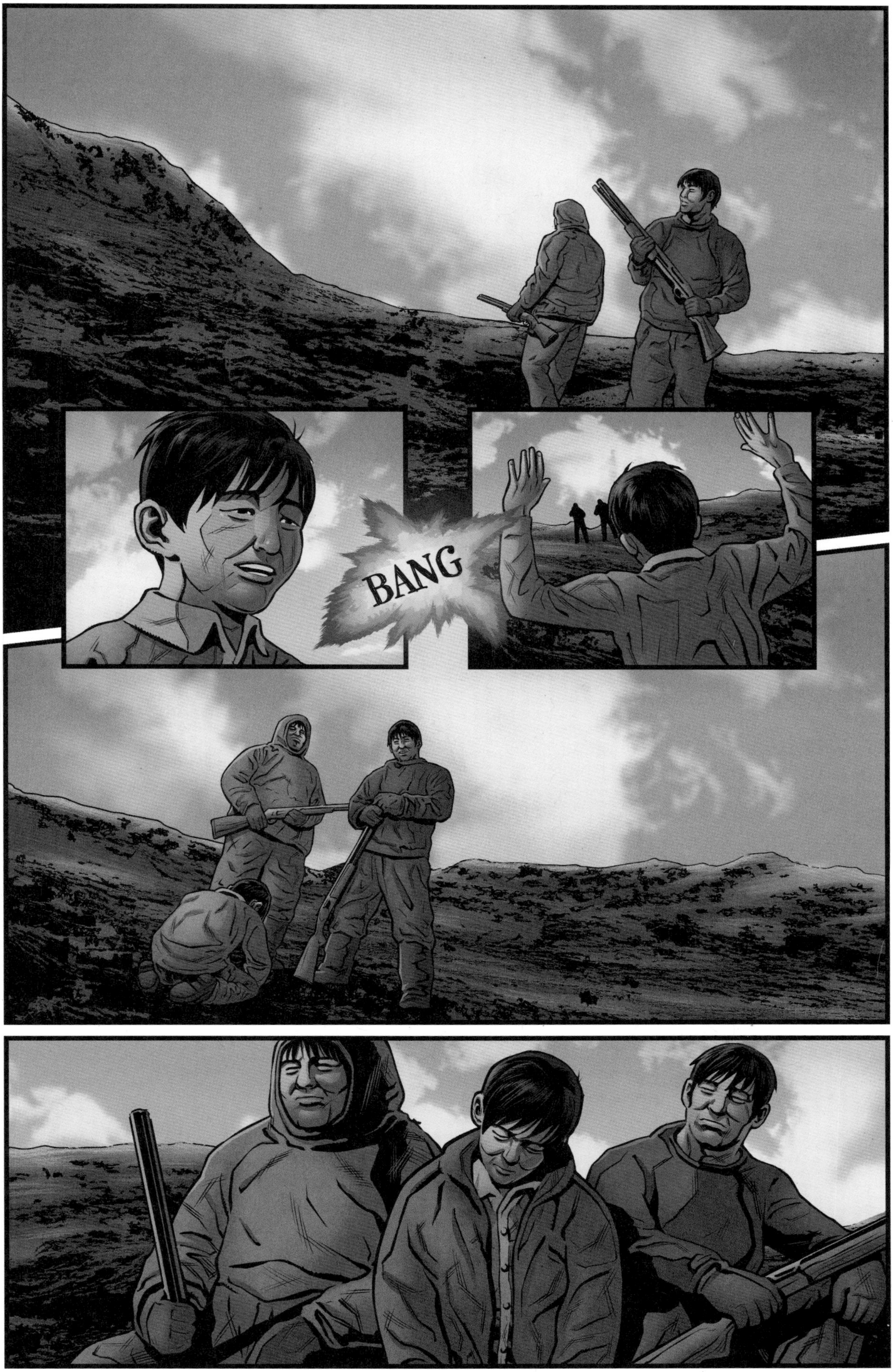
BANG

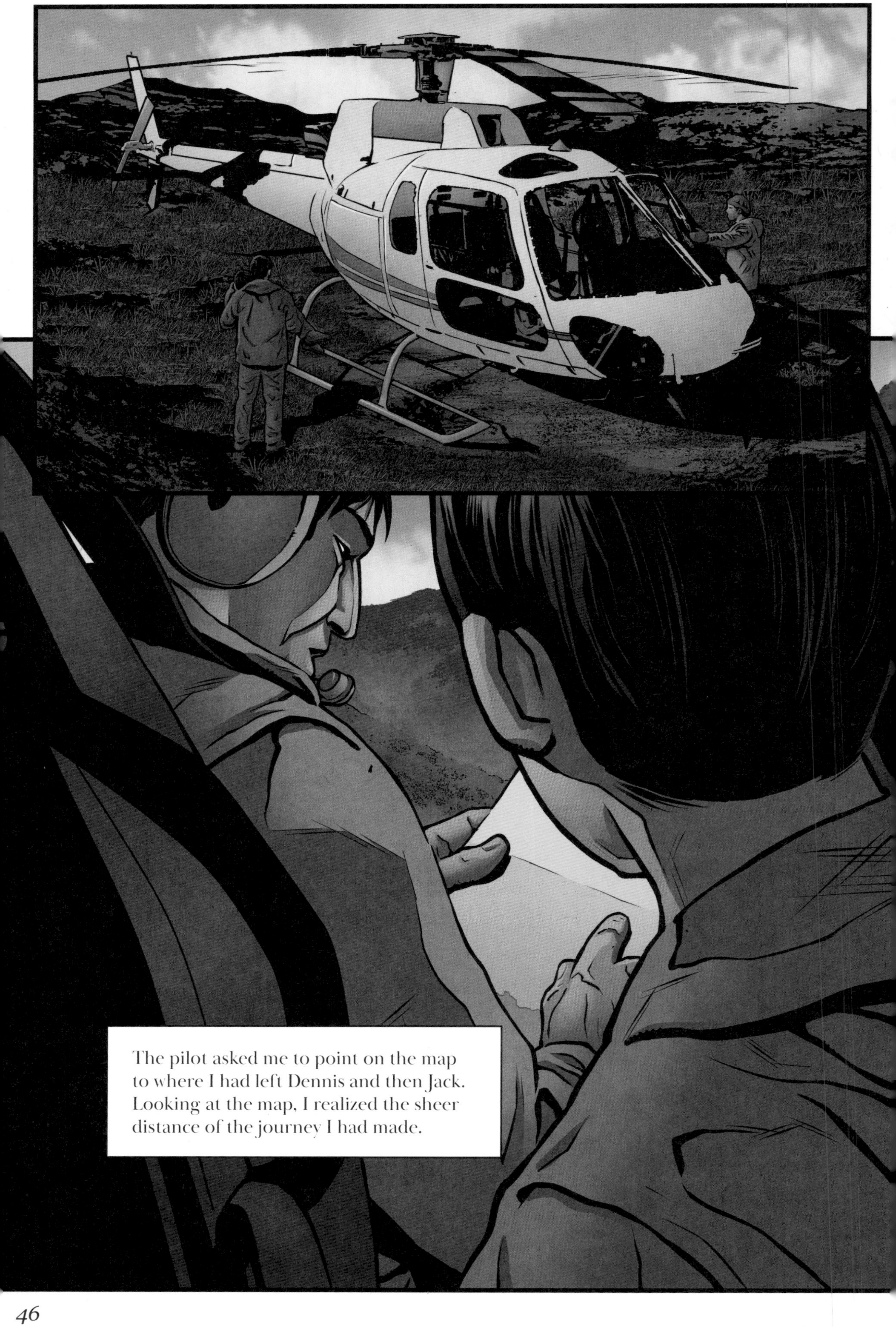
The pilot asked me to point on the map to where I had left Dennis and then Jack. Looking at the map, I realized the sheer distance of the journey I had made.

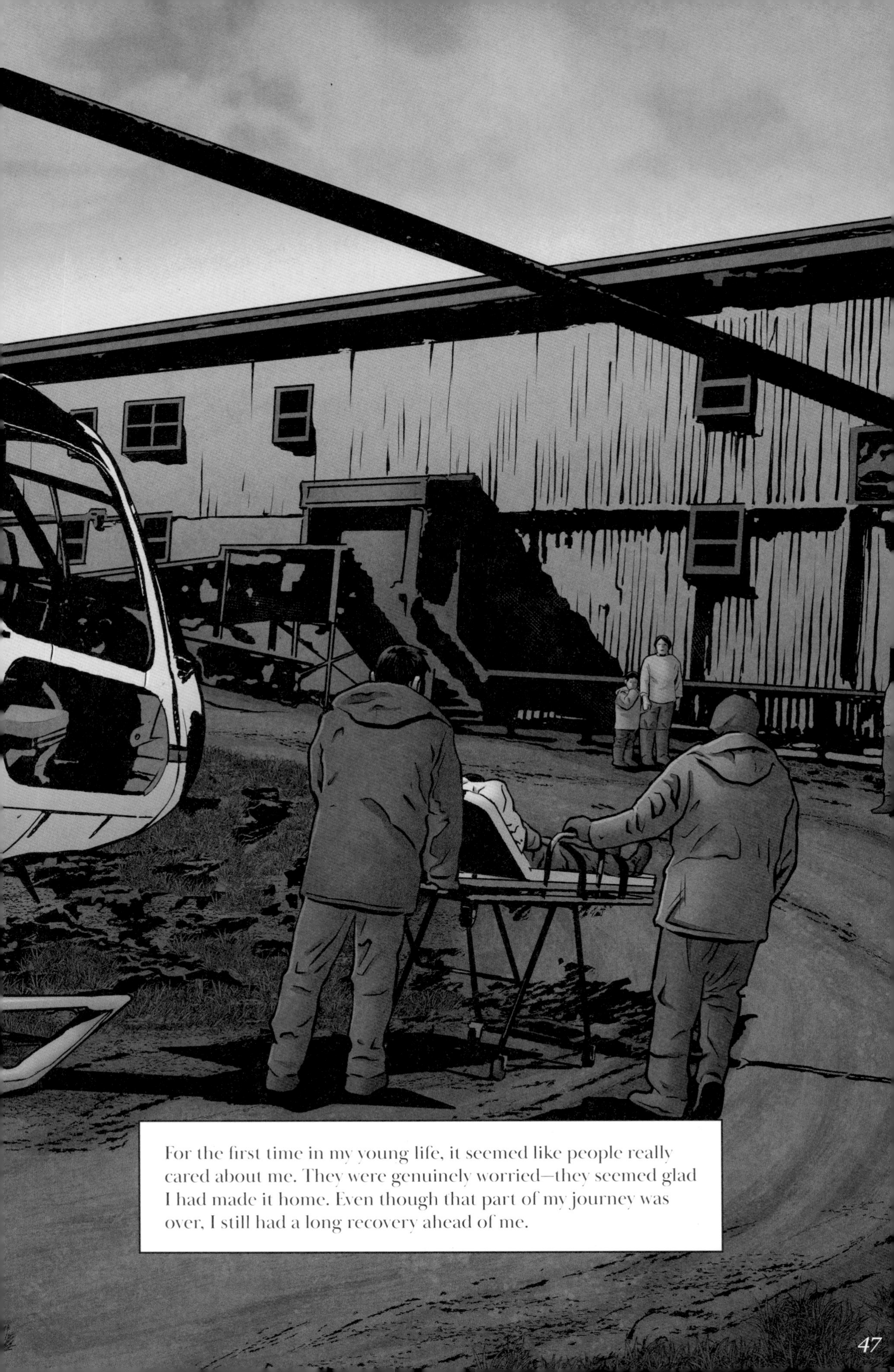
For the first time in my young life, it seemed like people really cared about me. They were genuinely worried—they seemed glad I had made it home. Even though that part of my journey was over, I still had a long recovery ahead of me.

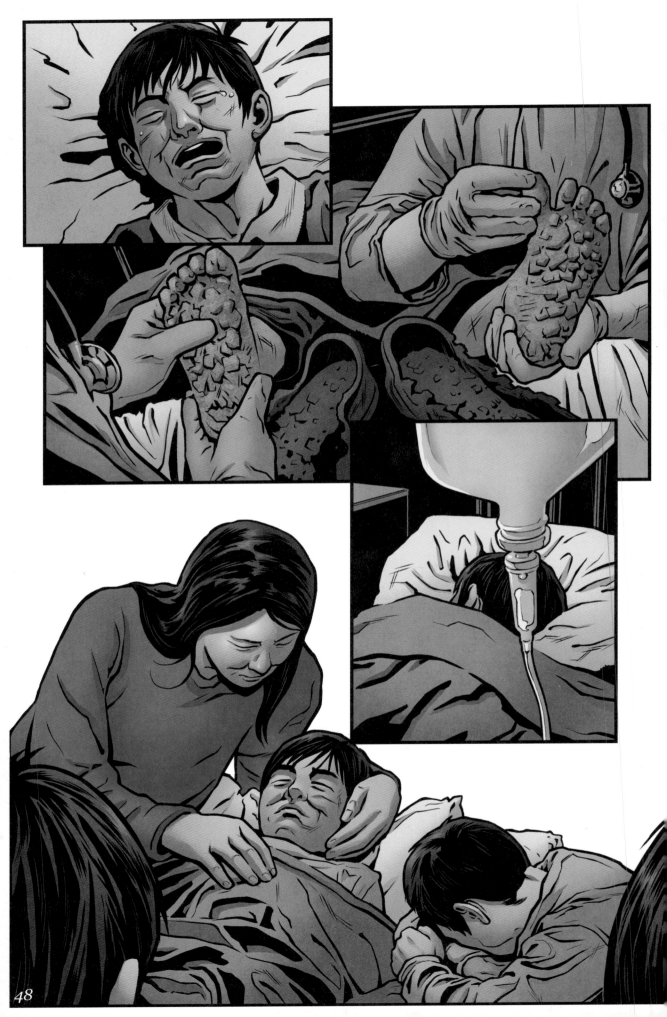

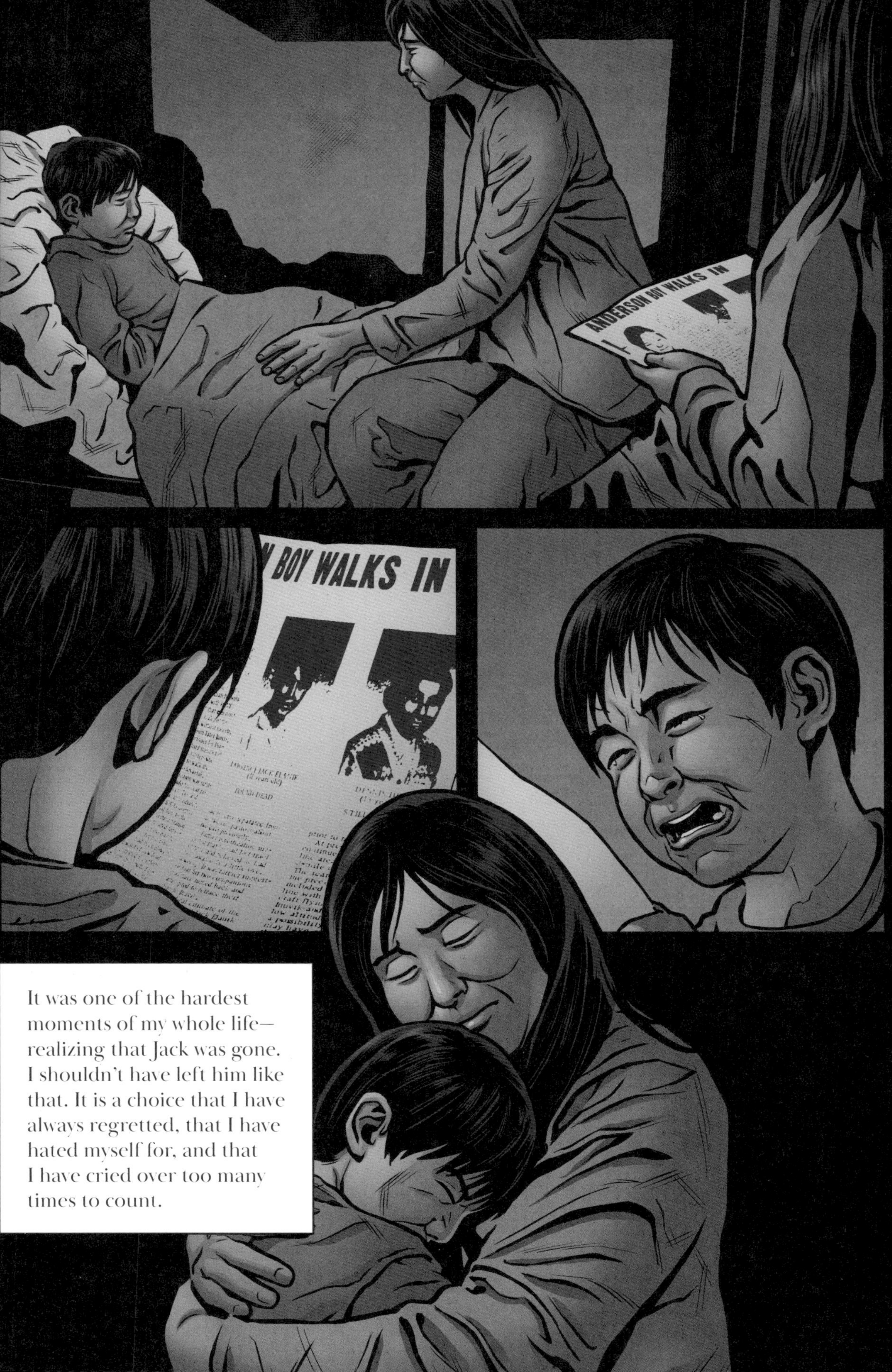
ANDERSON BOY WALKS IN
N BOY WALKS IN
It was one of the hardest moments of my whole life—realizing that Jack was gone. I shouldn't have left him like that. It is a choice that I have always regretted, that I have hated myself for, and that I have cried over too many times to count.

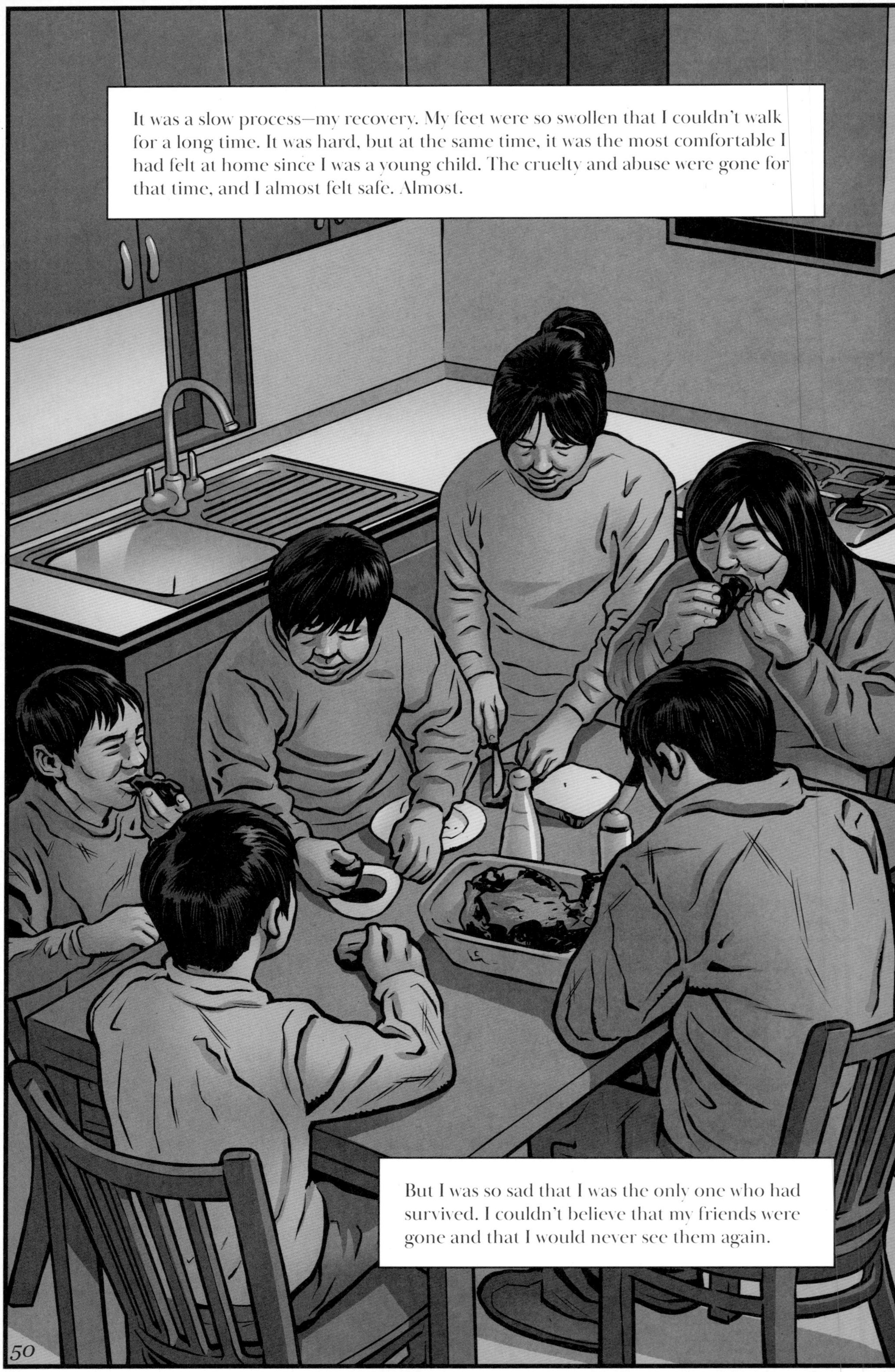
It was a slow process—my recovery. My feet were so swollen that I couldn't walk for a long time. It was hard, but at the same time, it was the most comfortable I had felt at home since I was a young child. The cruelty and abuse were gone for that time, and I almost felt safe. Almost.
But I was so sad that I was the only one who had survived. I couldn't believe that my friends were gone and that I would never see them again.

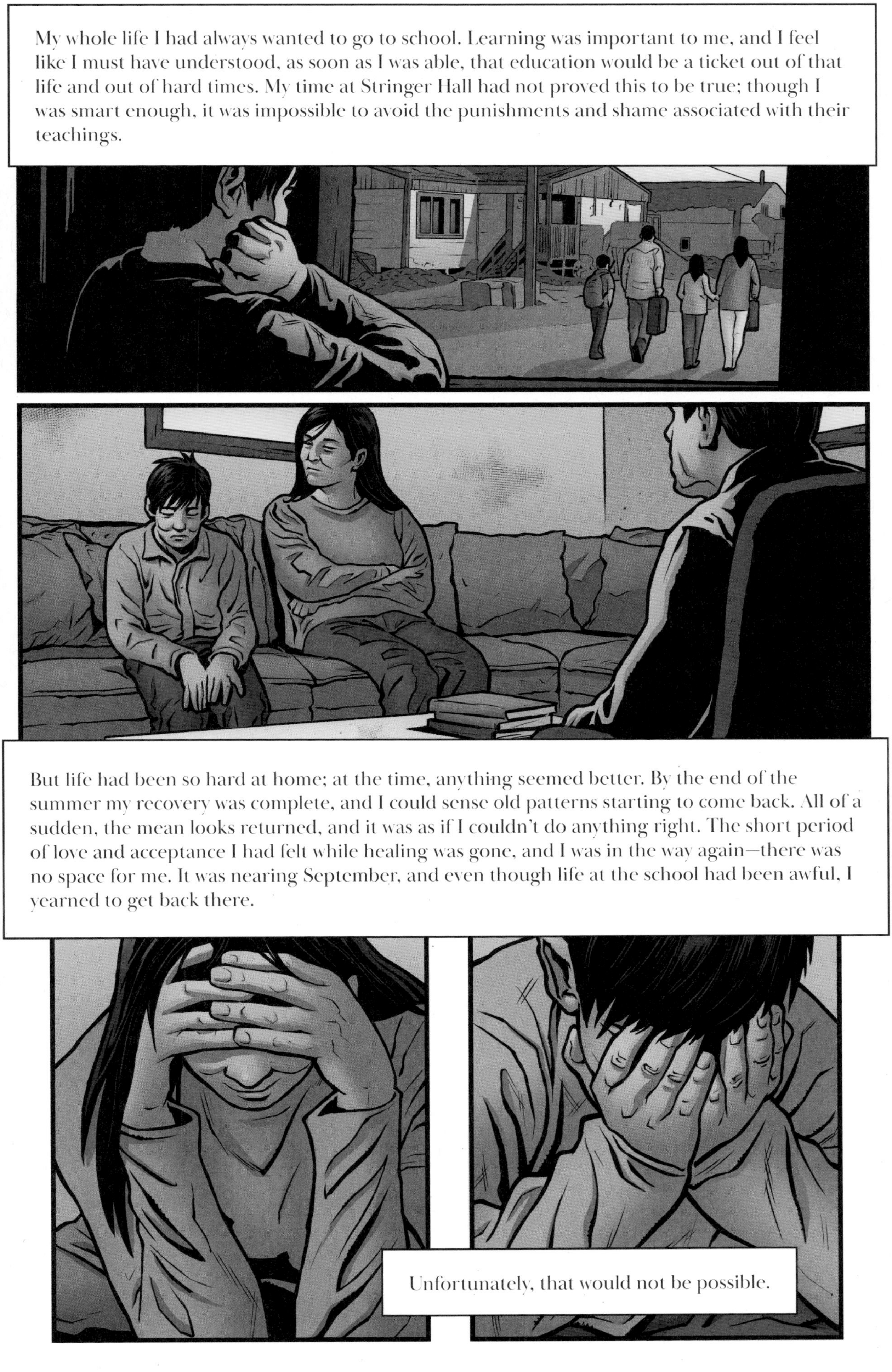
My whole life I had always wanted to go to school. Learning was important to me, and I feel like I must have understood, as soon as I was able, that education would be a ticket out of that life and out of hard times. My time at Stringer Hall had not proved this to be true; though I was smart enough, it was impossible to avoid the punishments and shame associated with their teachings.
But life had been so hard at home; at the time, anything seemed better. By the end of the summer my recovery was complete, and I could sense old patterns starting to come back. All of a sudden, the mean looks returned, and it was as if I couldn't do anything right. The short period of love and acceptance I had felt while healing was gone, and I was in the way again—there was no space for me. It was nearing September, and even though life at the school had been awful, I yearned to get back there.
Unfortunately, that would not be possible.

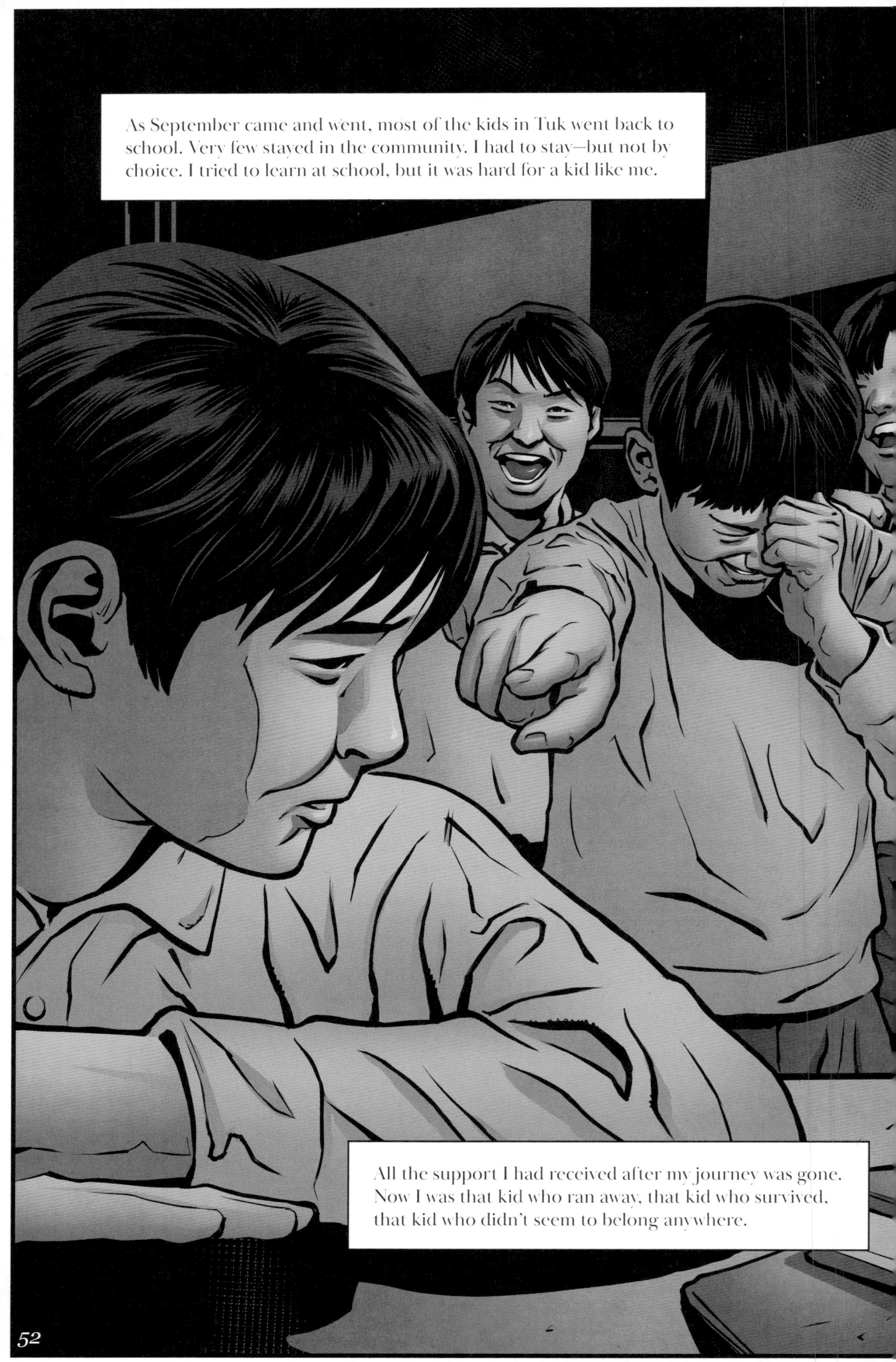
As September came and went, most of the kids in Tuk went back to school. Very few stayed in the community. I had to stay—but not by choice. I tried to learn at school, but it was hard for a kid like me.
All the support I had received after my journey was gone. Now I was that kid who ran away, that kid who survived, that kid who didn't seem to belong anywhere.

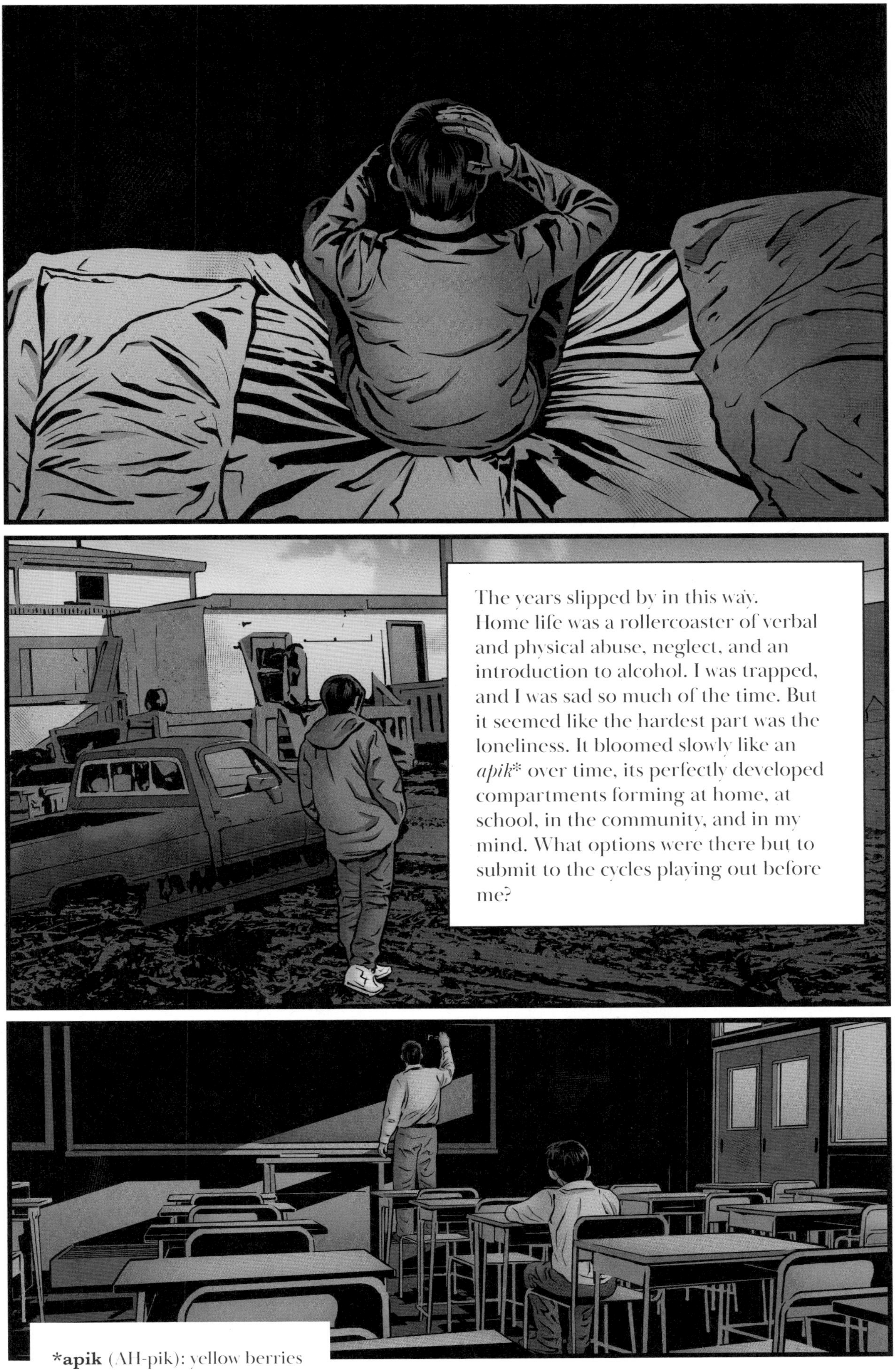
The years slipped by in this way. Home life was a rollercoaster of verbal and physical abuse, neglect, and an introduction to alcohol. I was trapped, and I was sad so much of the time. But it seemed like the hardest part was the loneliness. It bloomed slowly like an *apik** over time, its perfectly developed compartments forming at home, at school, in the community, and in my mind. What options were there but to submit to the cycles playing out before me?
***apik** (AH-pik): yellow berries

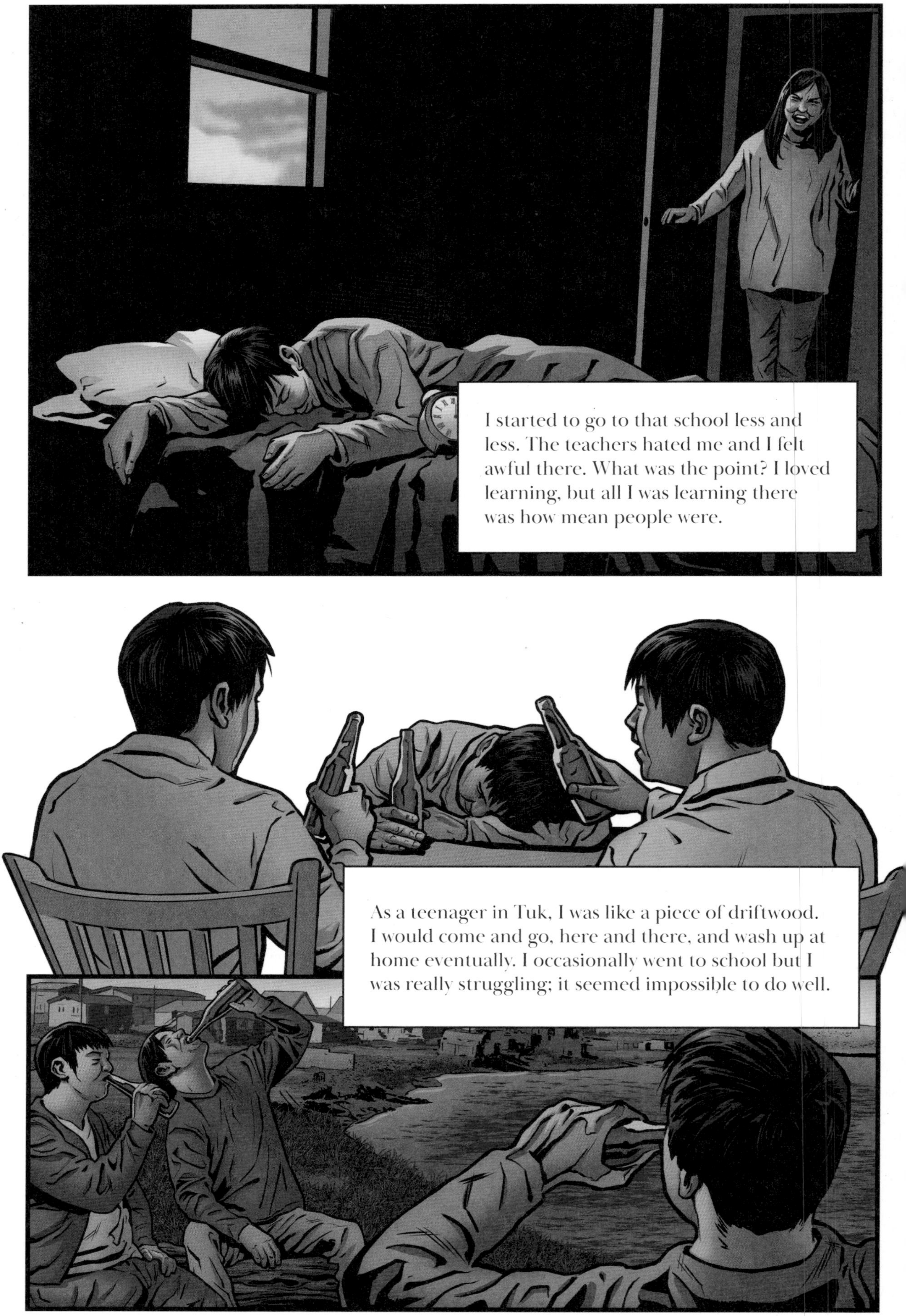
I started to go to that school less and less. The teachers hated me and I felt awful there. What was the point? I loved learning, but all I was learning there was how mean people were.
As a teenager in Tuk, I was like a piece of driftwood. I would come and go, here and there, and wash up at home eventually. I occasionally went to school but I was really struggling; it seemed impossible to do well.

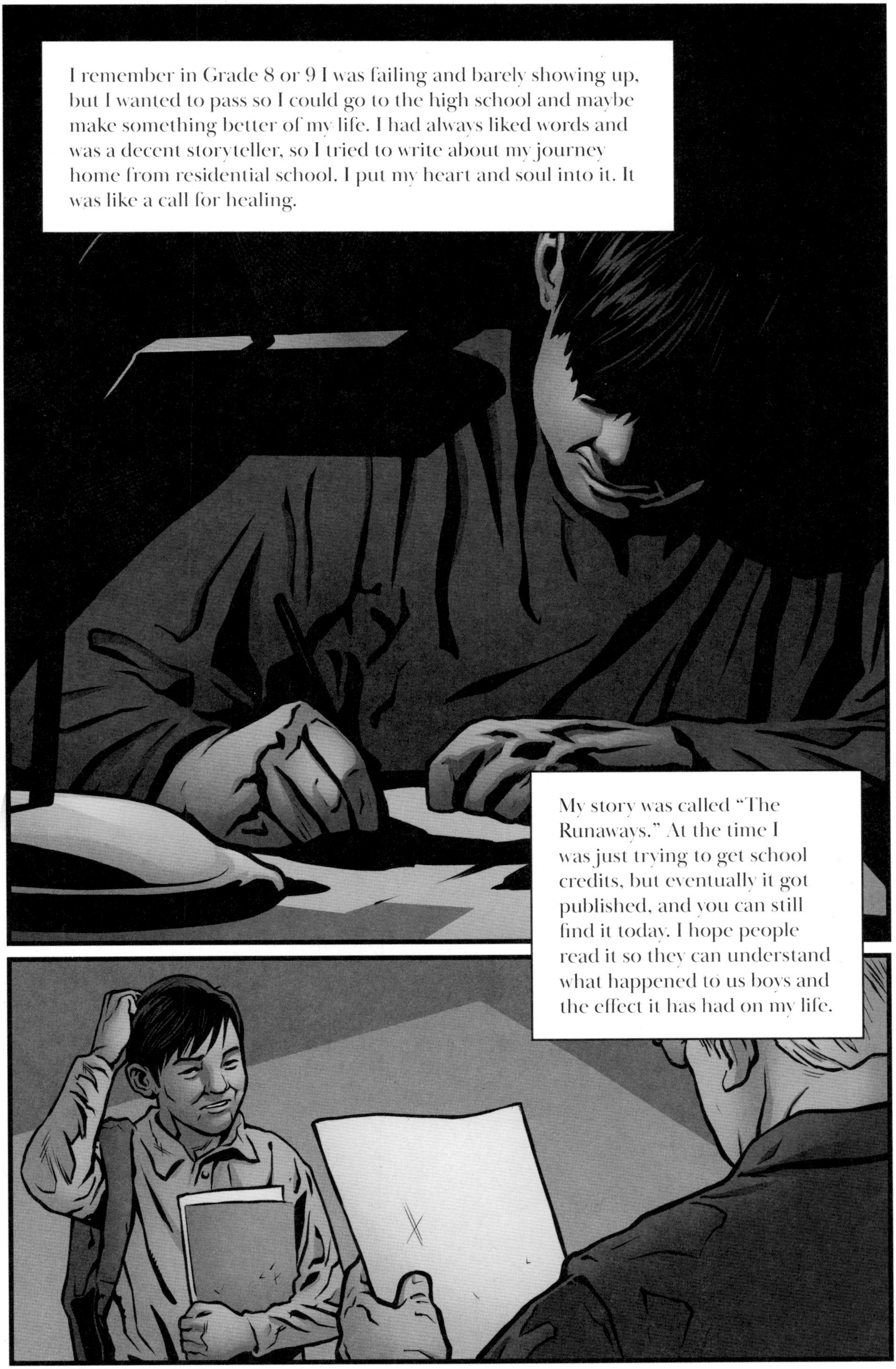
I remember in Grade 8 or 9 I was failing and barely showing up, but I wanted to pass so I could go to the high school and maybe make something better of my life. I had always liked words and was a decent storyteller, so I tried to write about my journey home from residential school. I put my heart and soul into it. It was like a call for healing.
My story was called "The Runaways." At the time I was just trying to get school credits, but eventually it got published, and you can still find it today. I hope people read it so they can understand what happened to us boys and the effect it has had on my life.

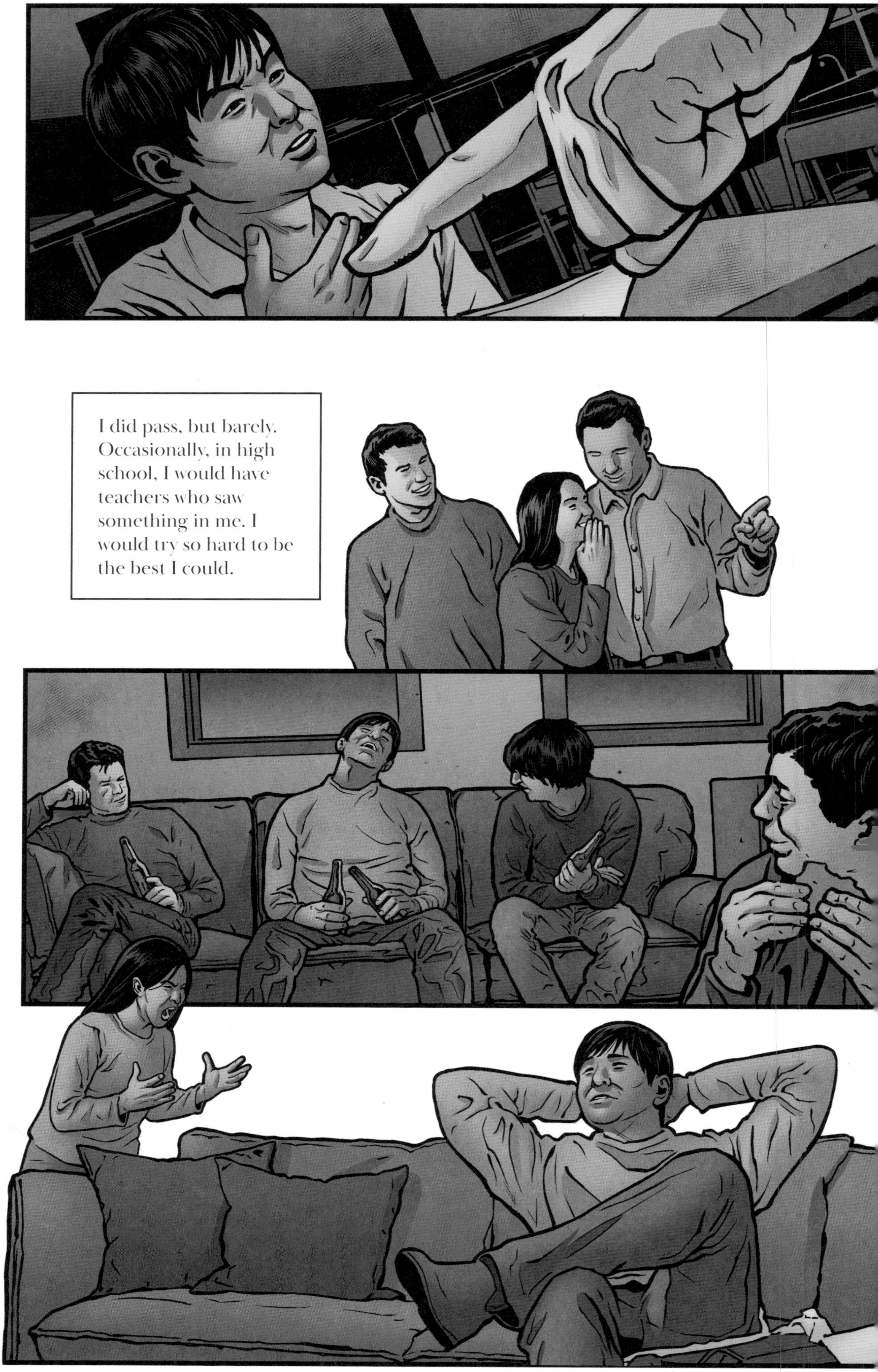
I did pass, but barely. Occasionally, in high school, I would have teachers who saw something in me. I would try so hard to be the best I could.

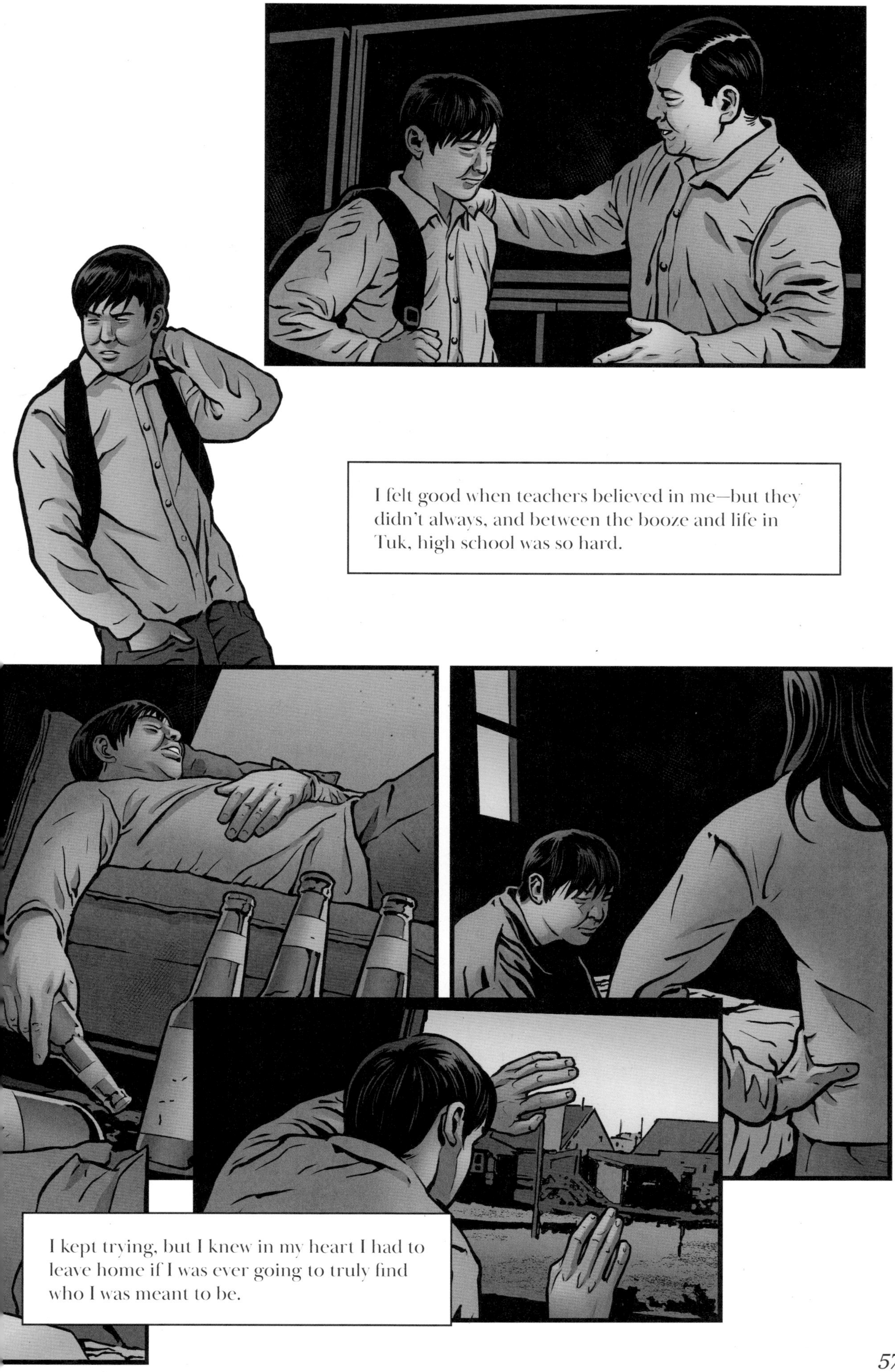
I felt good when teachers believed in me—but they didn't always, and between the booze and life in Tuk, high school was so hard.
I kept trying, but I knew in my heart I had to leave home if I was ever going to truly find who I was meant to be.

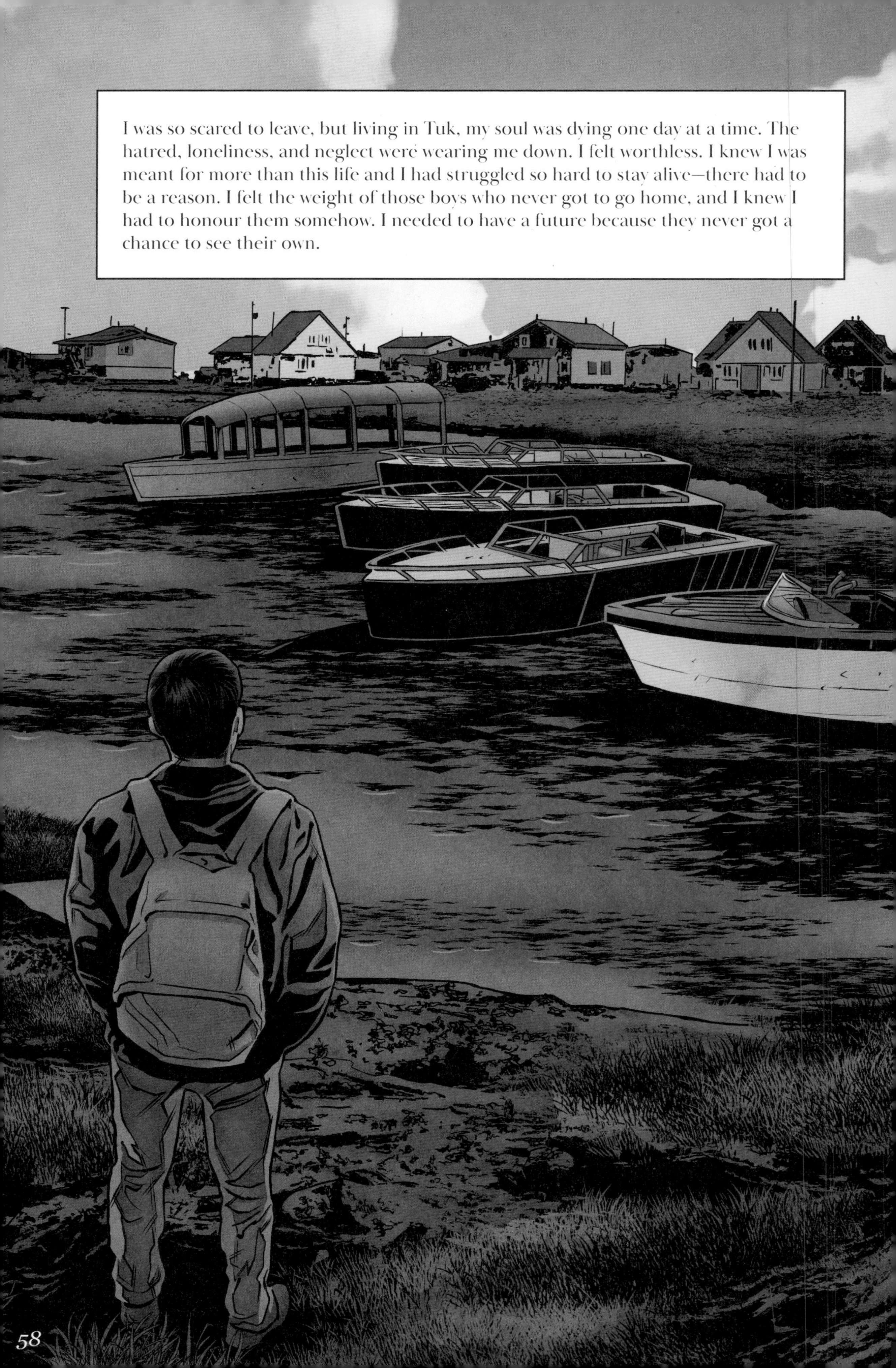
I was so scared to leave, but living in Tuk, my soul was dying one day at a time. The hatred, loneliness, and neglect were wearing me down. I felt worthless. I knew I was meant for more than this life and I had struggled so hard to stay alive—there had to be a reason. I felt the weight of those boys who never got to go home, and I knew I had to honour them somehow. I needed to have a future because they never got a chance to see their own.

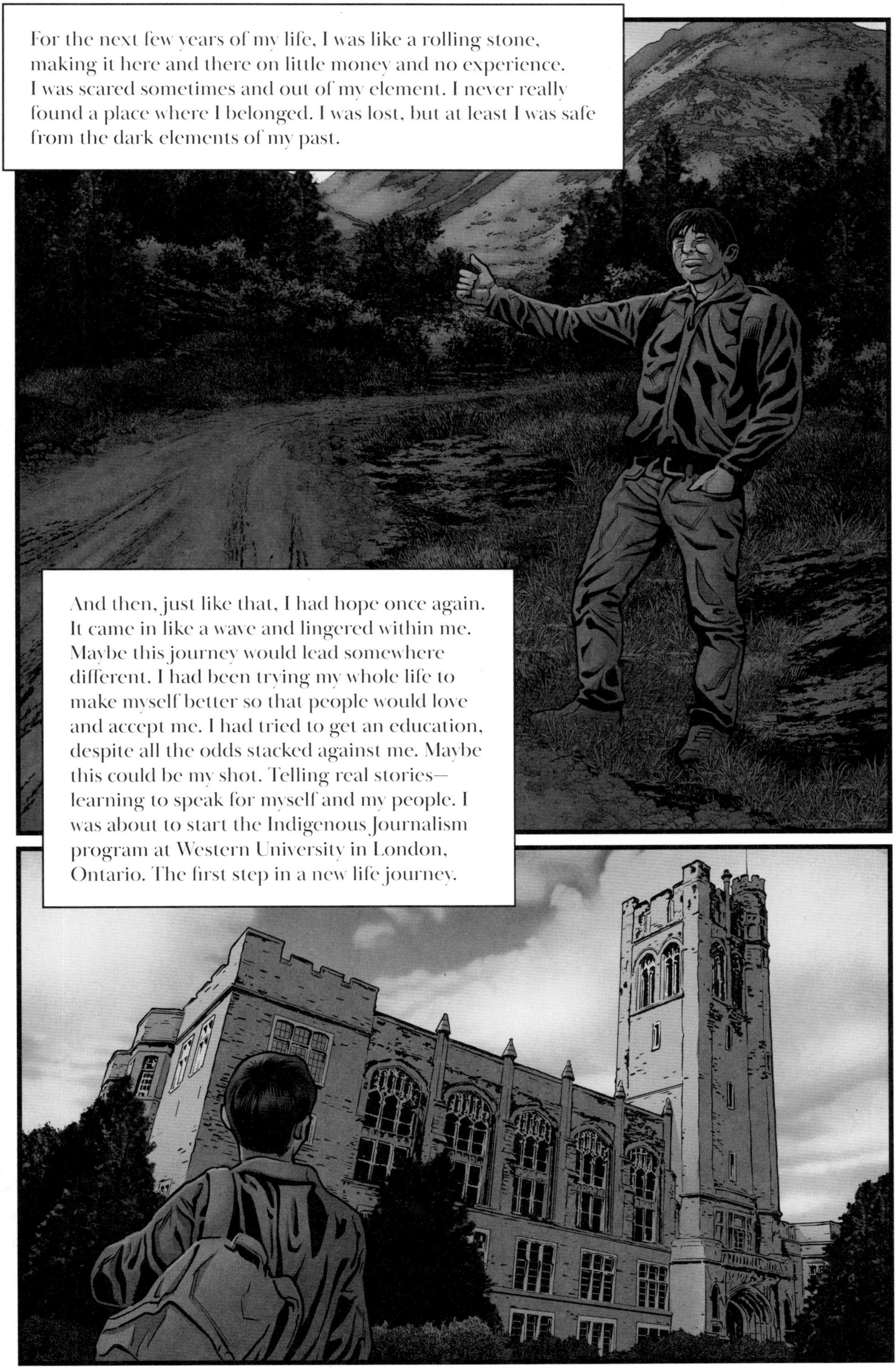
For the next few years of my life, I was like a rolling stone, making it here and there on little money and no experience. I was scared sometimes and out of my element. I never really found a place where I belonged. I was lost, but at least I was safe from the dark elements of my past.
And then, just like that, I had hope once again. It came in like a wave and lingered within me. Maybe this journey would lead somewhere different. I had been trying my whole life to make myself better so that people would love and accept me. I had tried to get an education, despite all the odds stacked against me. Maybe this could be my shot. Telling real stories—learning to speak for myself and my people. I was about to start the Indigenous Journalism program at Western University in London, Ontario. The first step in a new life journey.

Life was good in London. I felt safe there. For the first time, I felt welcomed and accepted. I was anonymous—no family ties, no history, no abuse. I found people who seemed to like me and want me around. I fell in with a group of students from the Six Nations Reserve. I liked them. They taught me about Iroquois culture, and I taught them about being Inuvialuit. The reciprocity of sharing knowledge reminded me of my community, and I felt accepted by them.

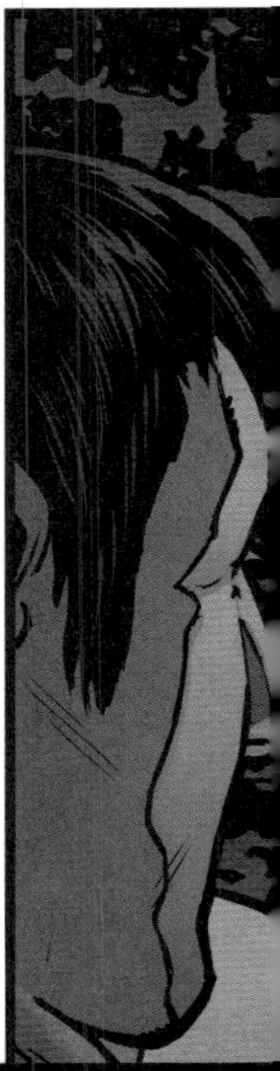

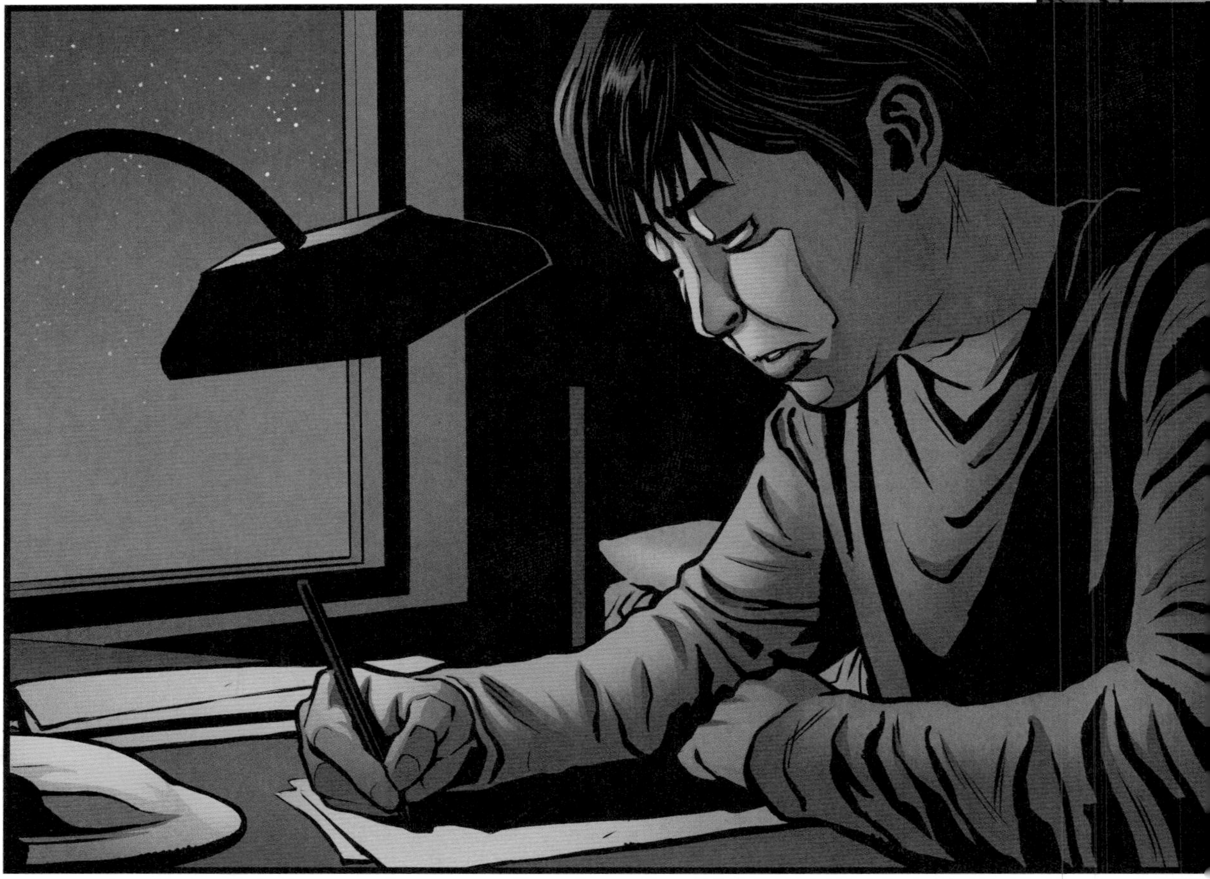

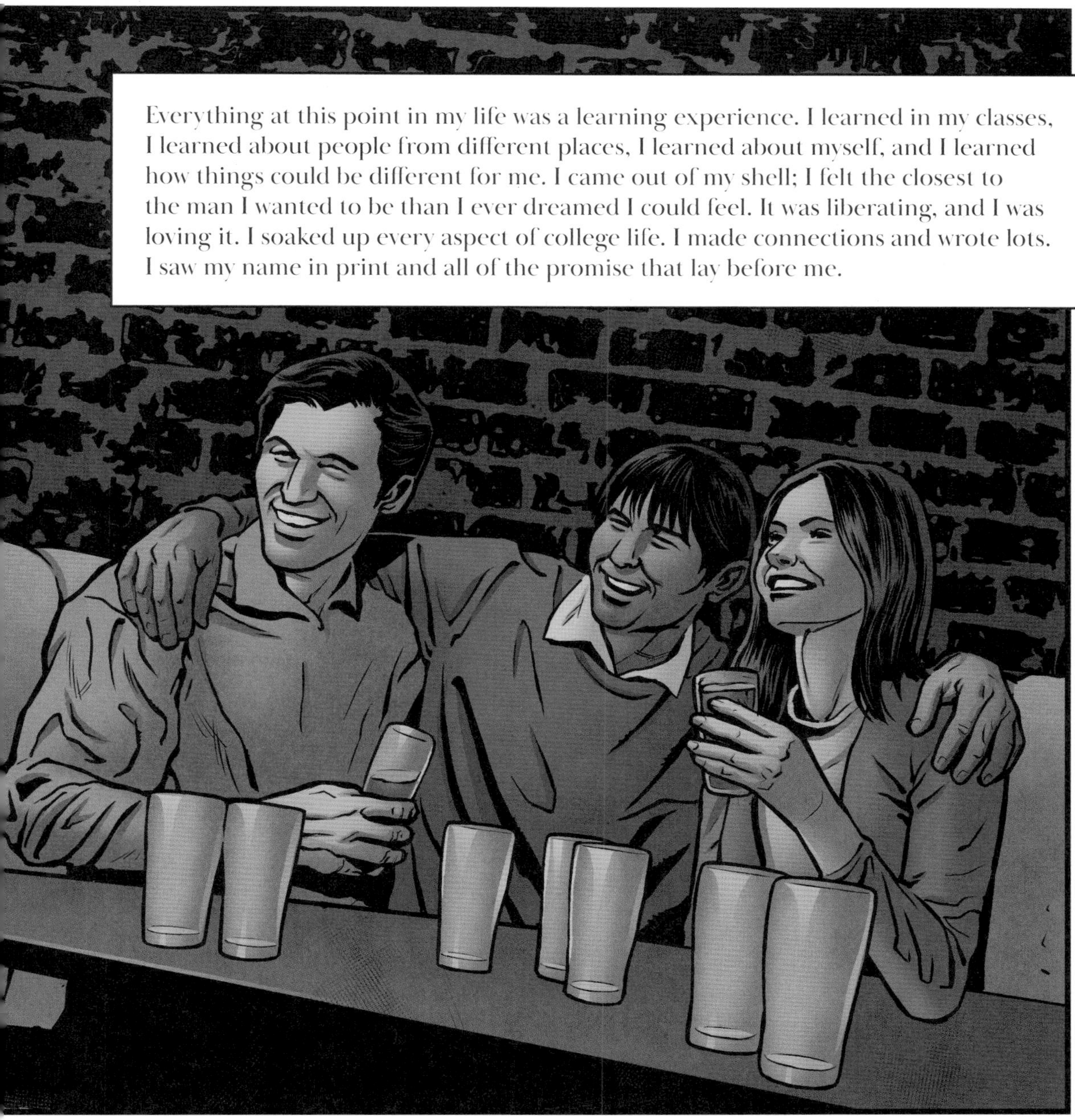
Everything at this point in my life was a learning experience. I learned in my classes, I learned about people from different places, I learned about myself, and I learned how things could be different for me. I came out of my shell; I felt the closest to the man I wanted to be than I ever dreamed I could feel. It was liberating, and I was loving it. I soaked up every aspect of college life. I made connections and wrote lots. I saw my name in print and all of the promise that lay before me.

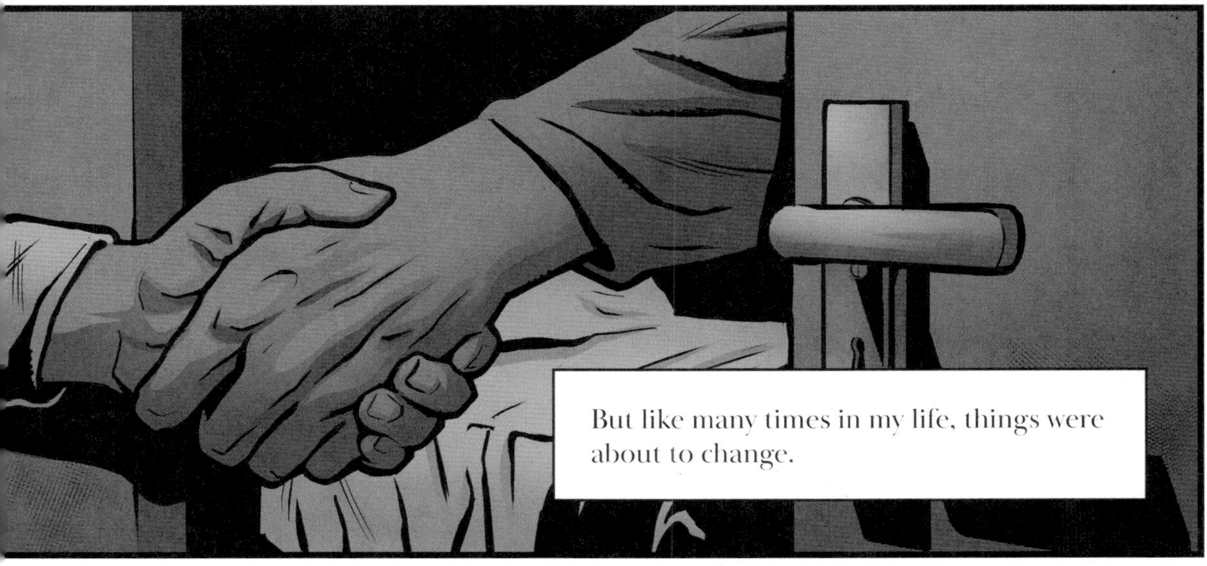
But like many times in my life, things were about to change.

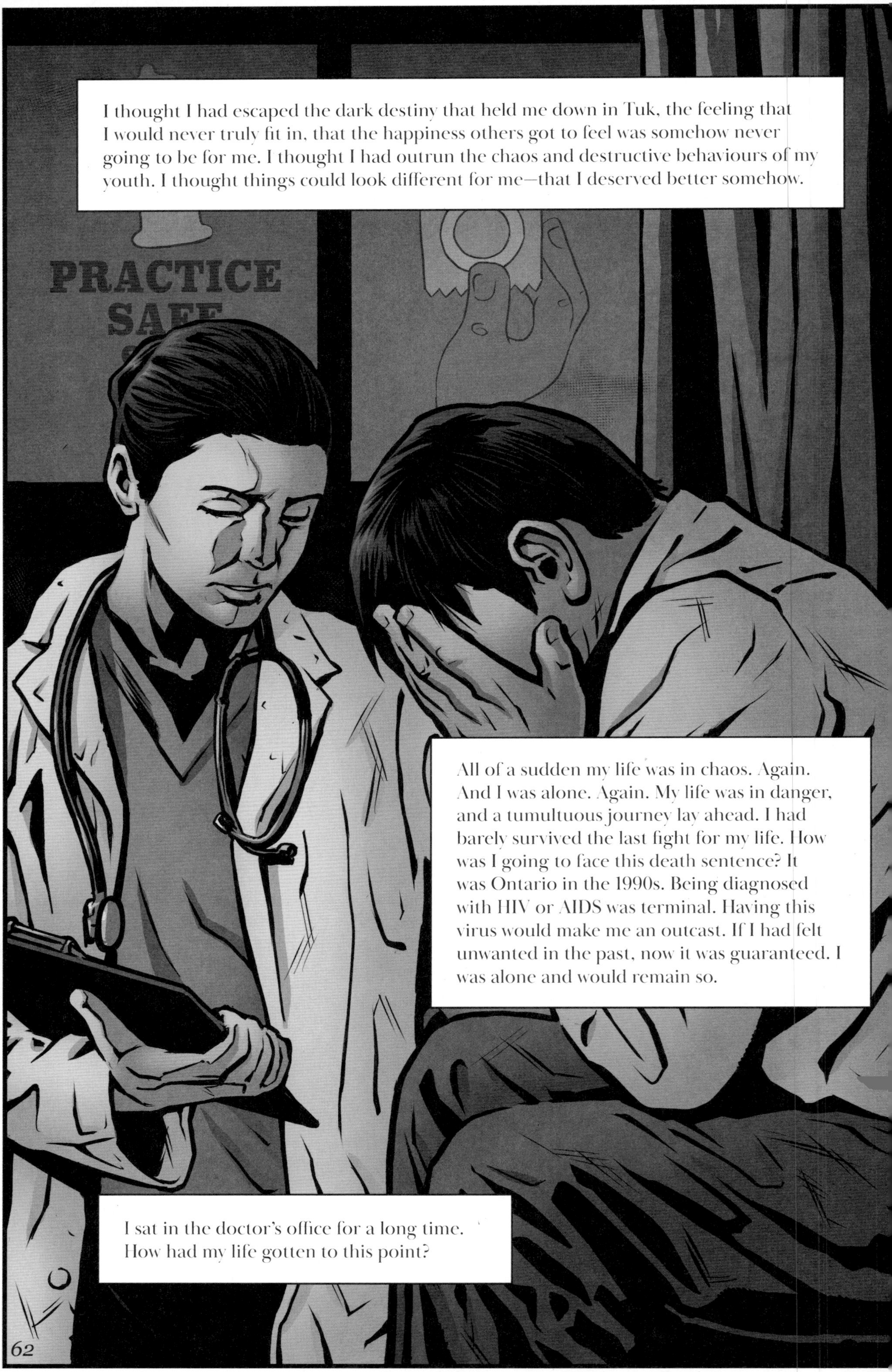
I thought I had escaped the dark destiny that held me down in Tuk, the feeling that I would never truly fit in, that the happiness others got to feel was somehow never going to be for me. I thought I had outrun the chaos and destructive behaviours of my youth. I thought things could look different for me—that I deserved better somehow.
PRACTICE
All of a sudden my life was in chaos. Again. And I was alone. Again. My life was in danger, and a tumultuous journey lay ahead. I had barely survived the last fight for my life. How was I going to face this death sentence? It was Ontario in the 1990s. Being diagnosed with HIV or AIDS was terminal. Having this virus would make me an outcast. If I had felt unwanted in the past, now it was guaranteed. I was alone and would remain so.
I sat in the doctor's office for a long time. How had my life gotten to this point?

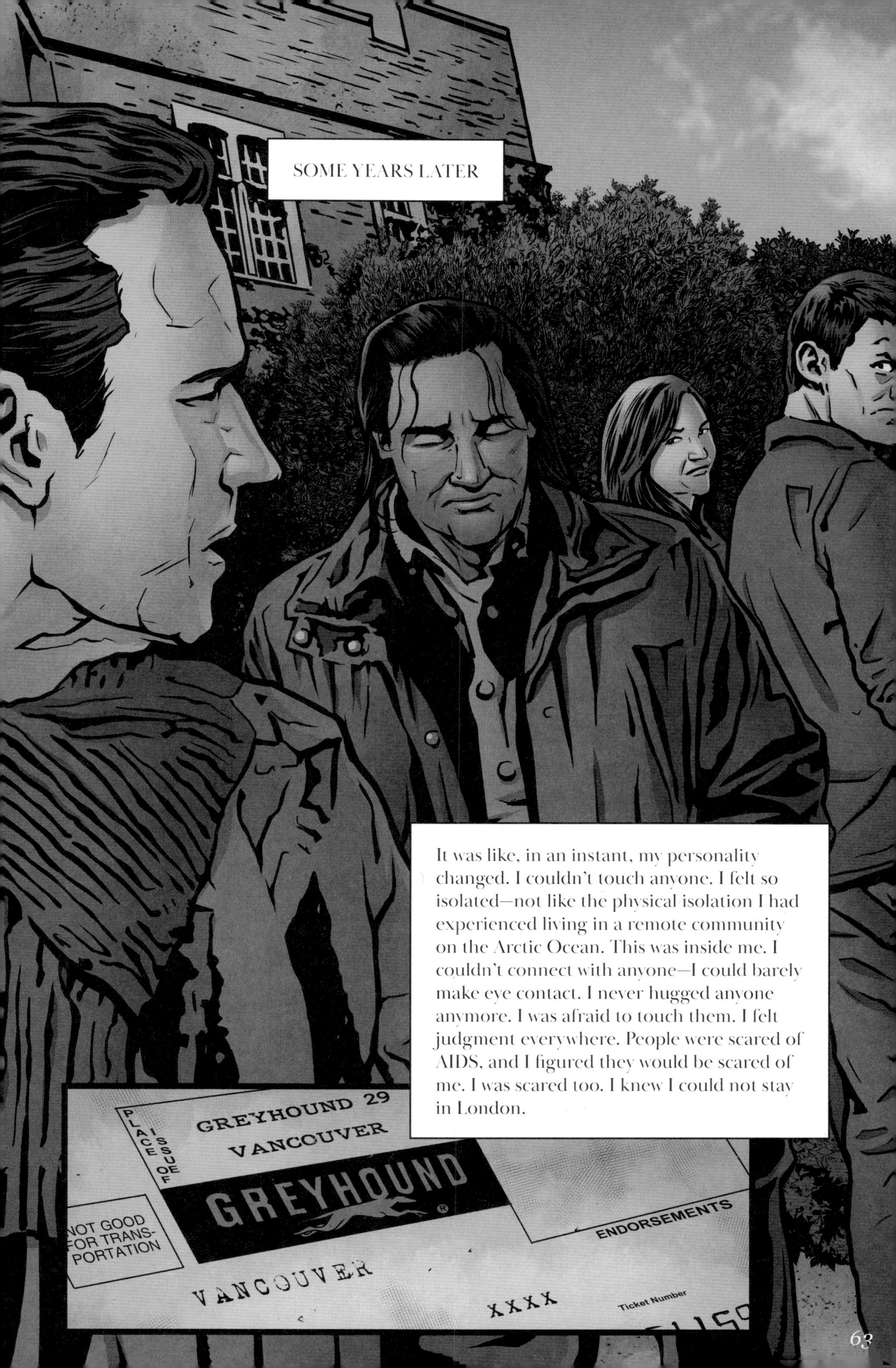
SOME YEARS LATER
It was like, in an instant, my personality changed. I couldn't touch anyone. I felt so isolated—not like the physical isolation I had experienced living in a remote community on the Arctic Ocean. This was inside me. I couldn't connect with anyone—I could barely make eye contact. I never hugged anyone anymore. I was afraid to touch them. I felt judgment everywhere. People were scared of AIDS, and I figured they would be scared of me. I was scared too. I knew I could not stay in London.
GREYHOUND 29
VANCOUVER
PLACE OF ISSUE
GREYHOUND
NOT GOOD FOR TRANSPORTATION
ENDORSEMENTS
VANCOUVER
XXXX
Ticket Number

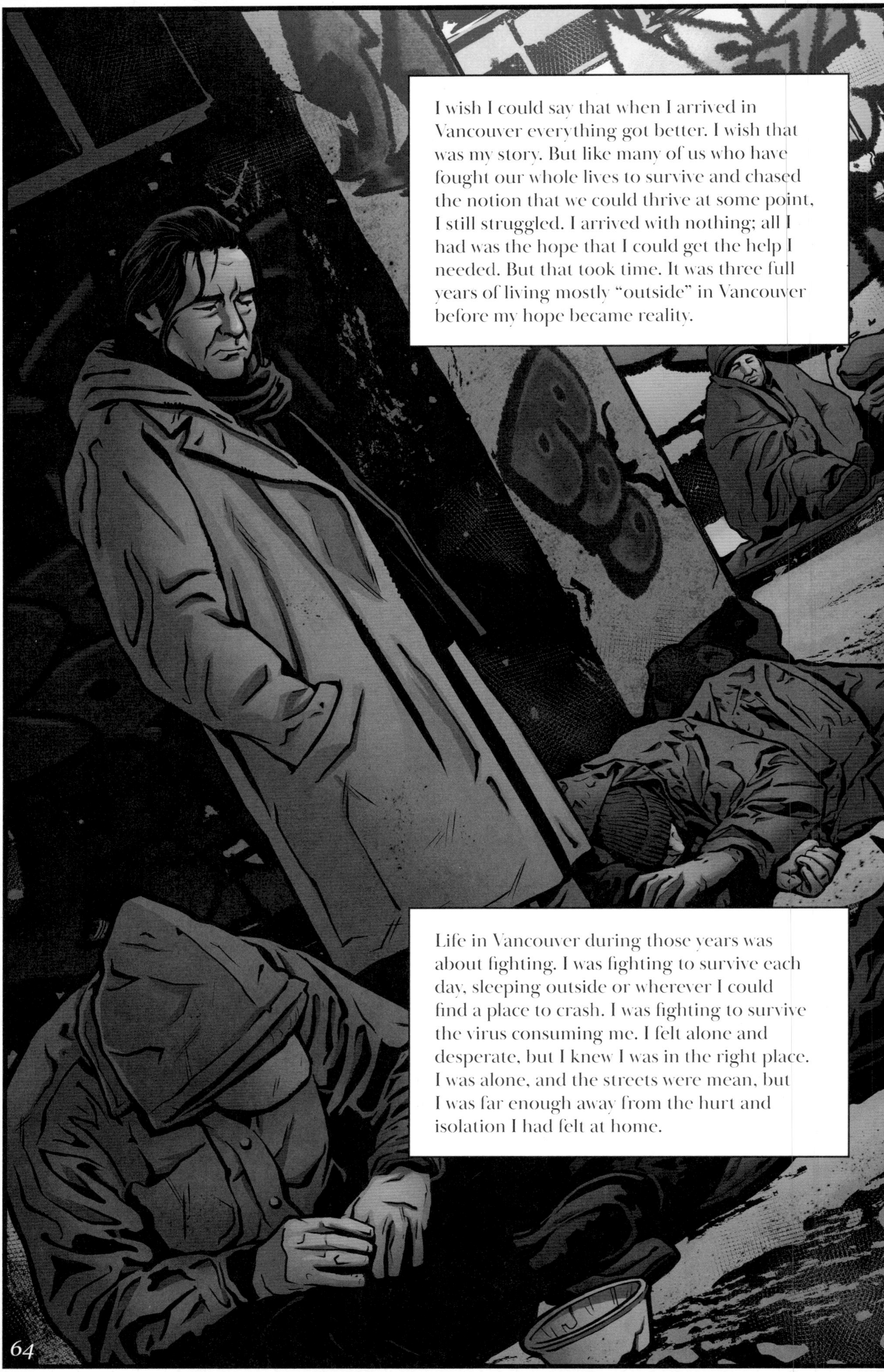
I wish I could say that when I arrived in Vancouver everything got better. I wish that was my story. But like many of us who have fought our whole lives to survive and chased the notion that we could thrive at some point, I still struggled. I arrived with nothing; all I had was the hope that I could get the help I needed. But that took time. It was three full years of living mostly "outside" in Vancouver before my hope became reality.
Life in Vancouver during those years was about fighting. I was fighting to survive each day, sleeping outside or wherever I could find a place to crash. I was fighting to survive the virus consuming me. I felt alone and desperate, but I knew I was in the right place. I was alone, and the streets were mean, but I was far enough away from the hurt and isolation I had felt at home.

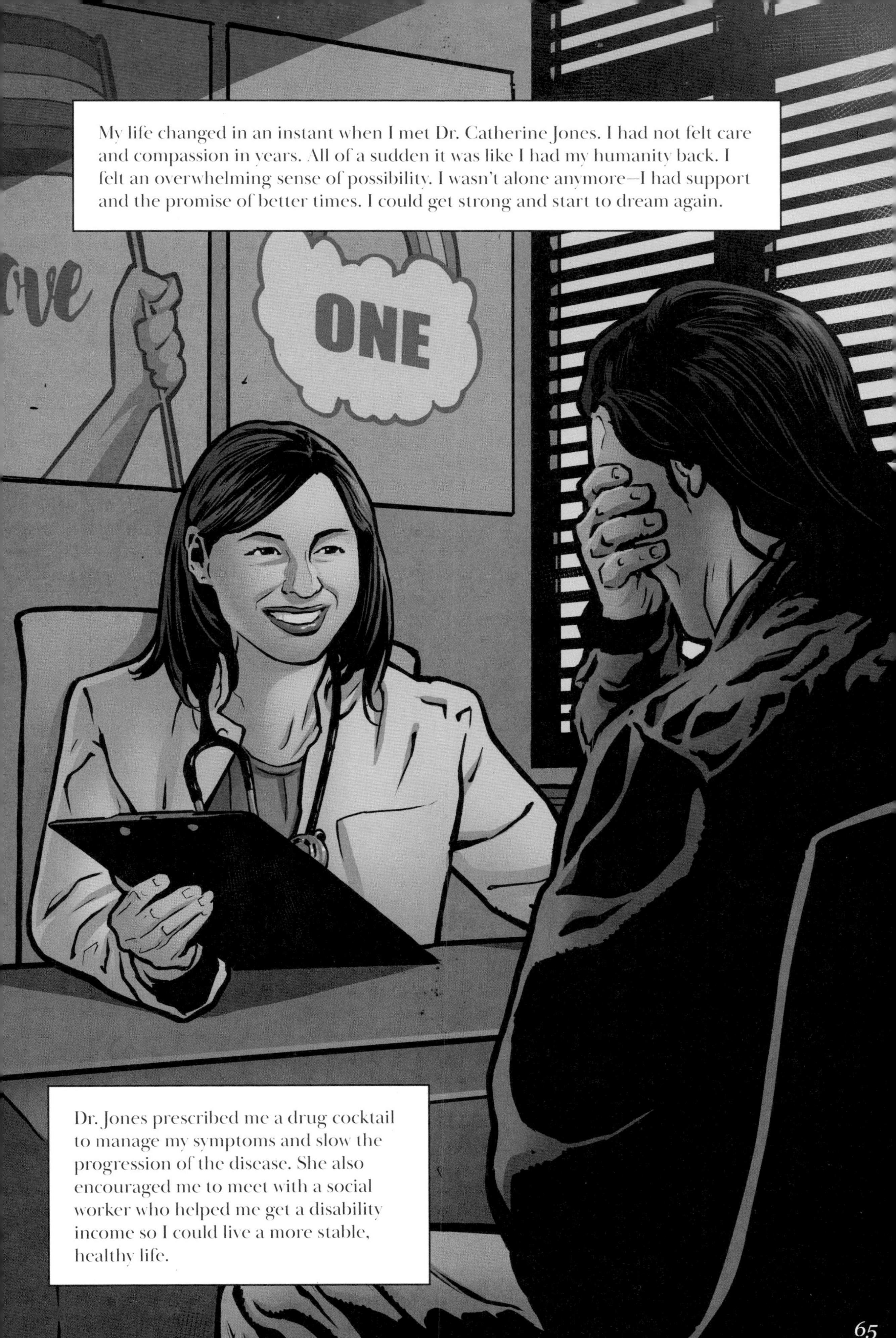
My life changed in an instant when I met Dr. Catherine Jones. I had not felt care and compassion in years. All of a sudden it was like I had my humanity back. I felt an overwhelming sense of possibility. I wasn't alone anymore—I had support and the promise of better times. I could get strong and start to dream again.
ONE
Dr. Jones prescribed me a drug cocktail to manage my symptoms and slow the progression of the disease. She also encouraged me to meet with a social worker who helped me get a disability income so I could live a more stable, healthy life.

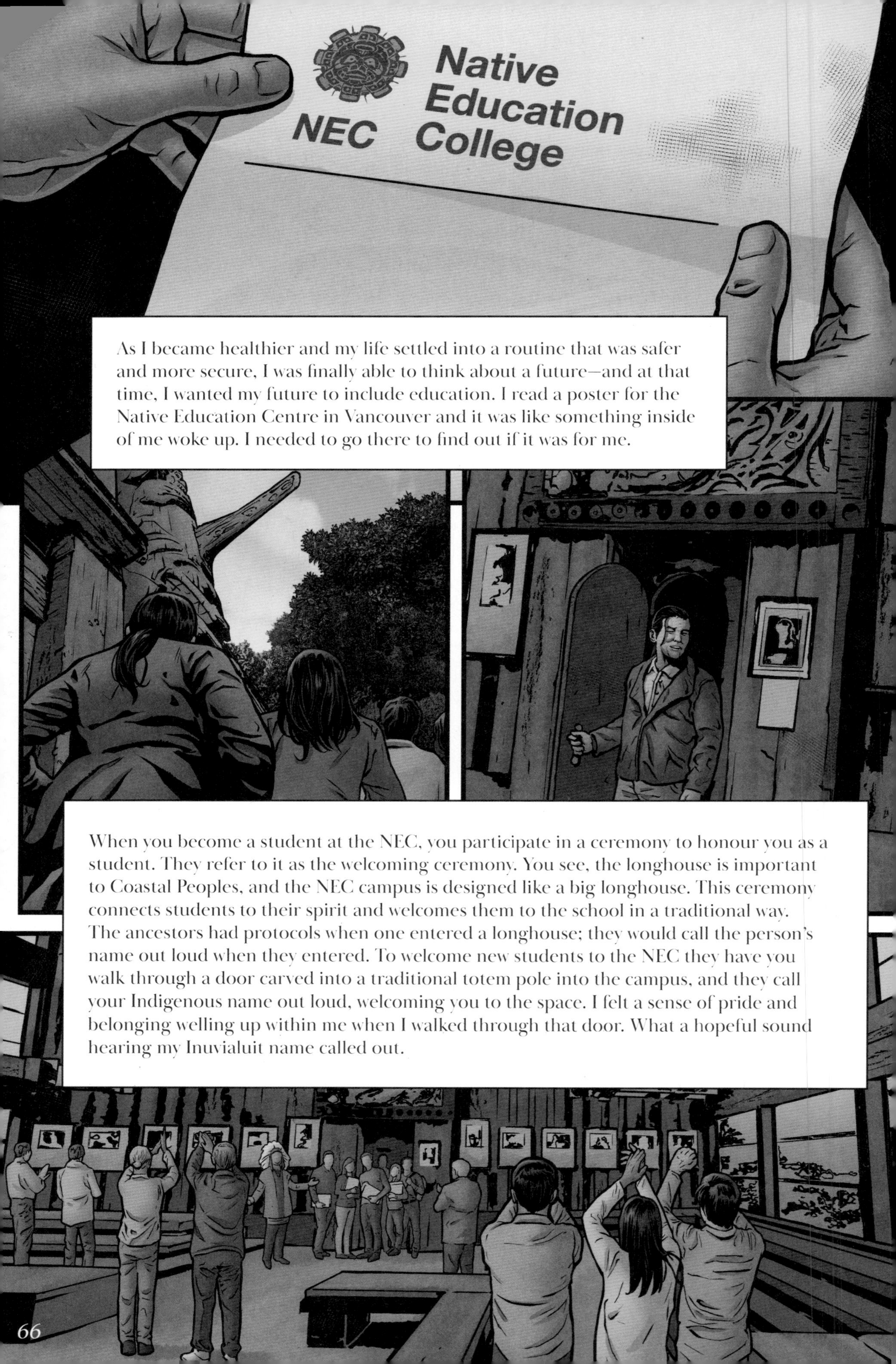
Native Education College
NEC
As I became healthier and my life settled into a routine that was safer and more secure, I was finally able to think about a future—and at that time, I wanted my future to include education. I read a poster for the Native Education Centre in Vancouver and it was like something inside of me woke up. I needed to go there to find out if it was for me.
When you become a student at the NEC, you participate in a ceremony to honour you as a student. They refer to it as the welcoming ceremony. You see, the longhouse is important to Coastal Peoples, and the NEC campus is designed like a big longhouse. This ceremony connects students to their spirit and welcomes them to the school in a traditional way. The ancestors had protocols when one entered a longhouse; they would call the person's name out loud when they entered. To welcome new students to the NEC they have you walk through a door carved into a traditional totem pole into the campus, and they call your Indigenous name out loud, welcoming you to the space. I felt a sense of pride and belonging welling up within me when I walked through that door. What a hopeful sound hearing my Inuvialuit name called out.

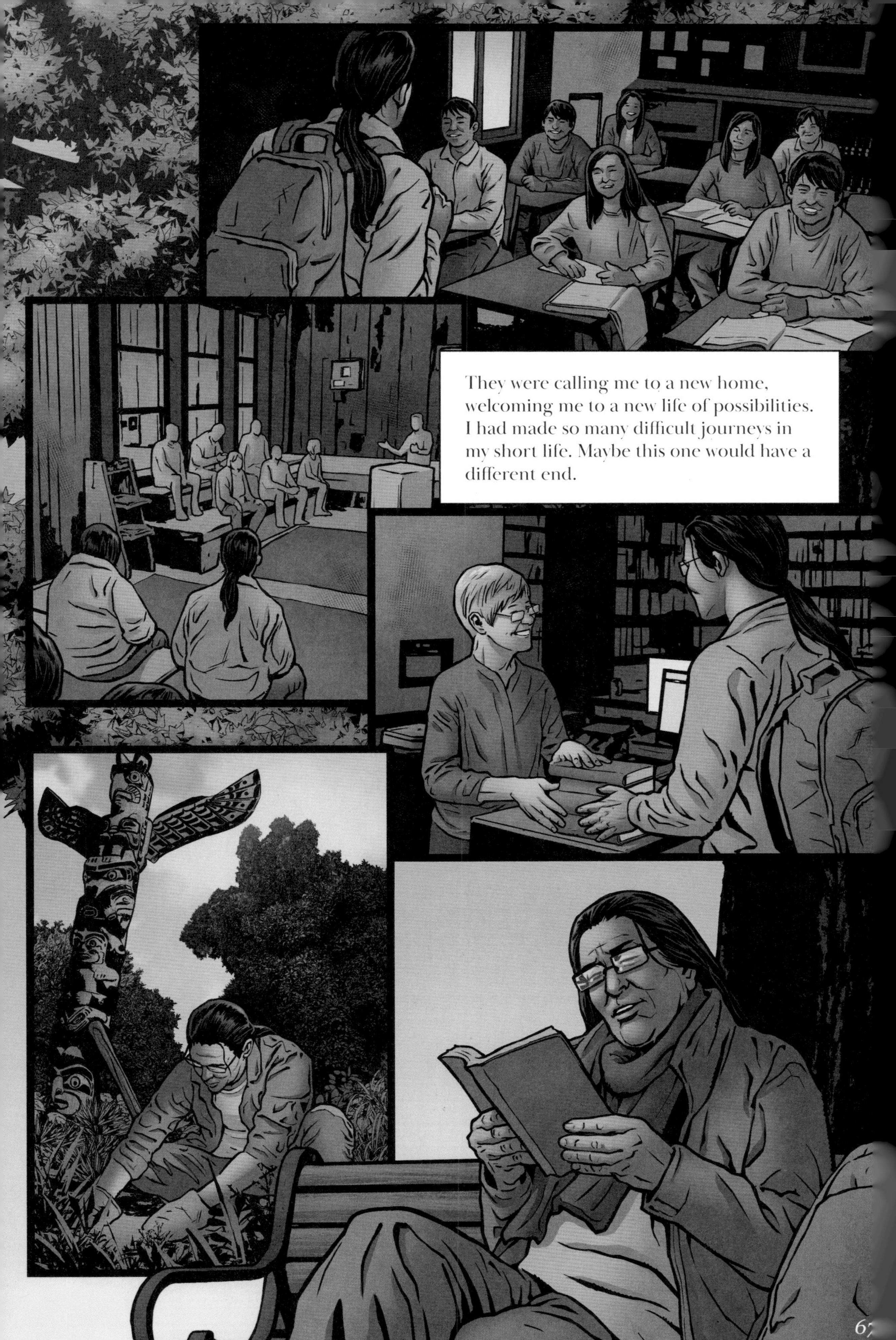
They were calling me to a new home, welcoming me to a new life of possibilities. I had made so many difficult journeys in my short life. Maybe this one would have a different end.

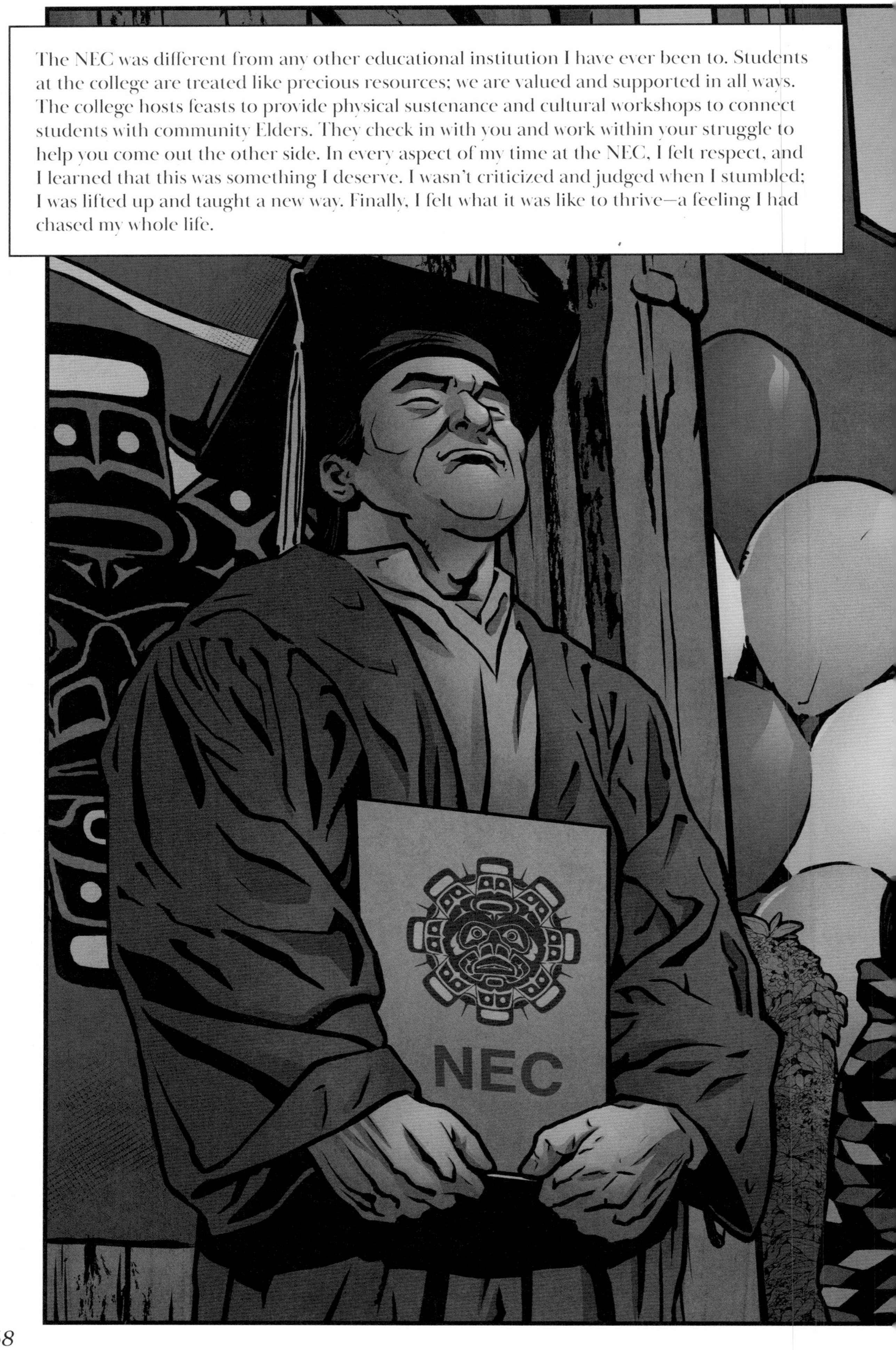
The NEC was different from any other educational institution I have ever been to. Students at the college are treated like precious resources; we are valued and supported in all ways. The college hosts feasts to provide physical sustenance and cultural workshops to connect students with community Elders. They check in with you and work within your struggle to help you come out the other side. In every aspect of my time at the NEC, I felt respect, and I learned that this was something I deserve. I wasn't criticized and judged when I stumbled; I was lifted up and taught a new way. Finally, I felt what it was like to thrive—a feeling I had chased my whole life.
NEC

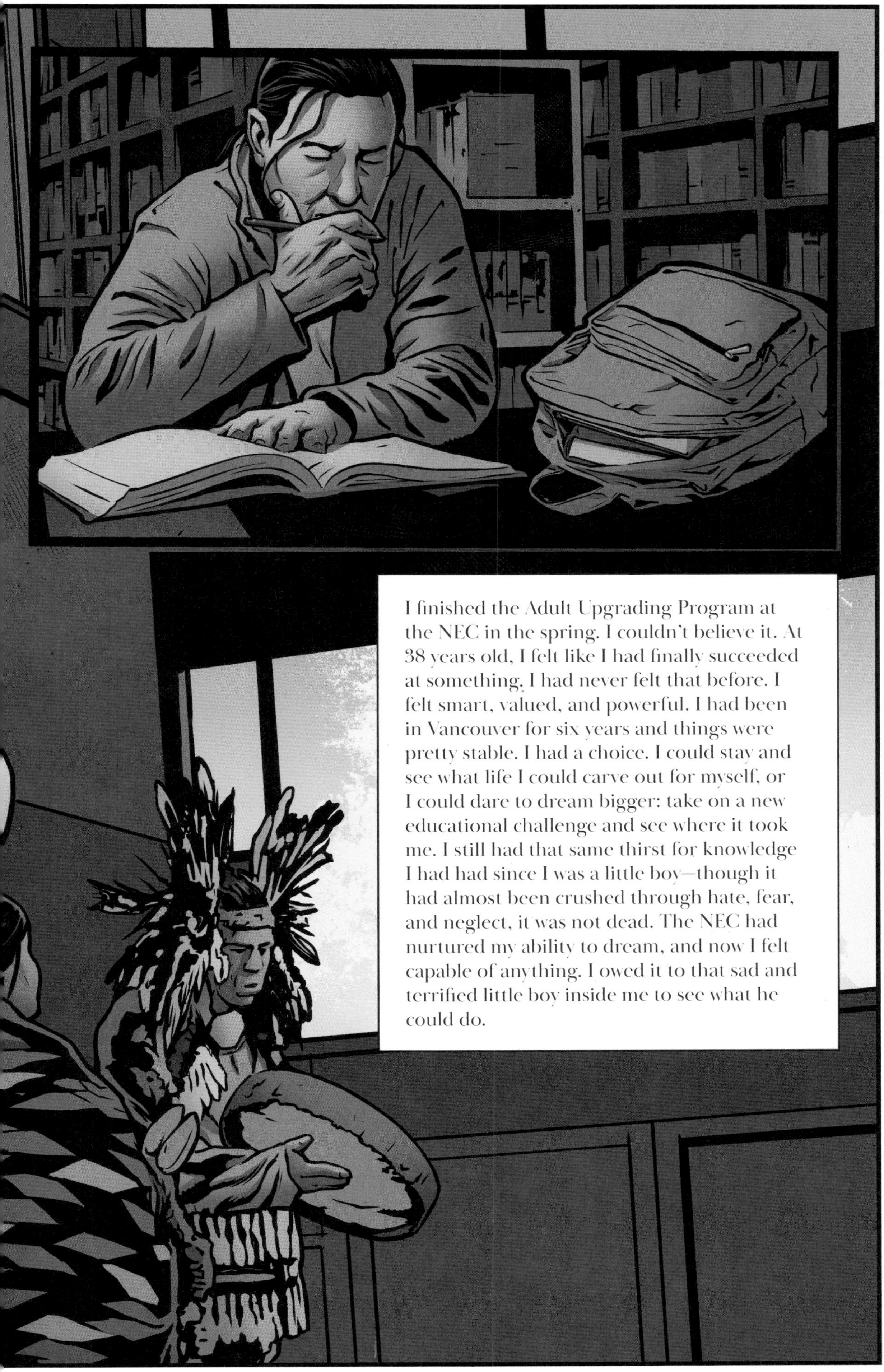
I finished the Adult Upgrading Program at the NEC in the spring. I couldn't believe it. At 38 years old, I felt like I had finally succeeded at something. I had never felt that before. I felt smart, valued, and powerful. I had been in Vancouver for six years and things were pretty stable. I had a choice. I could stay and see what life I could carve out for myself, or I could dare to dream bigger: take on a new educational challenge and see where it took me. I still had that same thirst for knowledge I had had since I was a little boy—though it had almost been crushed through hate, fear, and neglect, it was not dead. The NEC had nurtured my ability to dream, and now I felt capable of anything. I owed it to that sad and terrified little boy inside me to see what he could do.

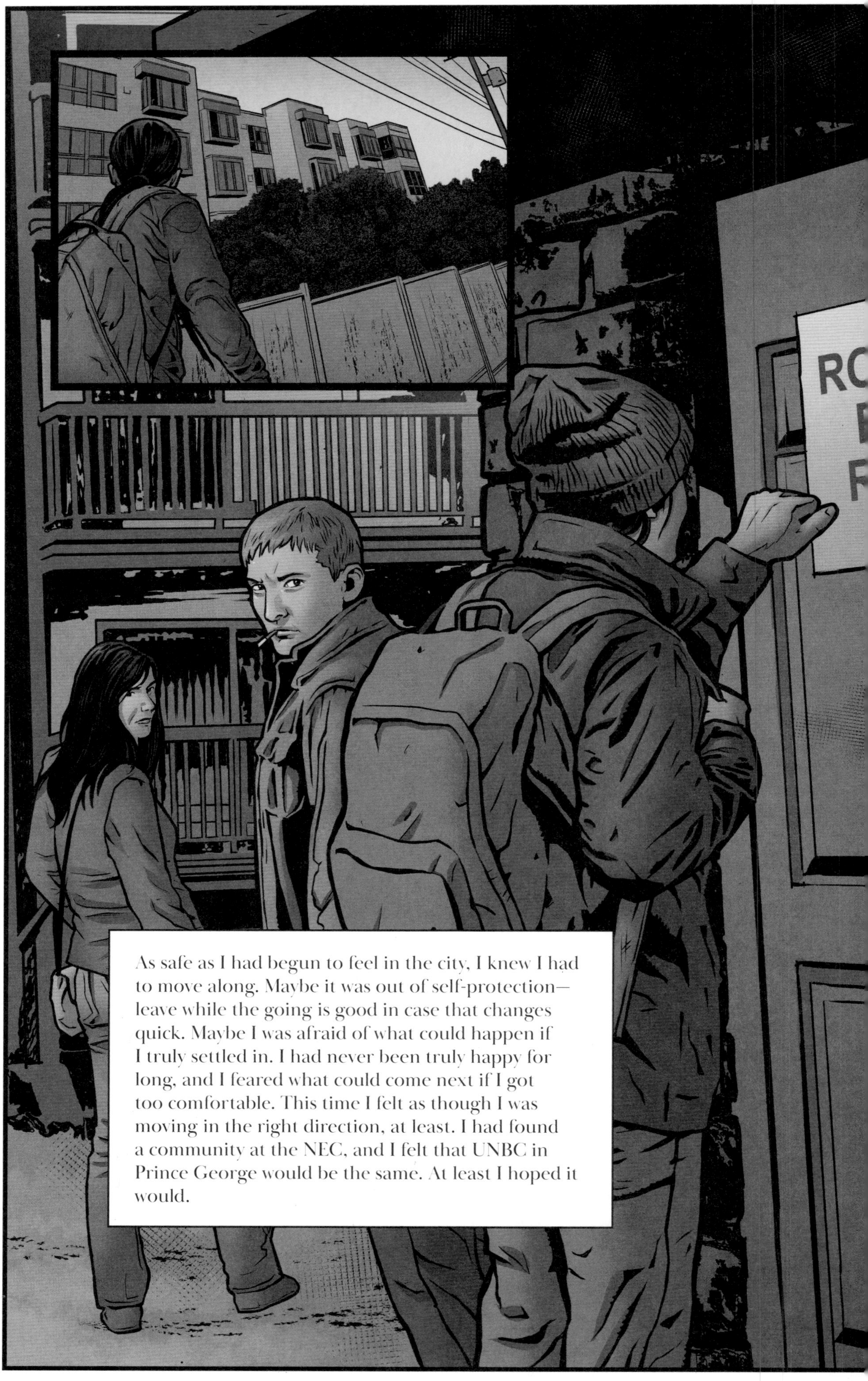
As safe as I had begun to feel in the city, I knew I had to move along. Maybe it was out of self-protection—leave while the going is good in case that changes quick. Maybe I was afraid of what could happen if I truly settled in. I had never been truly happy for long, and I feared what could come next if I got too comfortable. This time I felt as though I was moving in the right direction, at least. I had found a community at the NEC, and I felt that UNBC in Prince George would be the same. At least I hoped it would.

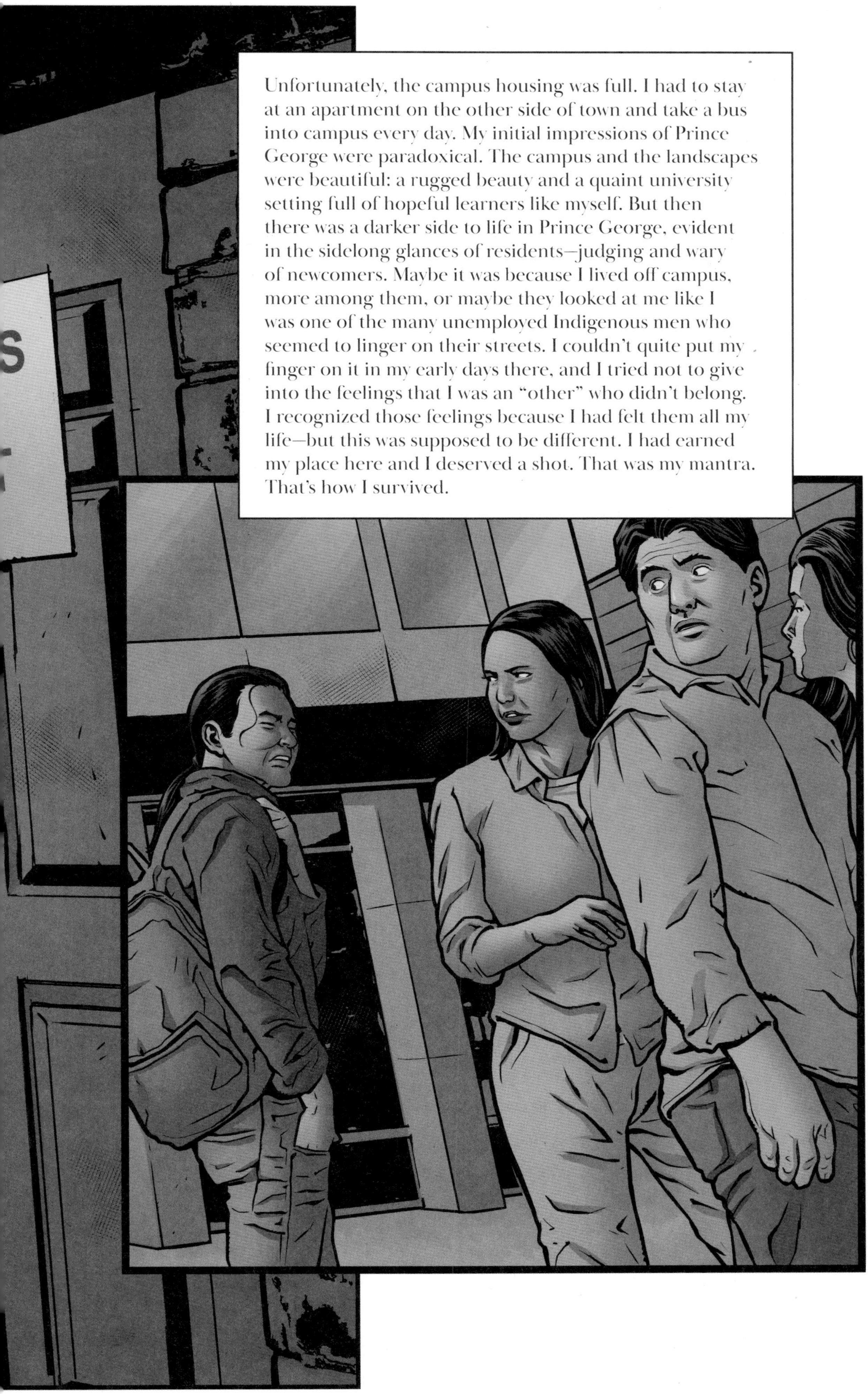
Unfortunately, the campus housing was full. I had to stay at an apartment on the other side of town and take a bus into campus every day. My initial impressions of Prince George were paradoxical. The campus and the landscapes were beautiful: a rugged beauty and a quaint university setting full of hopeful learners like myself. But then there was a darker side to life in Prince George, evident in the sidelong glances of residents—judging and wary of newcomers. Maybe it was because I lived off campus, more among them, or maybe they looked at me like I was one of the many unemployed Indigenous men who seemed to linger on their streets. I couldn't quite put my finger on it in my early days there, and I tried not to give into the feelings that I was an "other" who didn't belong. I recognized those feelings because I had felt them all my life—but this was supposed to be different. I had earned my place here and I deserved a shot. That was my mantra. That's how I survived.

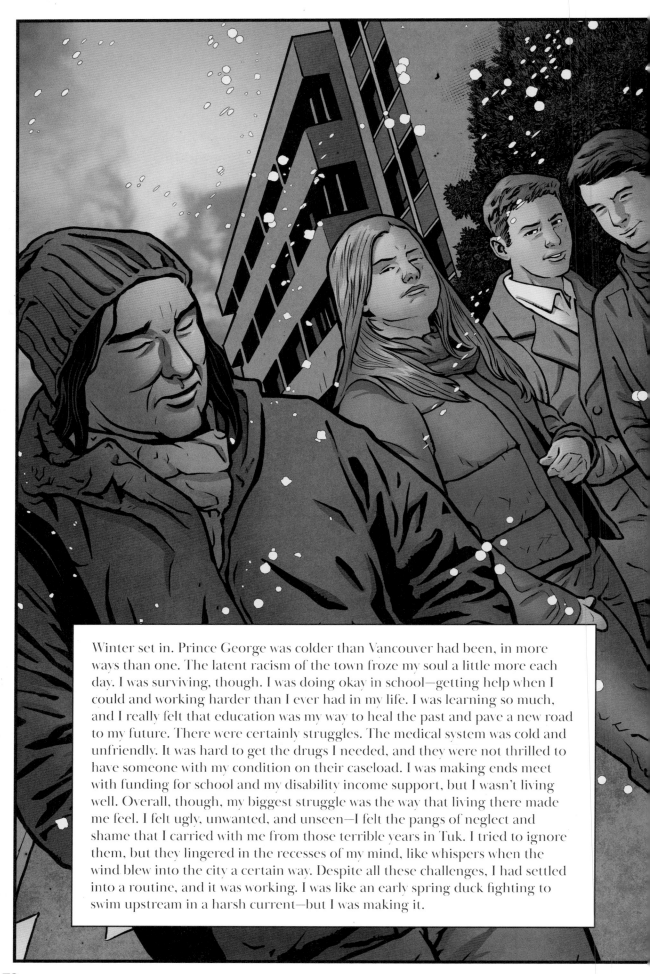

Winter set in. Prince George was colder than Vancouver had been, in more ways than one. The latent racism of the town froze my soul a little more each day. I was surviving, though. I was doing okay in school—getting help when I could and working harder than I ever had in my life. I was learning so much, and I really felt that education was my way to heal the past and pave a new road to my future. There were certainly struggles. The medical system was cold and unfriendly. It was hard to get the drugs I needed, and they were not thrilled to have someone with my condition on their caseload. I was making ends meet with funding for school and my disability income support, but I wasn't living well. Overall, though, my biggest struggle was the way that living there made me feel. I felt ugly, unwanted, and unseen—I felt the pangs of neglect and shame that I carried with me from those terrible years in Tuk. I tried to ignore them, but they lingered in the recesses of my mind, like whispers when the wind blew into the city a certain way. Despite all these challenges, I had settled into a routine, and it was working. I was like an early spring duck fighting to swim upstream in a harsh current—but I was making it.

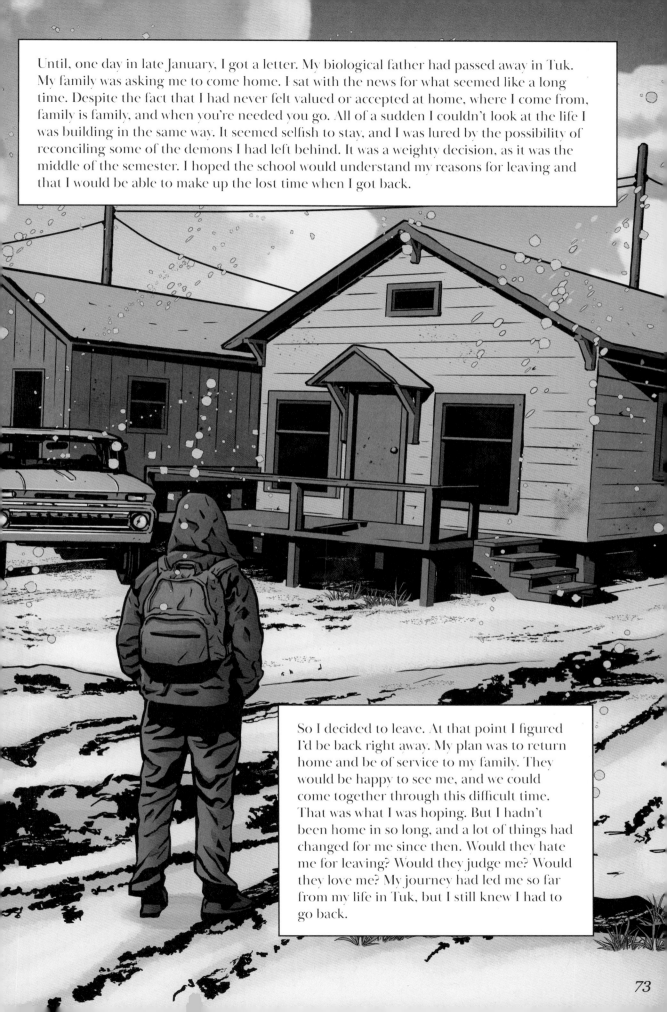

Until, one day in late January, I got a letter. My biological father had passed away in Tuk. My family was asking me to come home. I sat with the news for what seemed like a long time. Despite the fact that I had never felt valued or accepted at home, where I come from, family is family, and when you're needed you go. All of a sudden I couldn't look at the life I was building in the same way. It seemed selfish to stay, and I was lured by the possibility of reconciling some of the demons I had left behind. It was a weighty decision, as it was the middle of the semester. I hoped the school would understand my reasons for leaving and that I would be able to make up the lost time when I got back.

So I decided to leave. At that point I figured I'd be back right away. My plan was to return home and be of service to my family. They would be happy to see me, and we could come together through this difficult time. That was what I was hoping. But I hadn't been home in so long, and a lot of things had changed for me since then. Would they hate me for leaving? Would they judge me? Would they love me? My journey had led me so far from my life in Tuk, but I still knew I had to go back.

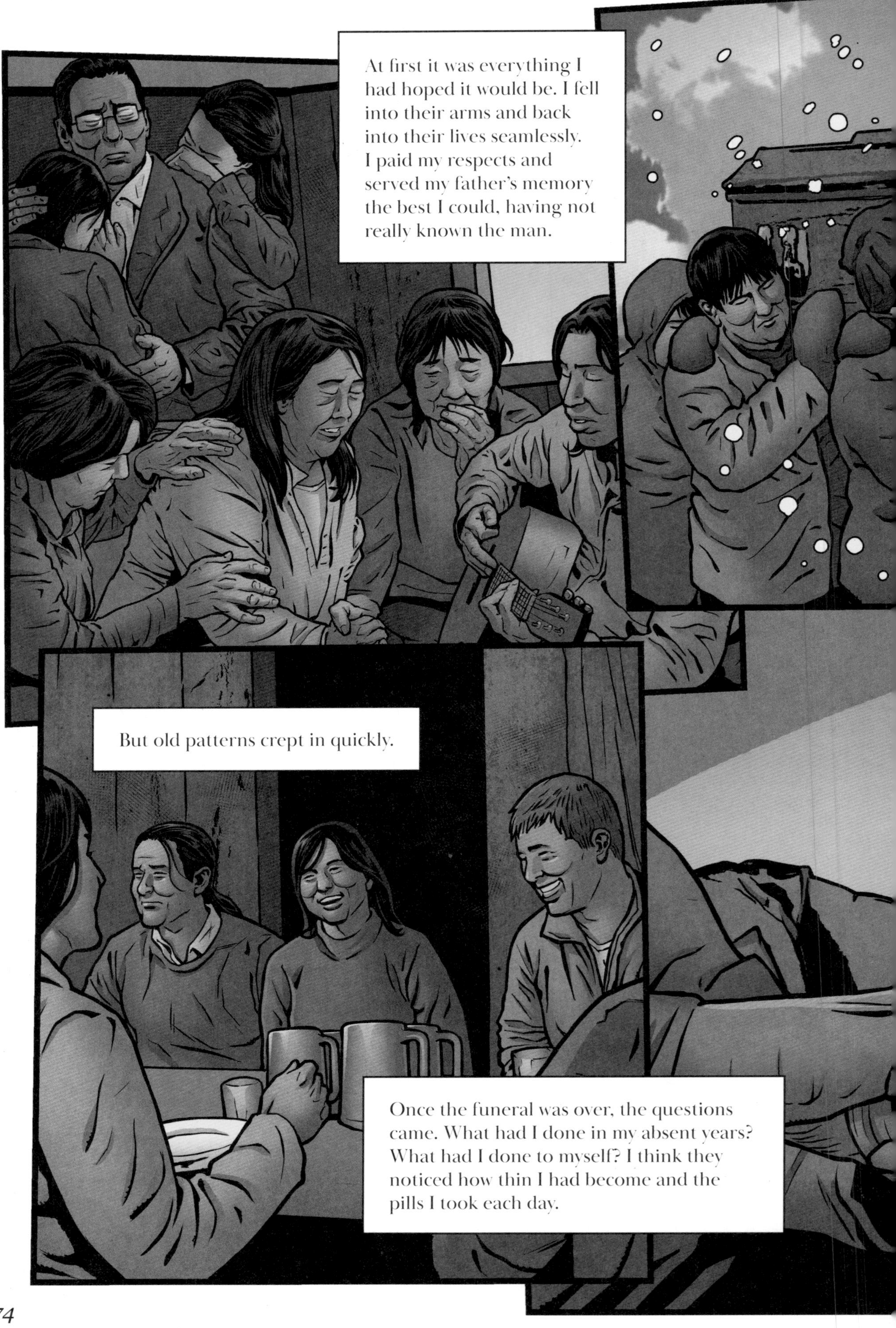
At first it was everything I had hoped it would be. I fell into their arms and back into their lives seamlessly. I paid my respects and served my father's memory the best I could, having not really known the man.
But old patterns crept in quickly.
Once the funeral was over, the questions came. What had I done in my absent years? What had I done to myself? I think they noticed how thin I had become and the pills I took each day.

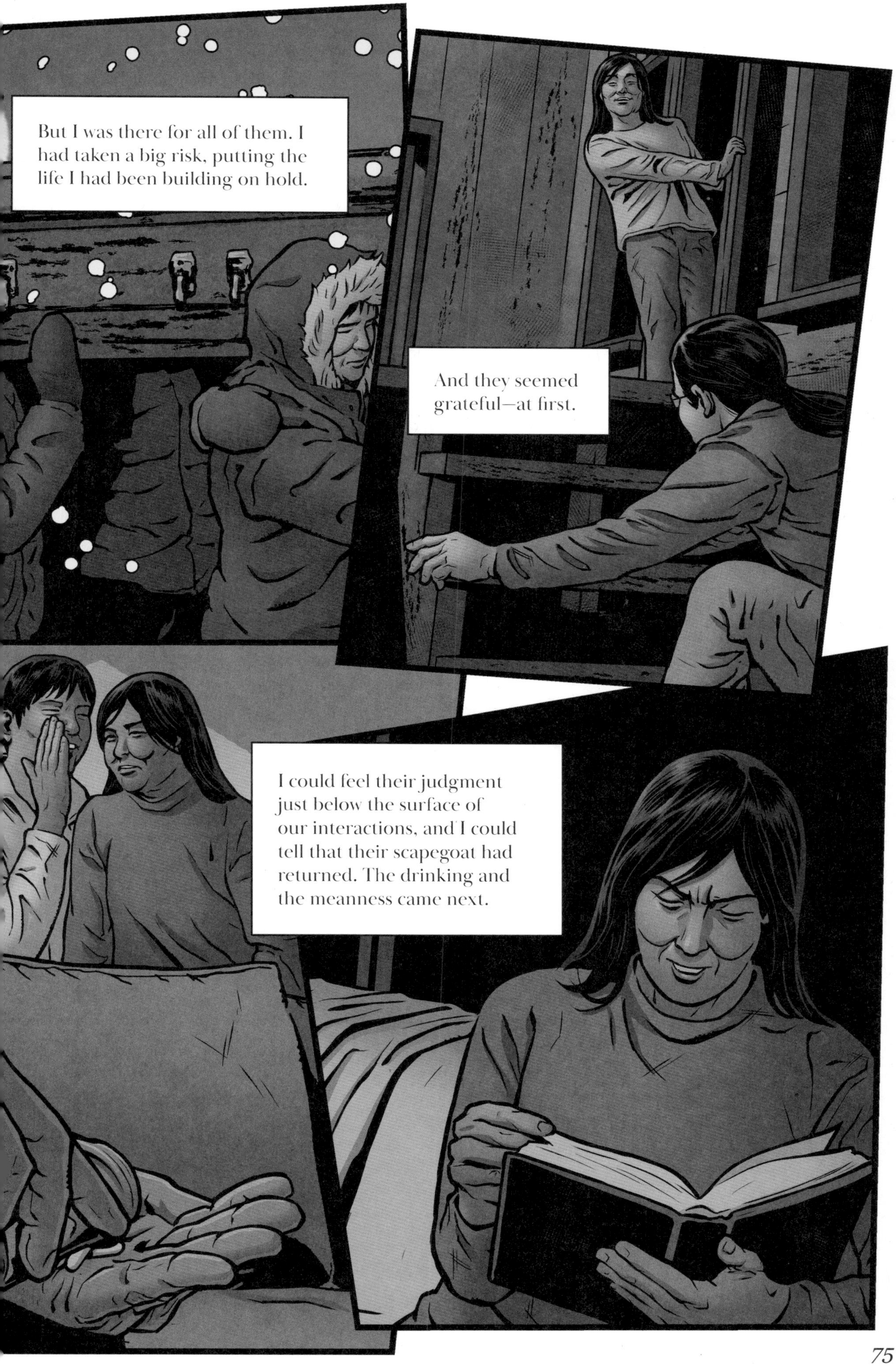
But I was there for all of them. I had taken a big risk, putting the life I had been building on hold.
And they seemed grateful—at first.
I could feel their judgment just below the surface of our interactions, and I could tell that their scapegoat had returned. The drinking and the meanness came next.

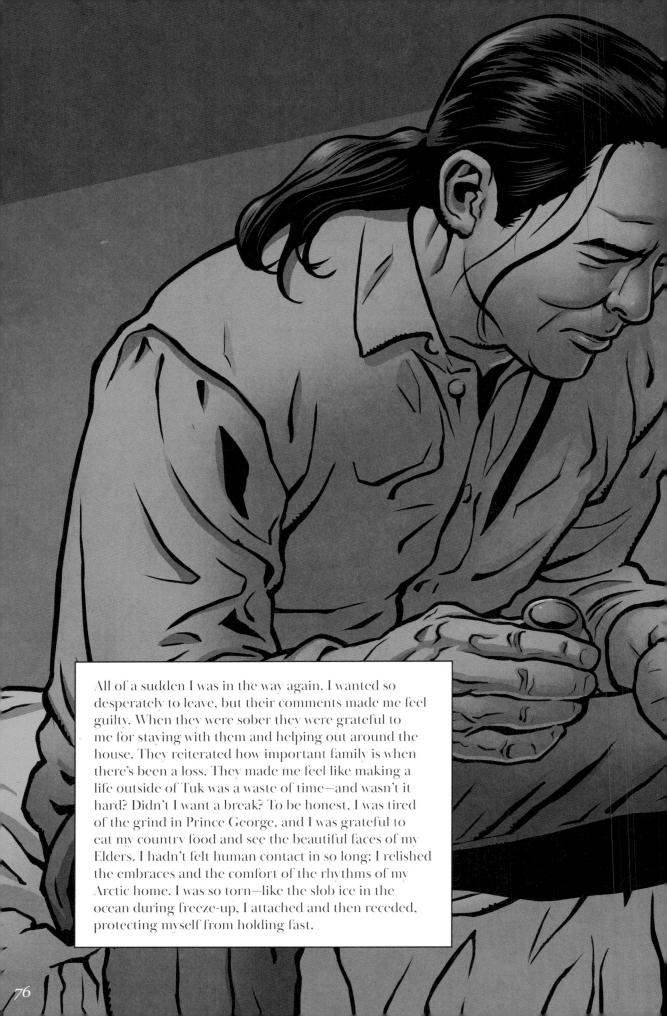

All of a sudden I was in the way again. I wanted so
desperately to leave, but their comments made me feel
guilty. When they were sober they were grateful to
me for staying with them and helping out around the
house. They reiterated how important family is when
there's been a loss. They made me feel like making a
life outside of Tuk was a waste of time—and wasn't it
hard? Didn't I want a break? To be honest, I was tired
of the grind in Prince George, and I was grateful to
eat my country food and see the beautiful faces of my
Elders. I hadn't felt human contact in so long; I relished
the embraces and the comfort of the rhythms of my
Arctic home. I was so torn—like the slob ice in the
ocean during freeze-up, I attached and then receded,
protecting myself from holding fast.

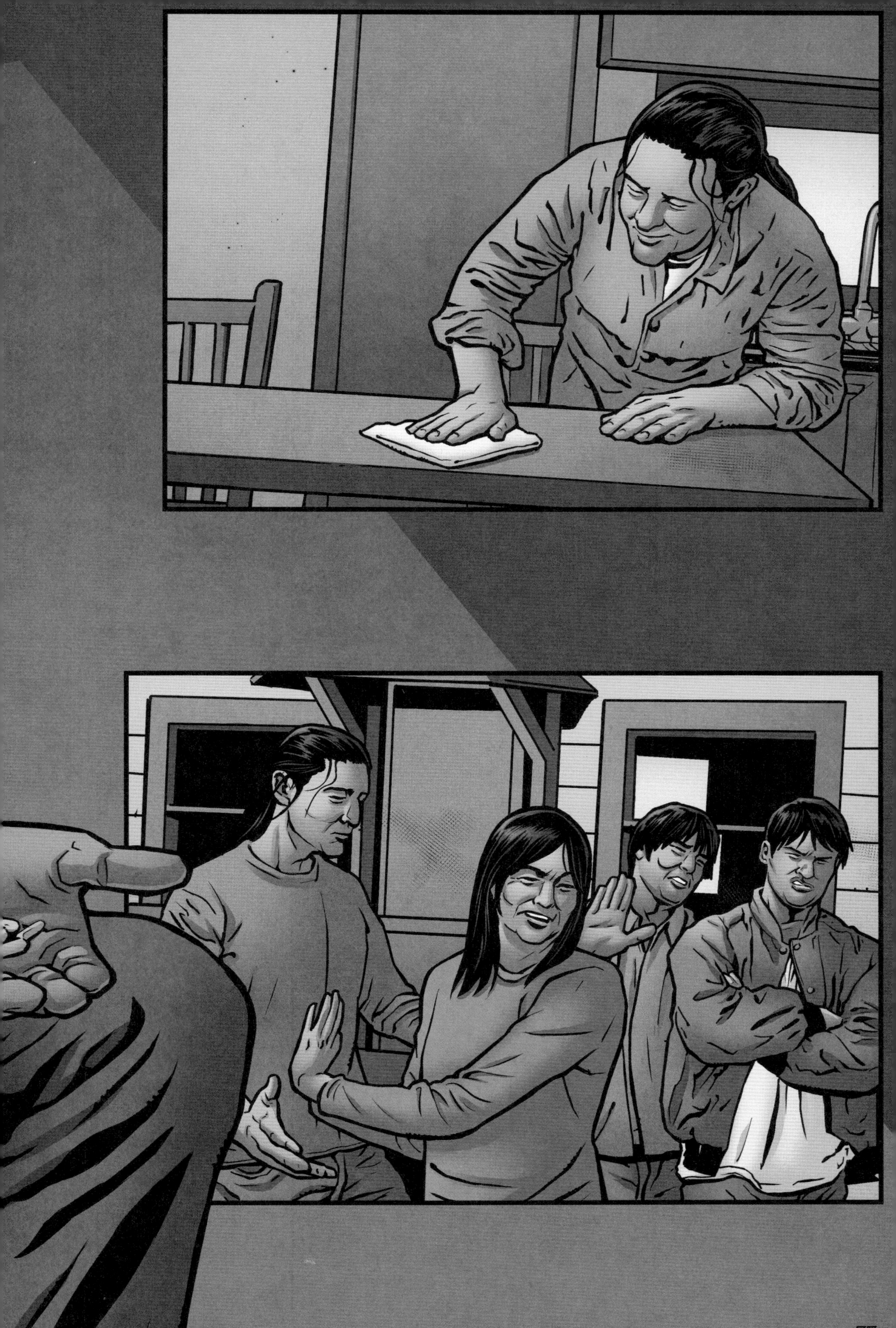

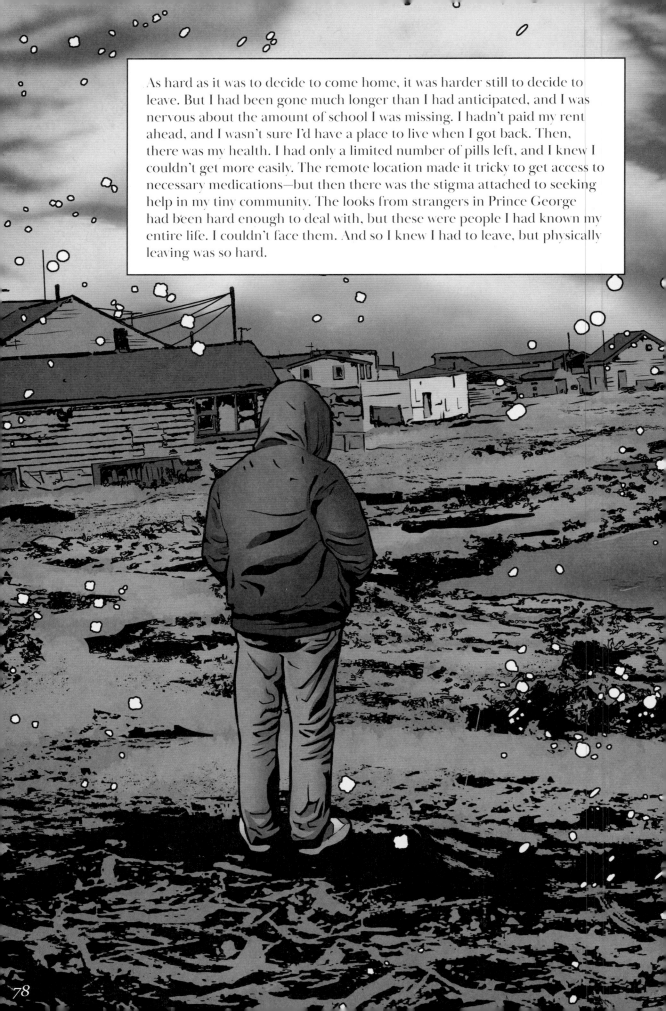

As hard as it was to decide to come home, it was harder still to decide to leave. But I had been gone much longer than I had anticipated, and I was nervous about the amount of school I was missing. I hadn't paid my rent ahead, and I wasn't sure I'd have a place to live when I got back. Then, there was my health. I had only a limited number of pills left, and I knew I couldn't get more easily. The remote location made it tricky to get access to necessary medications—but then there was the stigma attached to seeking help in my tiny community. The looks from strangers in Prince George had been hard enough to deal with, but these were people I had known my entire life. I couldn't face them. And so I knew I had to leave, but physically leaving was so hard.

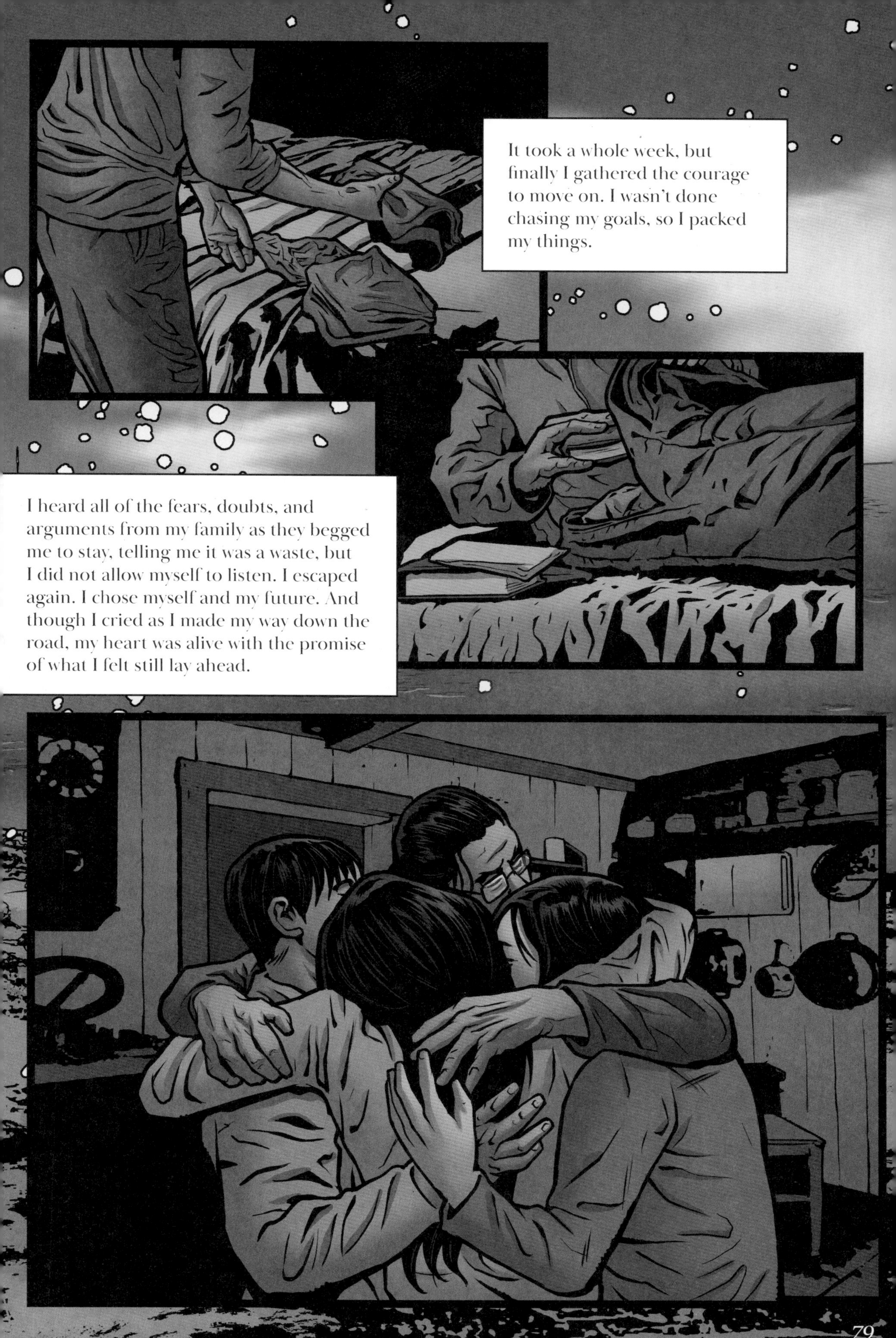
It took a whole week, but finally I gathered the courage to move on. I wasn't done chasing my goals, so I packed my things.
I heard all of the fears, doubts, and arguments from my family as they begged me to stay, telling me it was a waste, but I did not allow myself to listen. I escaped again. I chose myself and my future. And though I cried as I made my way down the road, my heart was alive with the promise of what I felt still lay ahead.

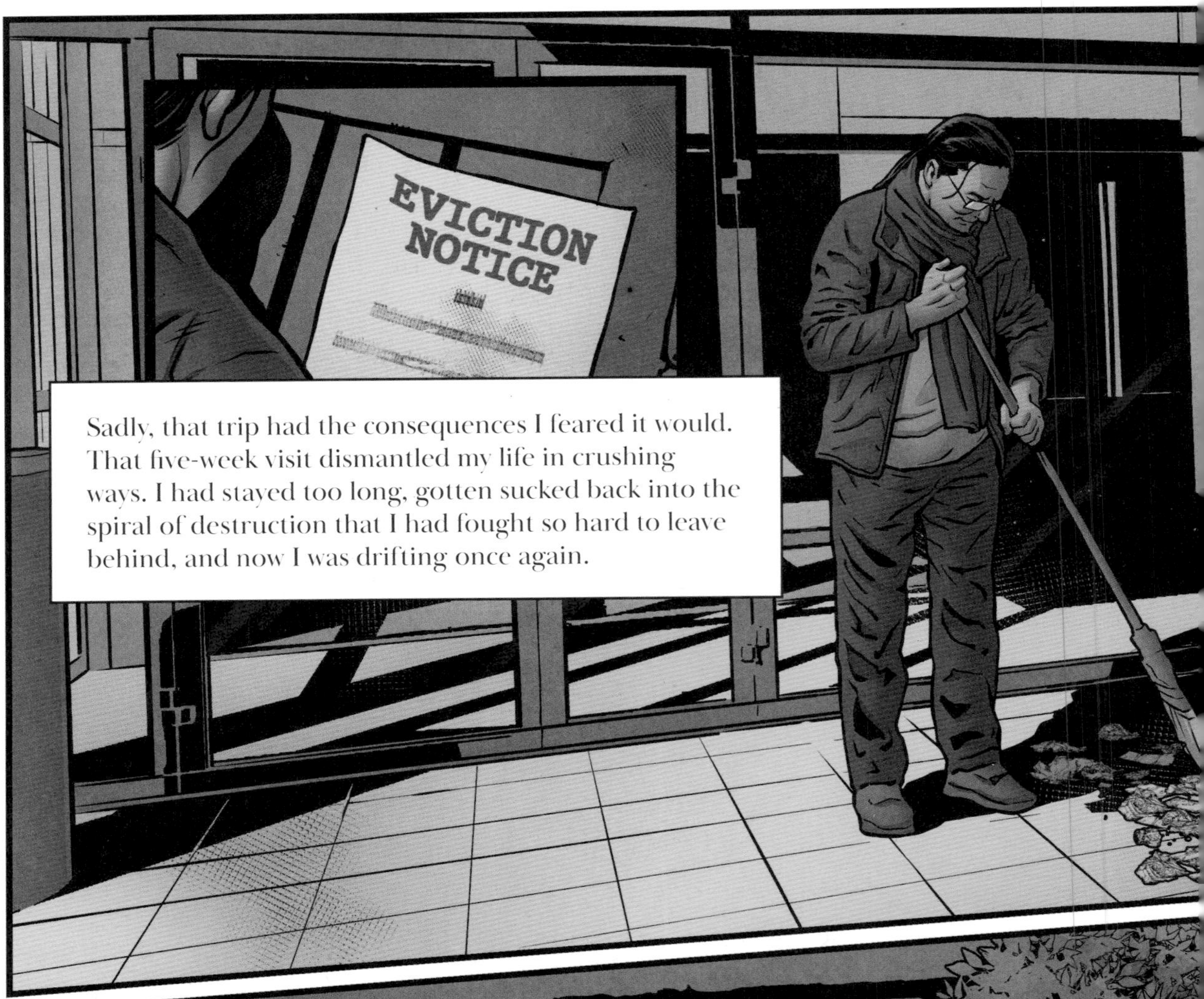
EVICTION NOTICE
Sadly, that trip had the consequences I feared it would. That five-week visit dismantled my life in crushing ways. I had stayed too long, gotten sucked back into the spiral of destruction that I had fought so hard to leave behind, and now I was drifting once again.

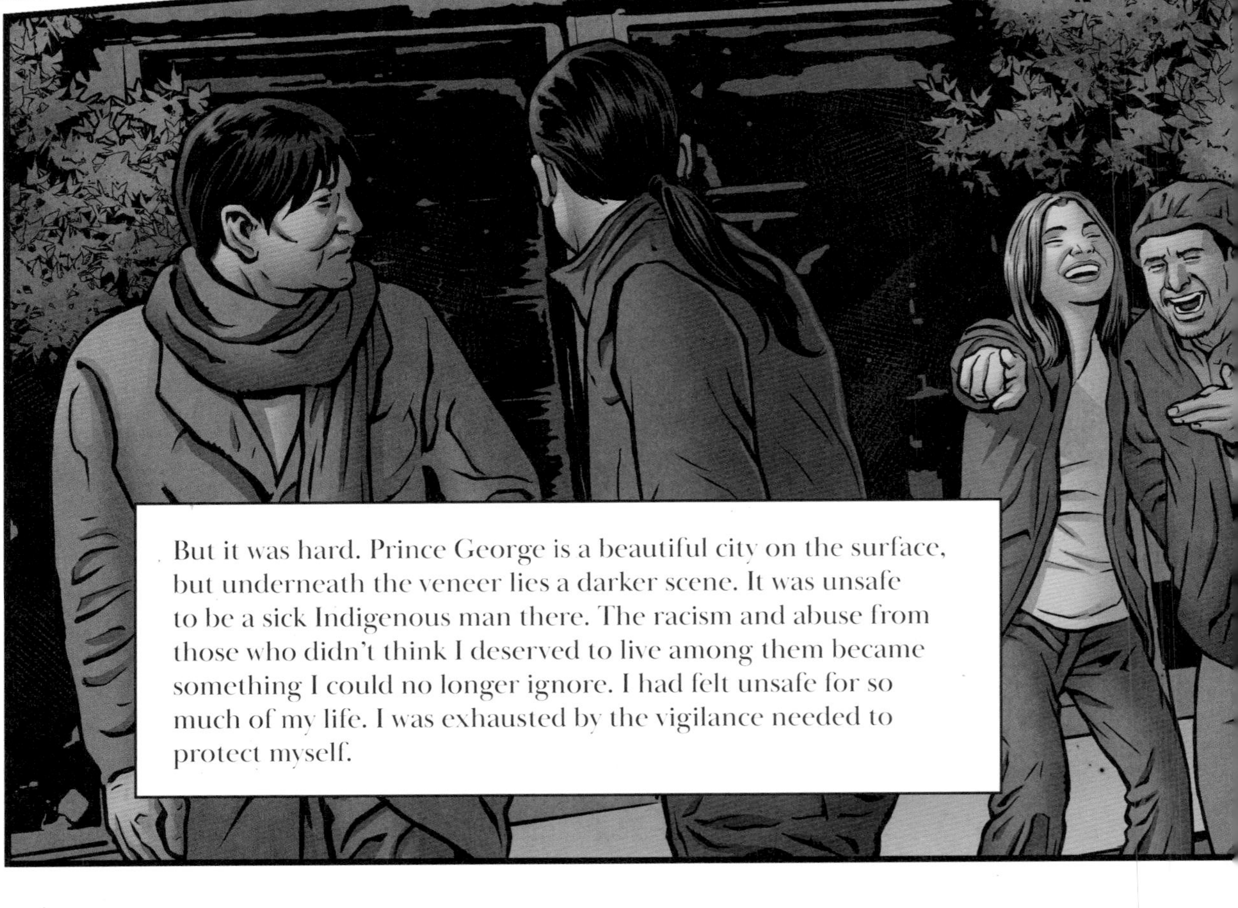
But it was hard. Prince George is a beautiful city on the surface, but underneath the veneer lies a darker scene. It was unsafe to be a sick Indigenous man there. The racism and abuse from those who didn't think I deserved to live among them became something I could no longer ignore. I had felt unsafe for so much of my life. I was exhausted by the vigilance needed to protect myself.

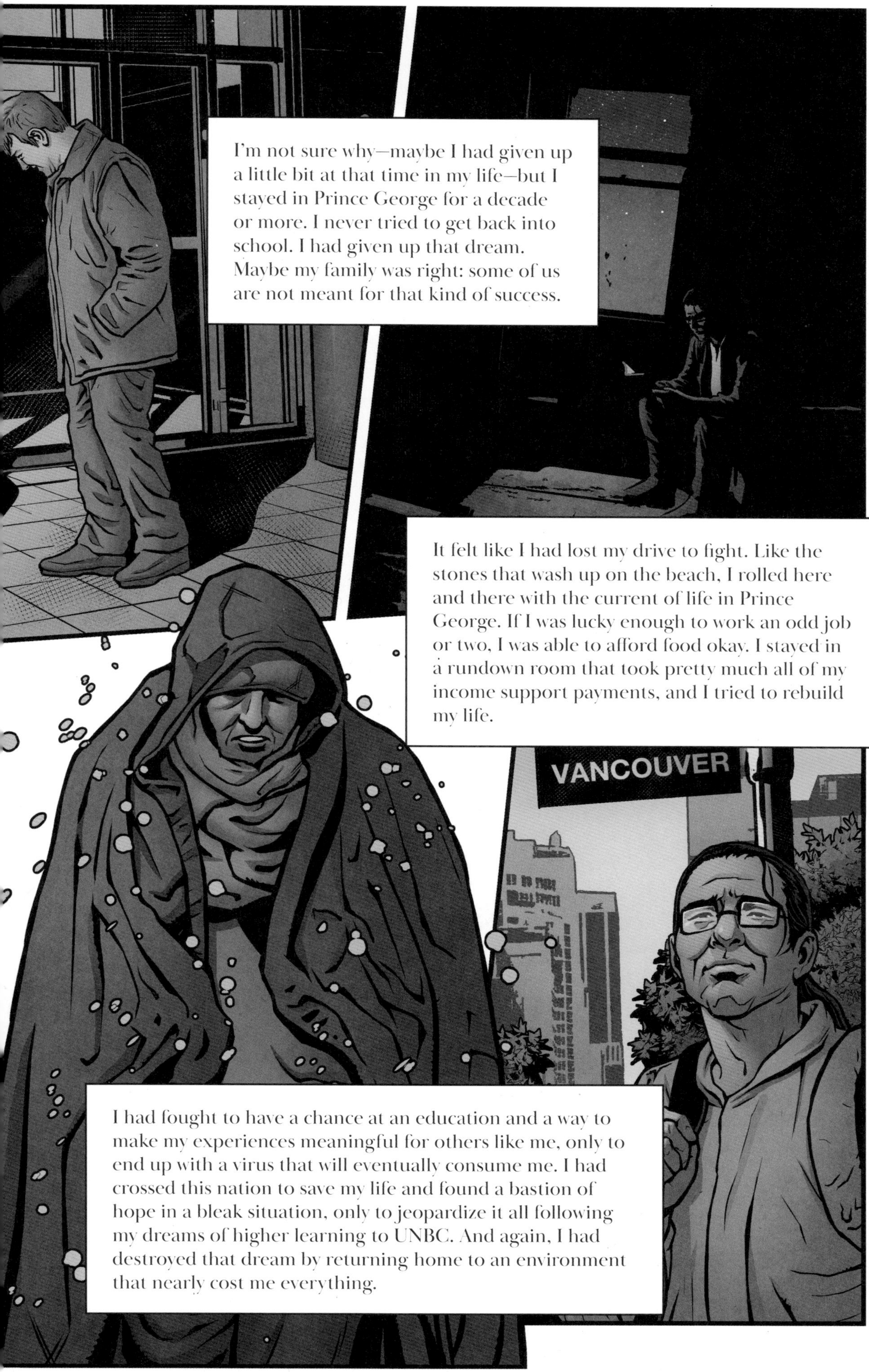
I'm not sure why—maybe I had given up a little bit at that time in my life—but I stayed in Prince George for a decade or more. I never tried to get back into school. I had given up that dream. Maybe my family was right: some of us are not meant for that kind of success.
It felt like I had lost my drive to fight. Like the stones that wash up on the beach, I rolled here and there with the current of life in Prince George. If I was lucky enough to work an odd job or two, I was able to afford food okay. I stayed in a rundown room that took pretty much all of my income support payments, and I tried to rebuild my life.
VANCOUVER
I had fought to have a chance at an education and a way to make my experiences meaningful for others like me, only to end up with a virus that will eventually consume me. I had crossed this nation to save my life and found a bastion of hope in a bleak situation, only to jeopardize it all following my dreams of higher learning to UNBC. And again, I had destroyed that dream by returning home to an environment that nearly cost me everything.

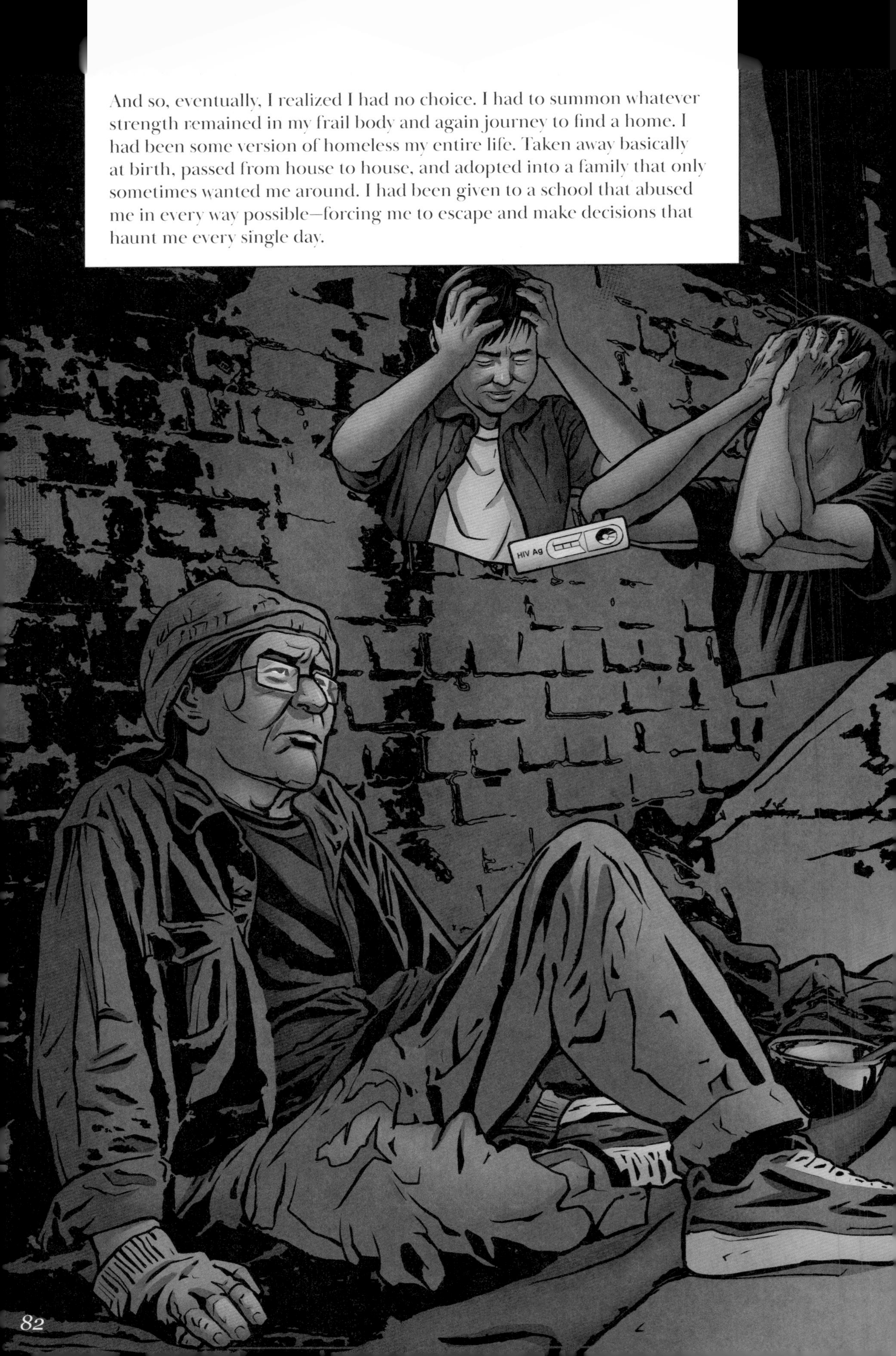
And so, eventually, I realized I had no choice. I had to summon whatever strength remained in my frail body and again journey to find a home. I had been some version of homeless my entire life. Taken away basically at birth, passed from house to house, and adopted into a family that only sometimes wanted me around. I had been given to a school that abused me in every way possible—forcing me to escape and make decisions that haunt me every single day.
HIV Ag

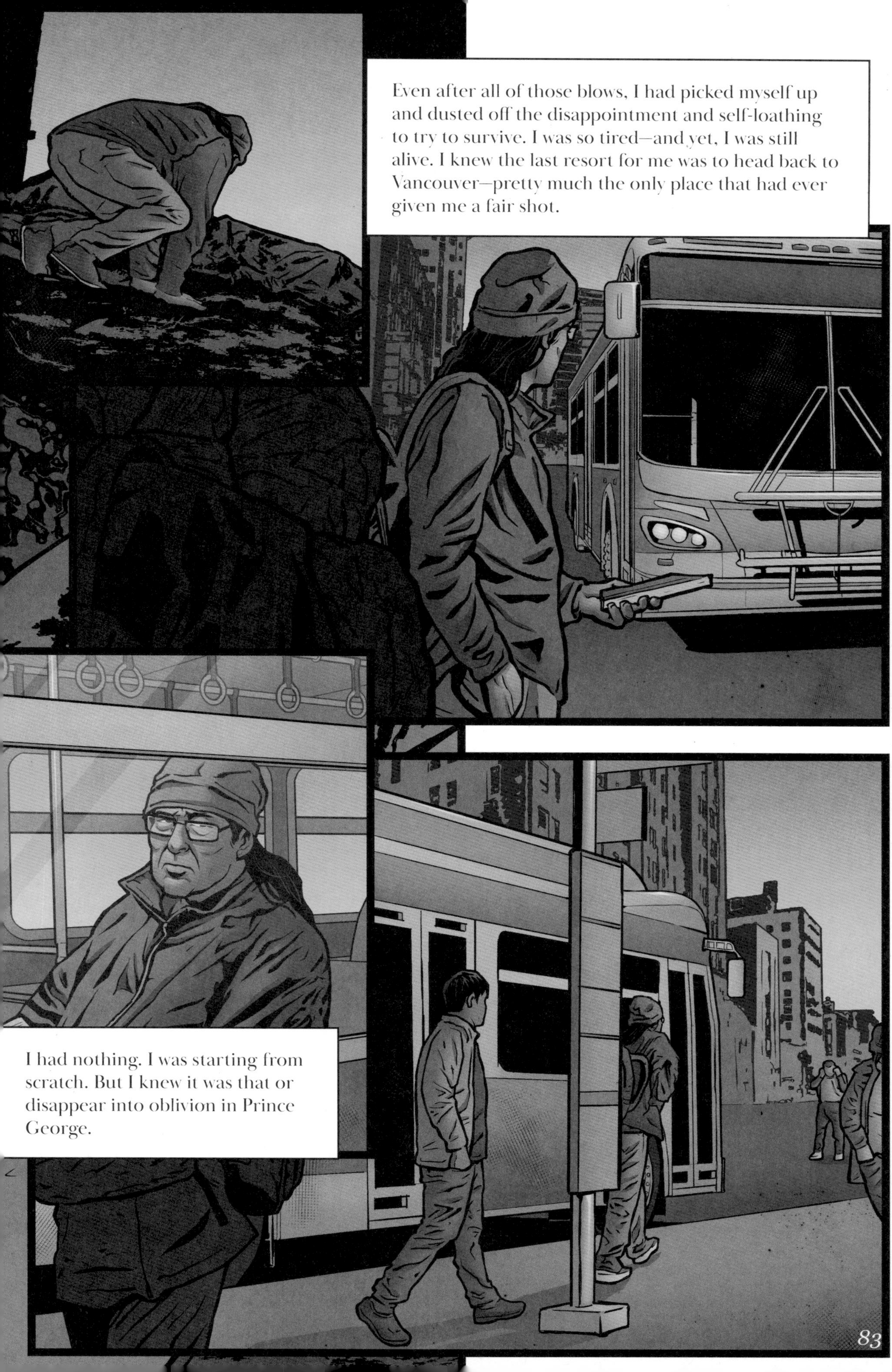
Even after all of those blows, I had picked myself up and dusted off the disappointment and self-loathing to try to survive. I was so tired—and yet, I was still alive. I knew the last resort for me was to head back to Vancouver—pretty much the only place that had ever given me a fair shot.
I had nothing. I was starting from scratch. But I knew it was that or disappear into oblivion in Prince George.

When I returned to Vancouver, I found myself in the same situation I had been in at 31 years old: broke, homeless, and in fear for my life. Luckily it was springtime and mild in the city, as I had to live "outside" for months. My disability income was interrupted for a period of time, and I could barely afford to feed myself. Fortunately I was back on the right medication and getting healthier by the day. There were other bright spots in this dark time in my life, and I will be forever grateful for these. I was reunited with Dr. Catherine Jones, and a friend I met on the street told me about a centre that caters to patients with my condition. I also eventually found a social worker who got me a permanent apartment in one of the nicest low-income housing units in the city. It was my own place that no one could take from me. For the first time in my whole life, I had a nice place to live and no fear of losing it.

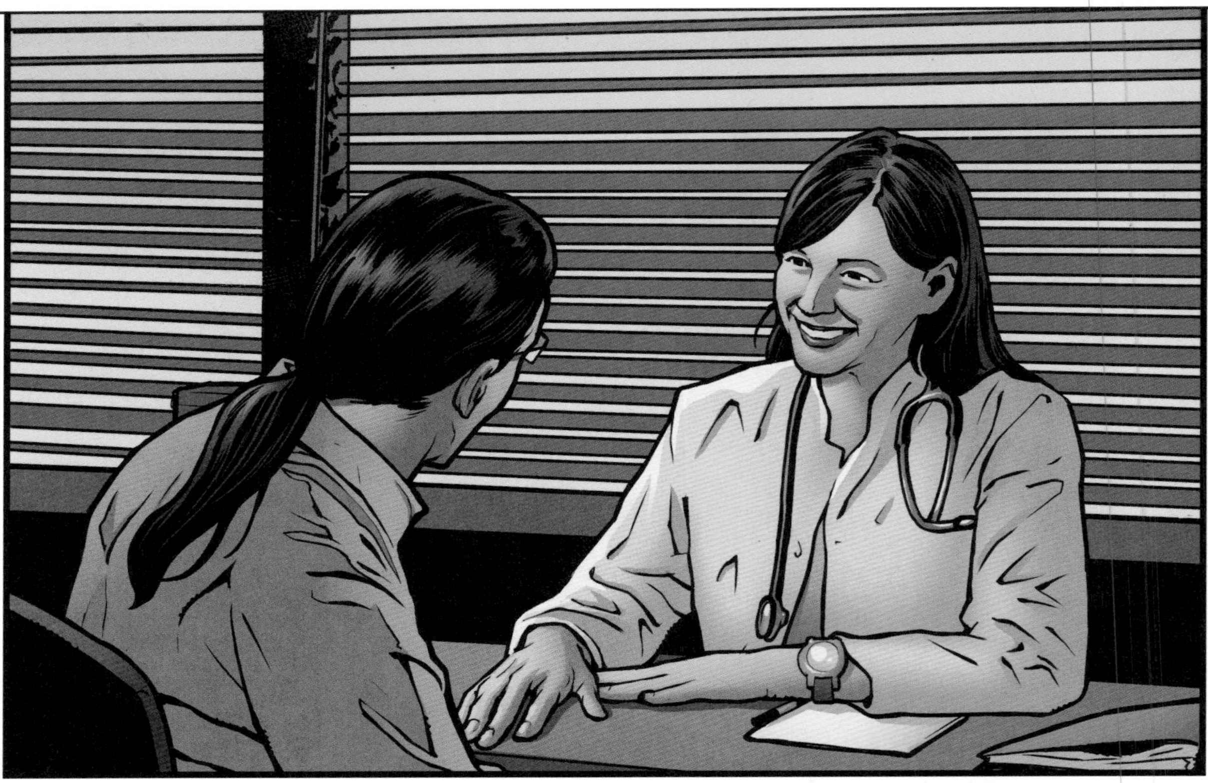

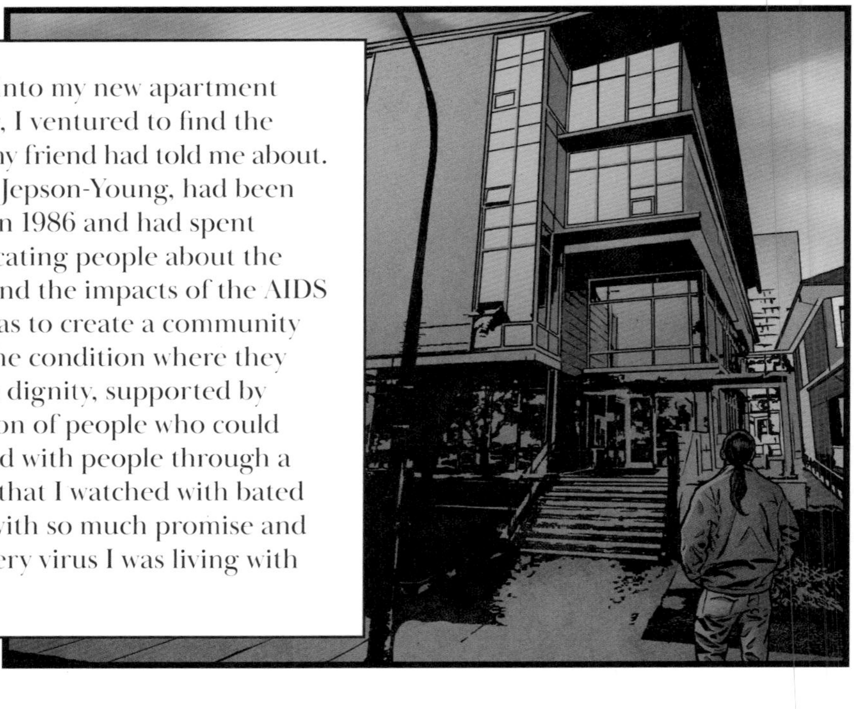

Shortly after I settled into my new apartment and life was stabilizing, I ventured to find the Dr. Peter Centre that my friend had told me about. A young doctor, Peter Jepson-Young, had been diagnosed with AIDS in 1986 and had spent the rest of his life educating people about the effects of the disease and the impacts of the AIDS epidemic. His vision was to create a community for those affected by the condition where they could live and die with dignity, supported by the love and compassion of people who could help. He had connected with people through a series of video diaries that I watched with bated breath. To see a man with so much promise and life battling with the very virus I was living with inspired me.

When I walked into the centre, I immediately felt love. It was everywhere. It was evident in the way that patients greeted each other, in the absence of the fear of touch, in the freedom of expression of care and compassion. It flowed through the smiles of the staff who greeted my personhood along with the physical body they saw before them. I am a man who never felt at home in any home I had ever lived—I had never felt the kind of belonging that so many are privileged to feel from birth. That was not the life I was born into, and I had never found it on this Earth up until the moment I walked into the Dr. Peter Centre. I was greeted by the support team at the centre. They wanted to know about who I was and what my experience living with the virus had been like. They supported me and honoured my story, and I knew right away that they accepted me and were ready to love me. I felt that from the first day. As I learned about the services they offered, I immediately began to feel the tensions in my body ease, and I realized that the calm energy flowing within me was the feeling of safety. I was safe there, and all of a sudden I knew that and felt it deeply. What a relief after more than half a century of living in fear to feel that level of protection against what had seemed like an endless storm.

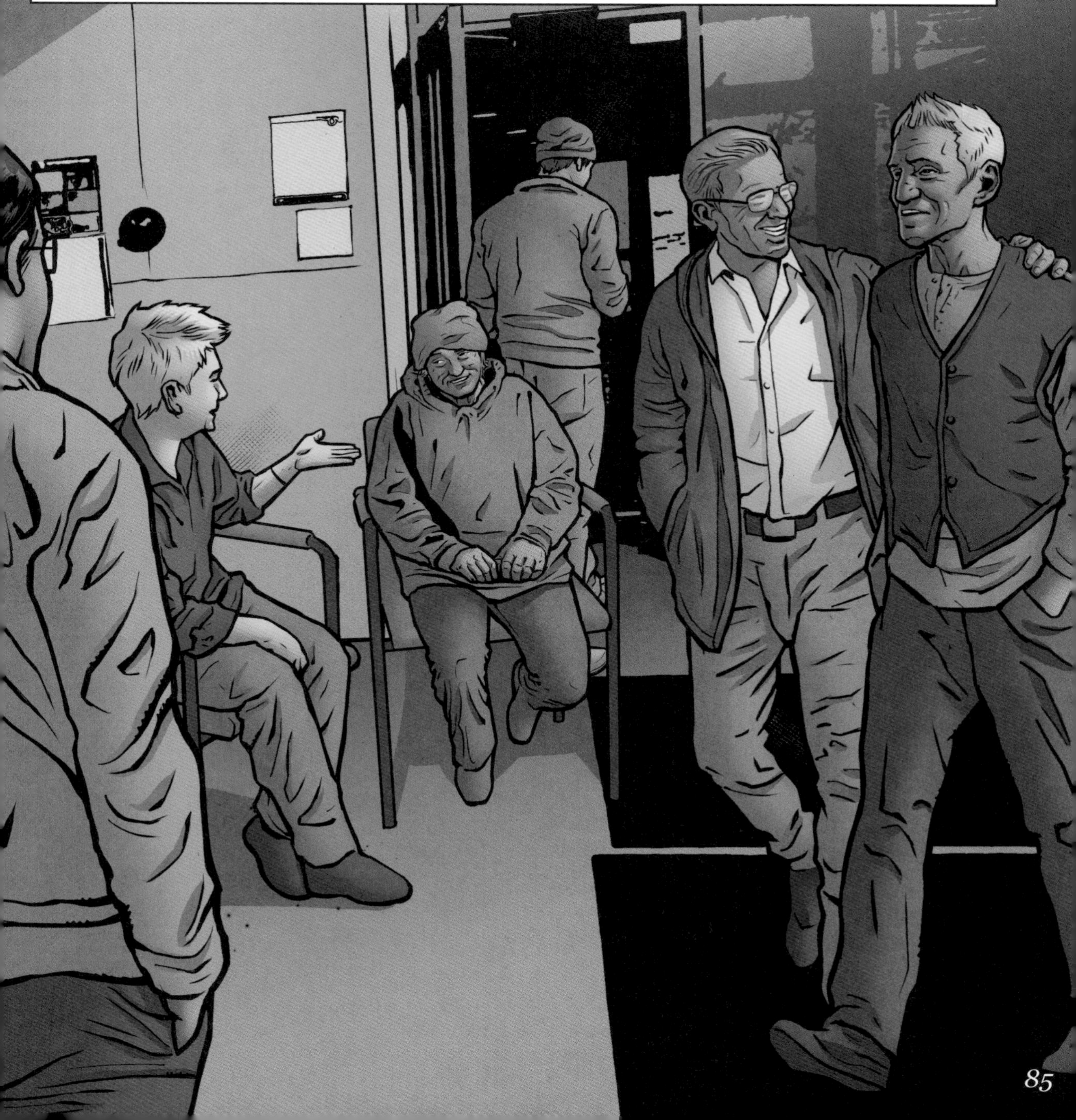

The Dr. Peter Centre operates with a wrap-around care approach. They provide nutritious meals that align with a diet rich in the foods and nutrients that people affected by HIV and AIDS need—cost free and at consistent times. They provide assistance with accessing community services like social workers, housing, health care, and counselling. The centre recognizes that people are endowed with valuable gifts and talents and that these nurture our spirits and are necessary for a quality life. They recognize that they serve a large Indigenous population in the city and invite input and knowledge to inform their ever-evolving process. I was lucky enough to do some contract work with them on making their injection sites culturally appropriate and also to facilitate Indigenous craft sessions that connected me to skills I had forgotten I knew. The centre has music rooms and a studio that allows patients to connect with their creative talents and soothe their wounds through art. Most of all, the centre gives us back our humanity and allows us to feel love and community with each other.

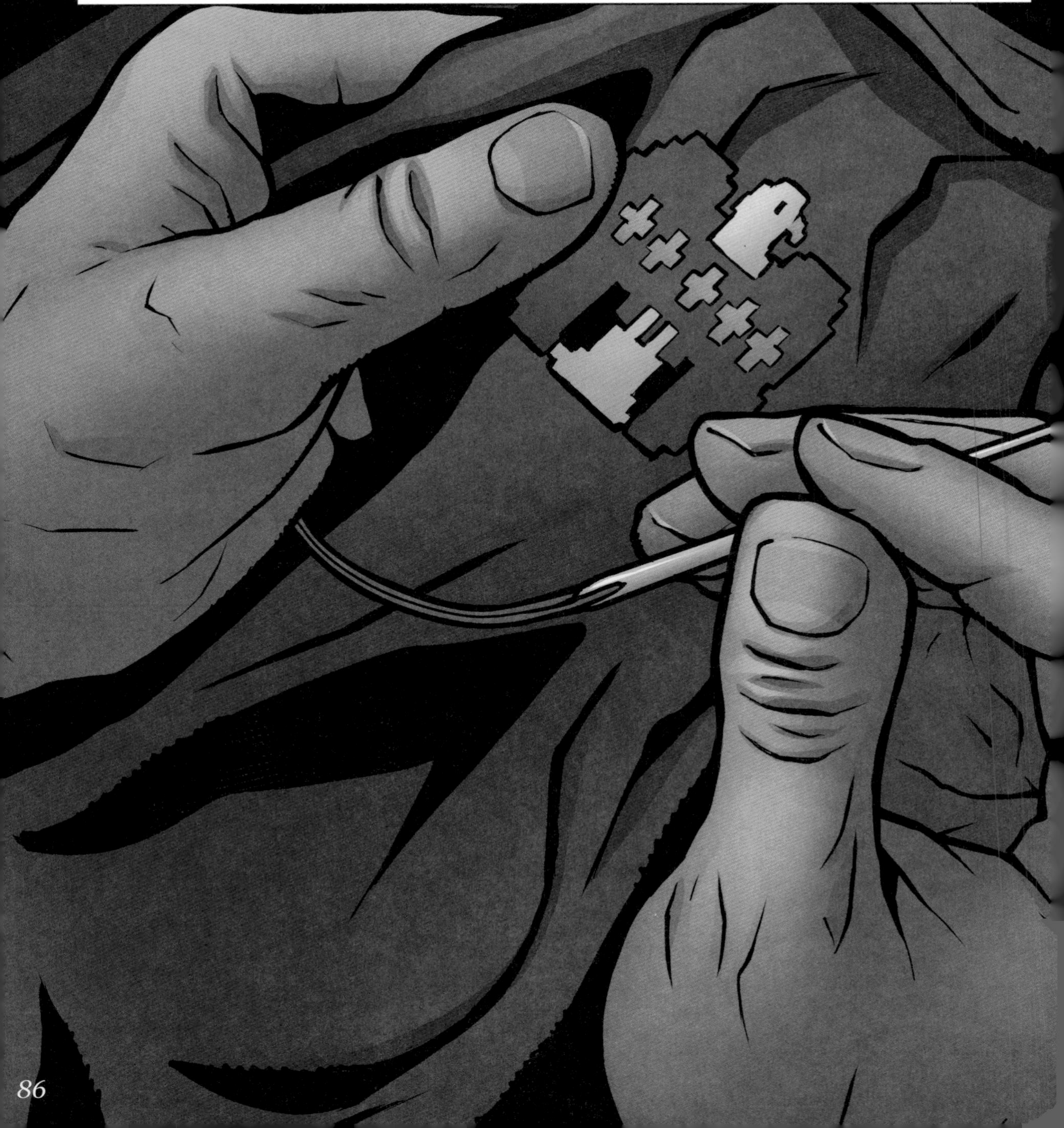

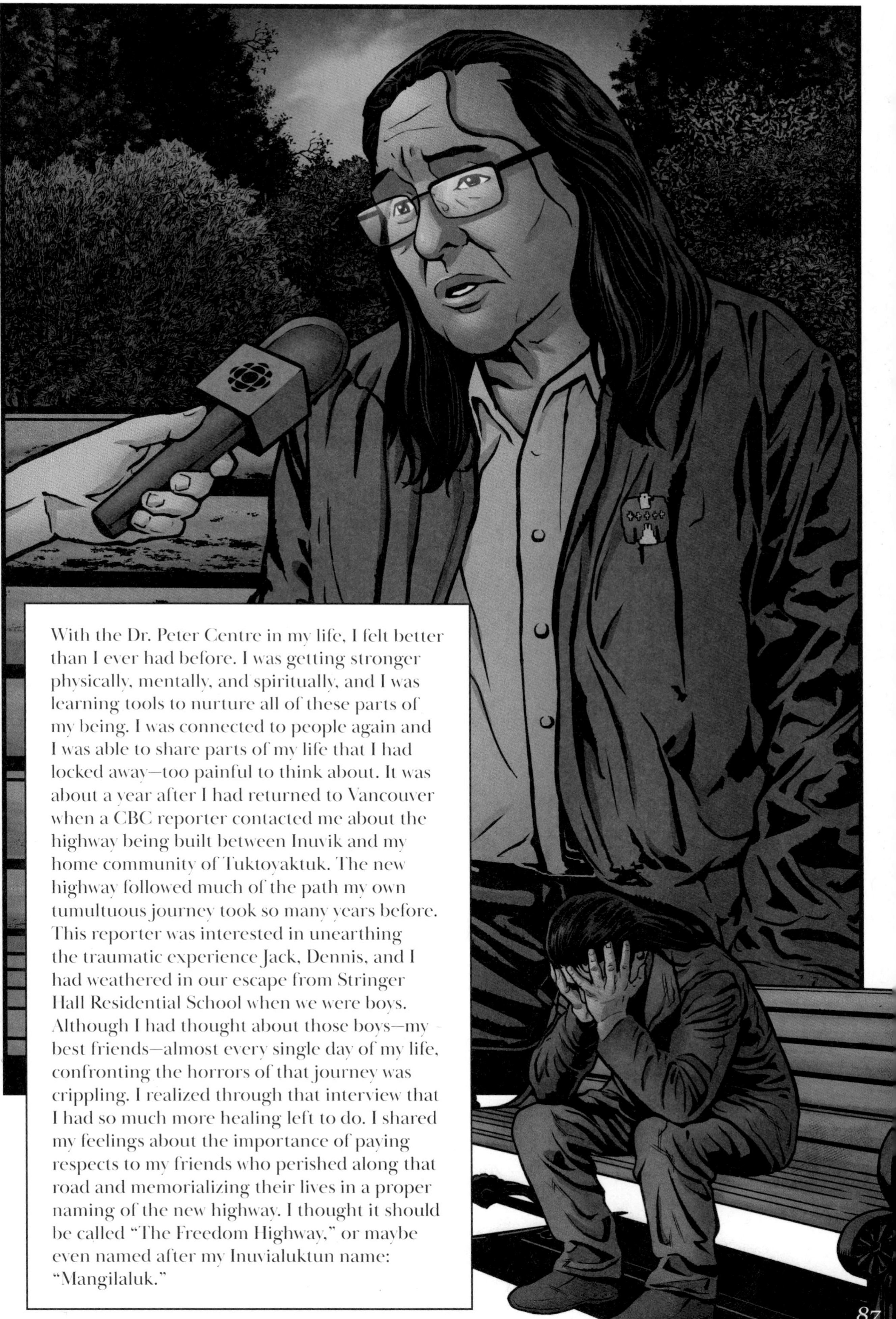
With the Dr. Peter Centre in my life, I felt better than I ever had before. I was getting stronger physically, mentally, and spiritually, and I was learning tools to nurture all of these parts of my being. I was connected to people again and I was able to share parts of my life that I had locked away—too painful to think about. It was about a year after I had returned to Vancouver when a CBC reporter contacted me about the highway being built between Inuvik and my home community of Tuktoyaktuk. The new highway followed much of the path my own tumultuous journey took so many years before. This reporter was interested in unearthing the traumatic experience Jack, Dennis, and I had weathered in our escape from Stringer Hall Residential School when we were boys. Although I had thought about those boys—my best friends—almost every single day of my life, confronting the horrors of that journey was crippling. I realized through that interview that I had so much more healing left to do. I shared my feelings about the importance of paying respects to my friends who perished along that road and memorializing their lives in a proper naming of the new highway. I thought it should be called "The Freedom Highway," or maybe even named after my Inuvialuktun name: "Mangilaluk."

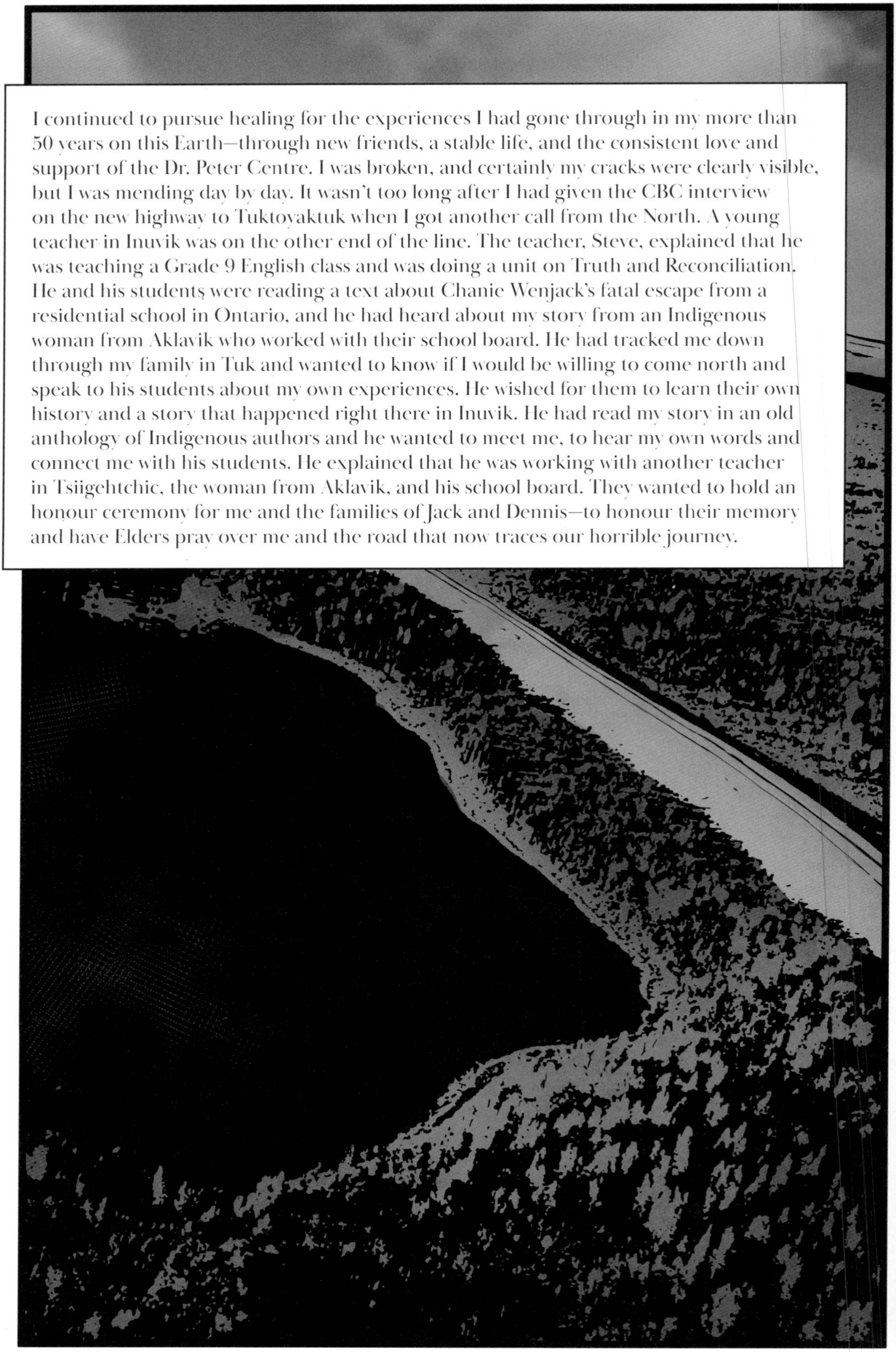
I continued to pursue healing for the experiences I had gone through in my more than 50 years on this Earth—through new friends, a stable life, and the consistent love and support of the Dr. Peter Centre. I was broken, and certainly my cracks were clearly visible, but I was mending day by day. It wasn't too long after I had given the CBC interview on the new highway to Tuktoyaktuk when I got another call from the North. A young teacher in Inuvik was on the other end of the line. The teacher, Steve, explained that he was teaching a Grade 9 English class and was doing a unit on Truth and Reconciliation. He and his students were reading a text about Chanie Wenjack's fatal escape from a residential school in Ontario, and he had heard about my story from an Indigenous woman from Aklavik who worked with their school board. He had tracked me down through my family in Tuk and wanted to know if I would be willing to come north and speak to his students about my own experiences. He wished for them to learn their own history and a story that happened right there in Inuvik. He had read my story in an old anthology of Indigenous authors and he wanted to meet me, to hear my own words and connect me with his students. He explained that he was working with another teacher in Tsiigehtchic, the woman from Aklavik, and his school board. They wanted to hold an honour ceremony for me and the families of Jack and Dennis—to honour their memory and have Elders pray over me and the road that now traces our horrible journey.

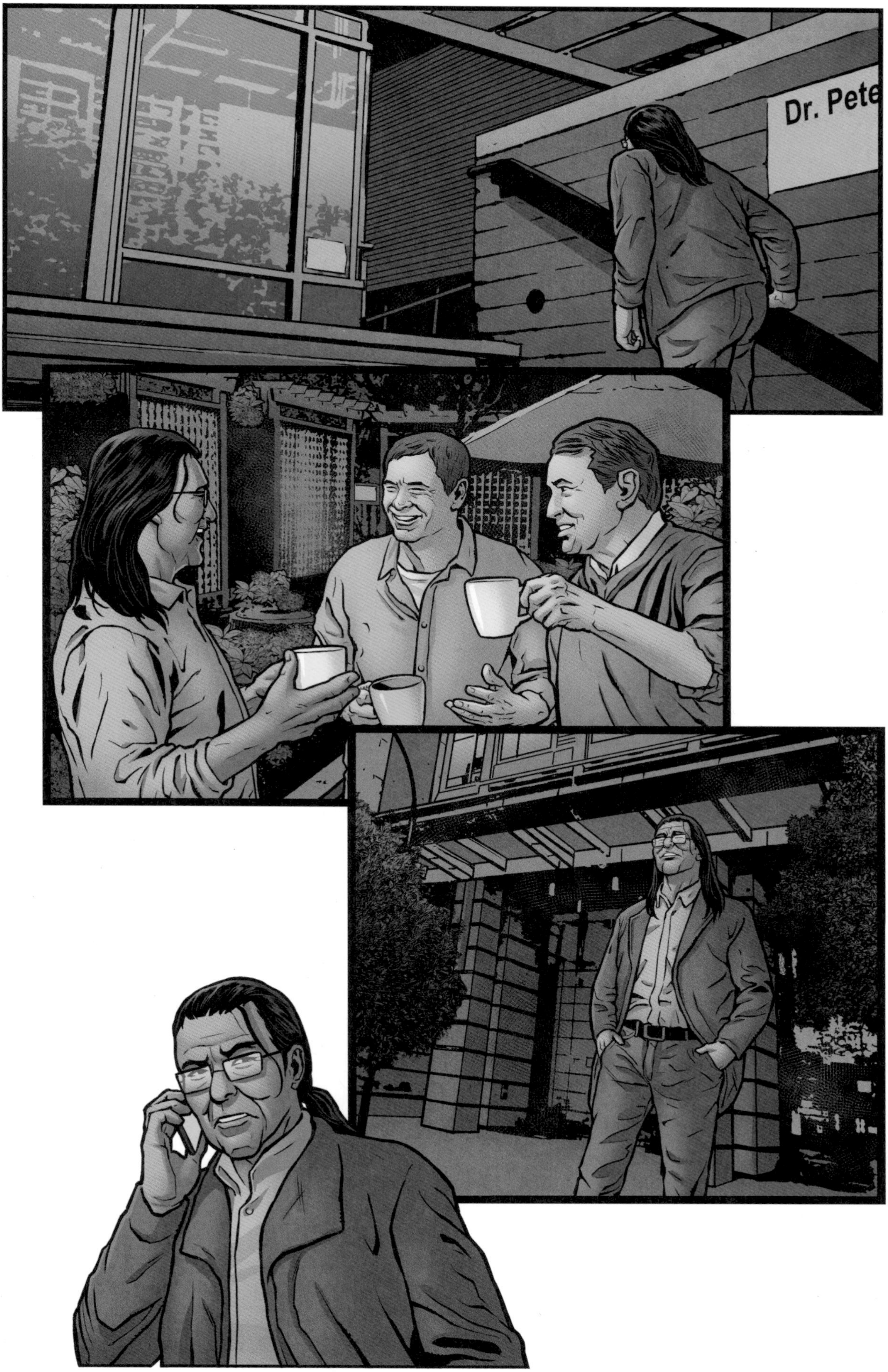
Dr. Pete

After I hung up the phone, I sat for a very long time. It was like time slowed. I breathed in and out, trying to slow the pounding in my chest and clear my mind. Immediately I felt fear and panic at the prospect of returning home. I couldn't imagine talking to students and telling my story. I couldn't imagine going back to Inuvik and spending time in the memory of the most devastating time in my life. I couldn't imagine facing family after the last time I left home. I had changed and was finally finding myself. Could I risk undoing that work—getting sucked back in? When time resumed once more and my mind was less muddled, I thought about what the teacher had been saying. His school board would fly me to Inuvik and I would speak to students about my life and the time I spent at Stringer Hall and my escape to Tuk. The community would host a reconciliation ceremony—an honour ceremony—to address what happened to us and offer healing and support. Jack's and Dennis's families would be there, as well as members of my own family. Then I would travel to Tuk for a few days to see my family before returning to Vancouver. Everything would be taken care of; all I would have to do was get on the plane. I knew I wasn't ready. But suddenly I realized the power of teaching students that something awful had happened to me, that I had fought my whole life to feel safe, and that I could help them learn and feel that they are loved and safe in their lives. It was like I felt strength return to my body, filling my veins with hope. Despite my fears, I had to do it. I had to go.

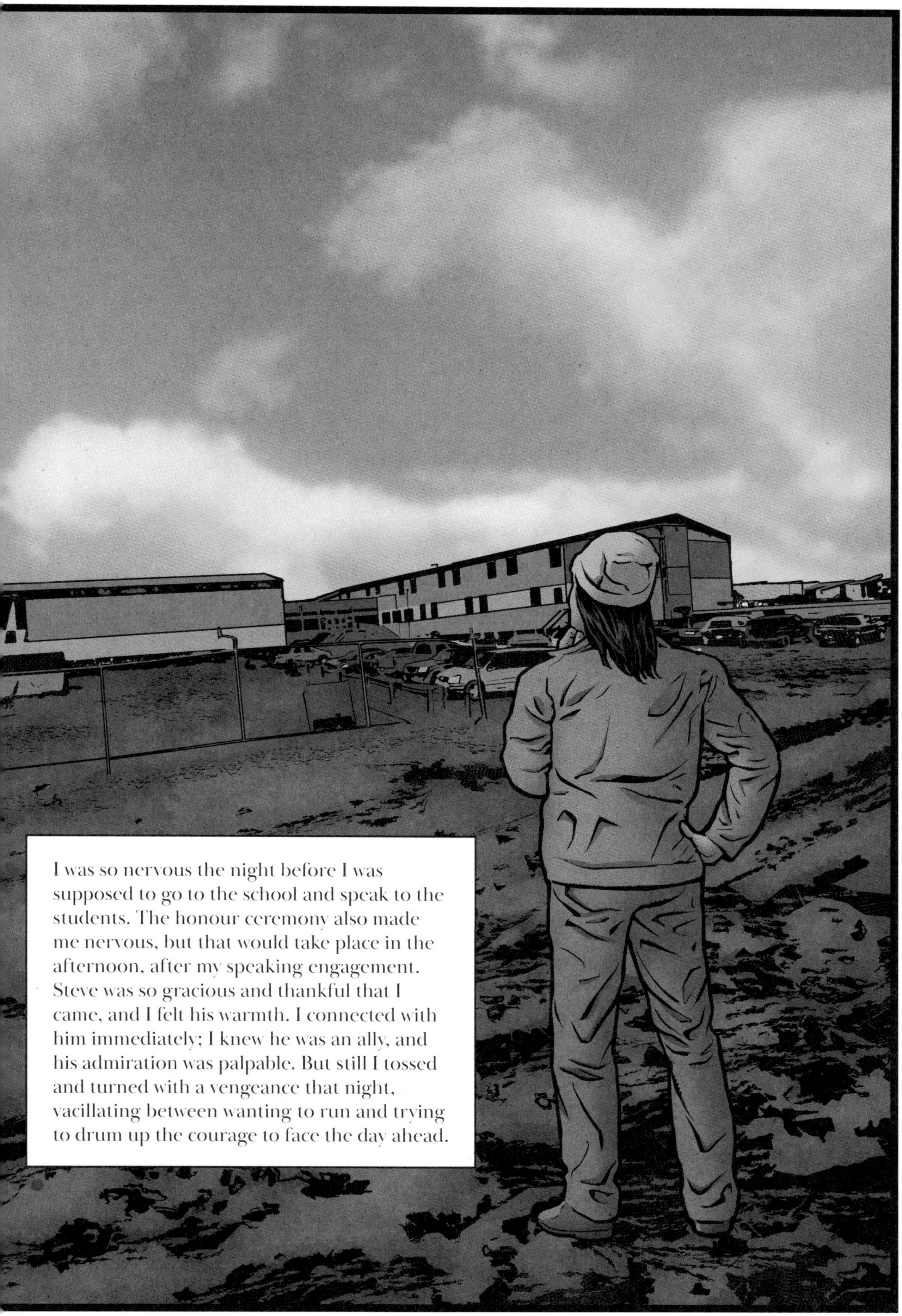
I was so nervous the night before I was supposed to go to the school and speak to the students. The honour ceremony also made me nervous, but that would take place in the afternoon, after my speaking engagement. Steve was so gracious and thankful that I came, and I felt his warmth. I connected with him immediately; I knew he was an ally, and his admiration was palpable. But still I tossed and turned with a vengeance that night, vacillating between wanting to run and trying to drum up the courage to face the day ahead.

Earlier that morning, the Indigenous woman who works with the school board had met with me to explain the honour ceremony. She was so kind and soft spoken; I connected with her immediately, just like I had with Steve. Her spirit filled me up—fortifying me for what lay ahead. She explained that Elders in her home community and some in Tuktoyaktuk had made prayer bundles and prayed over them for the participants in the ceremony to throw into the fire. That there would be Elders and drummers and dancers from Inuvik and Tuk to celebrate and honour me. Members of Dennis's and Jack's families would be in attendance so they could participate in honouring their fallen boys. There would be dignitatries from Inuvik and Tuk, as well as 30 Grade 9 students who had written letters to me that they would present to me at the ceremony. I was awestruck by their generosity and by the fact that so many people were willing to pause their lives to celebrate mine.

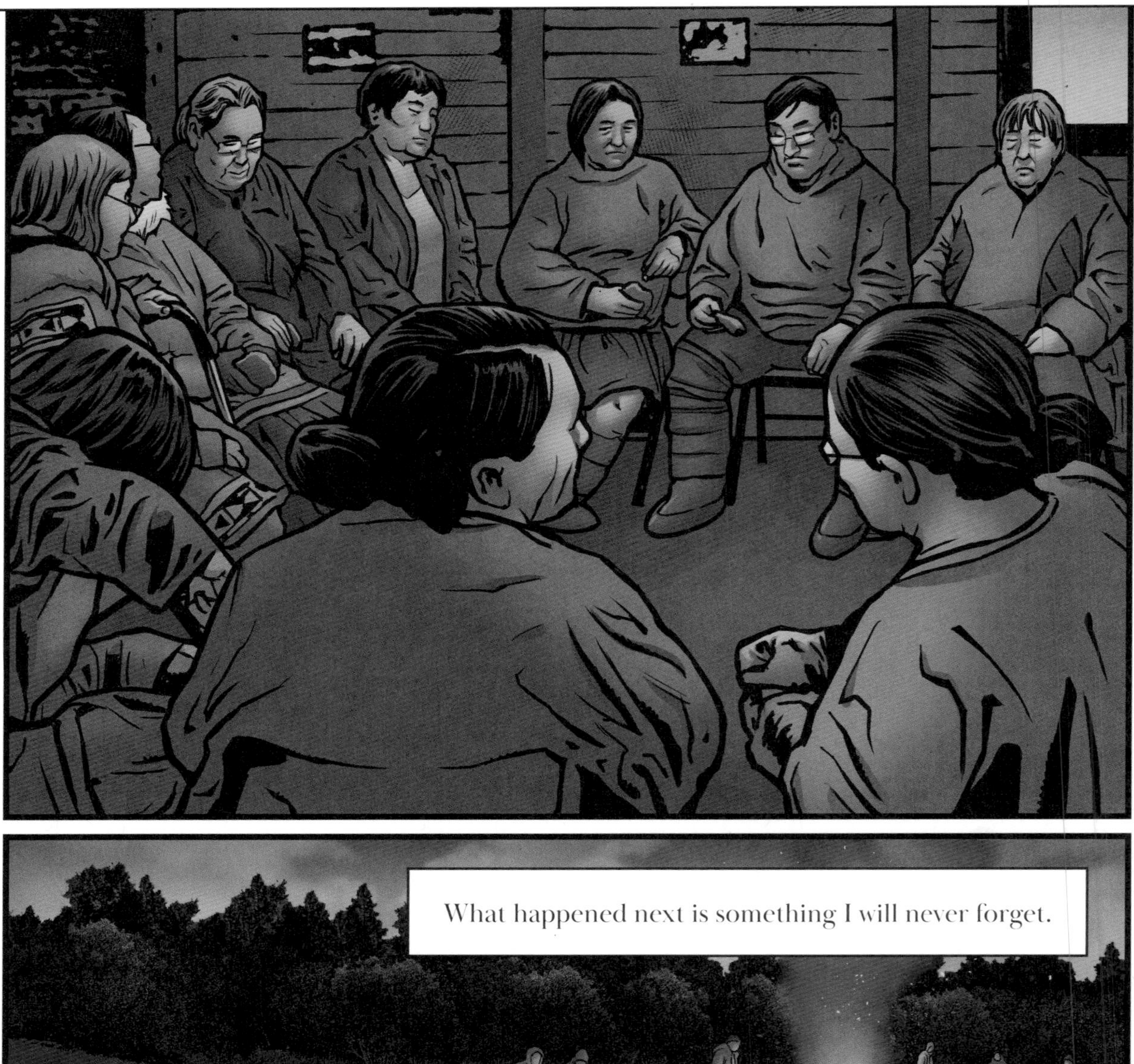

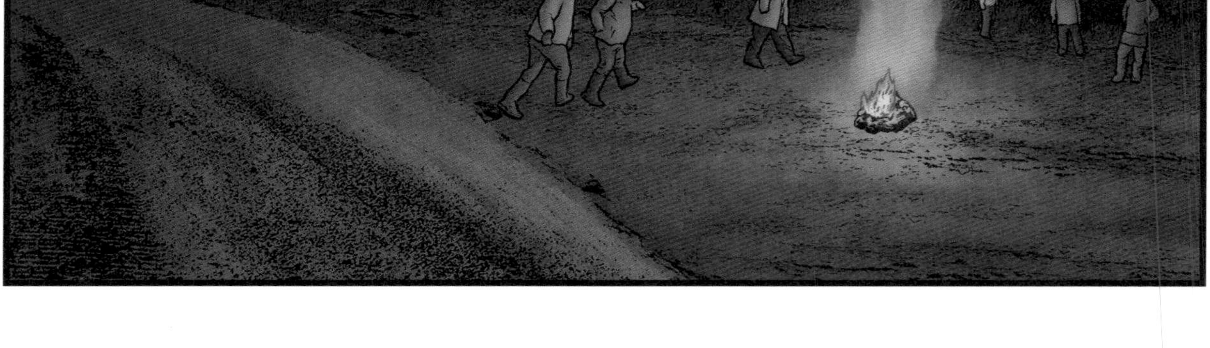
What happened next is something I will never forget.

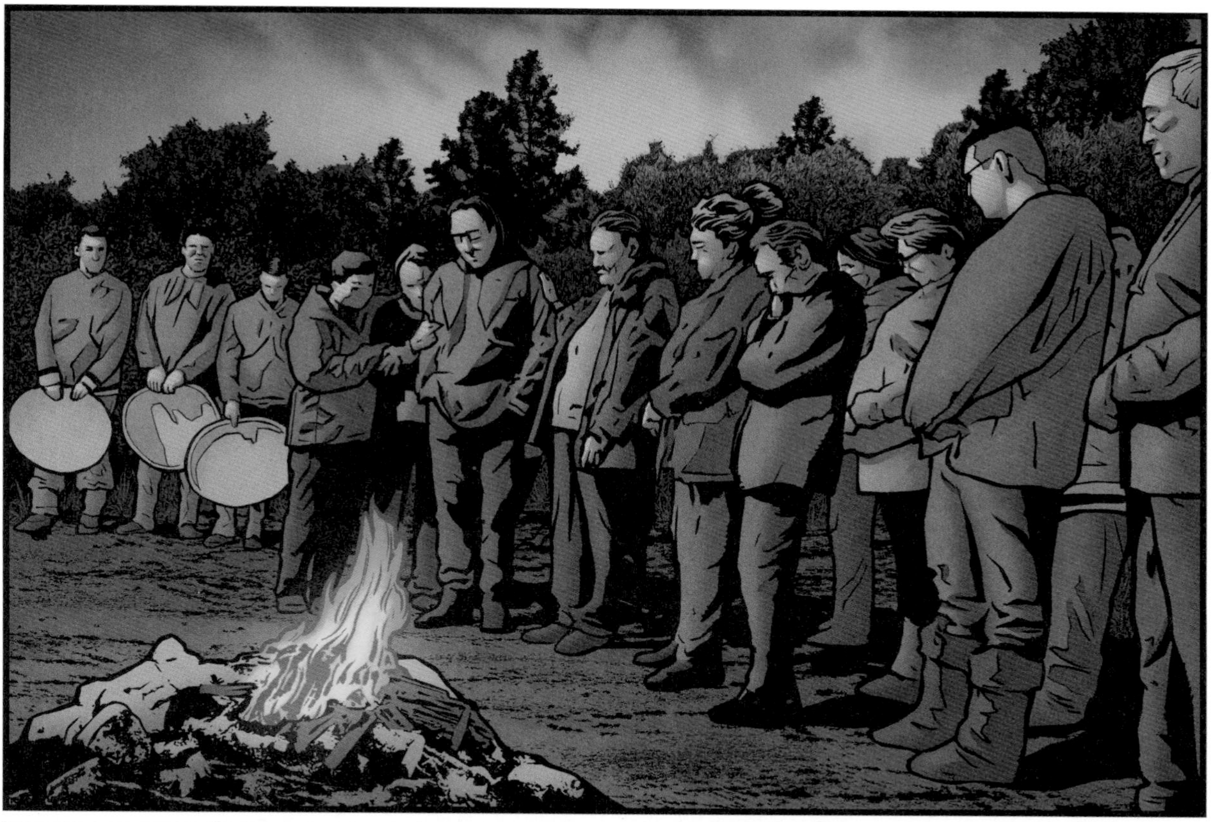
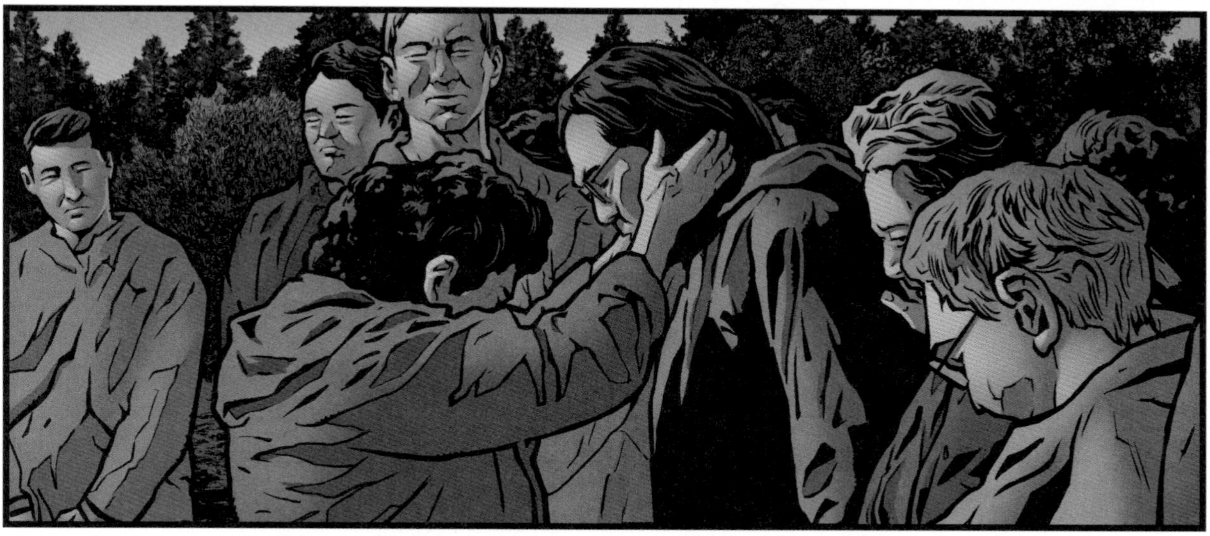
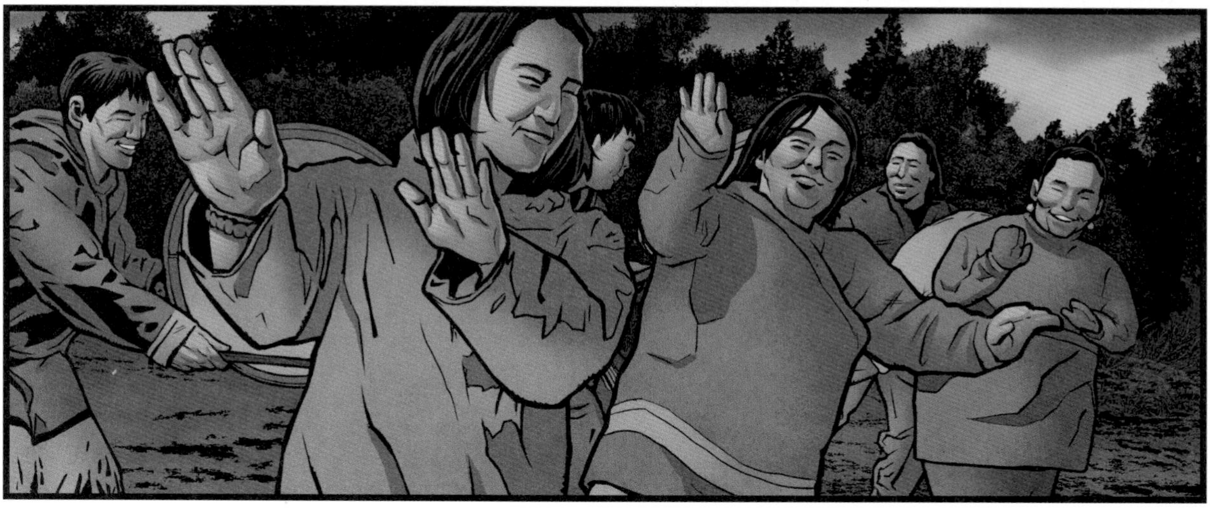

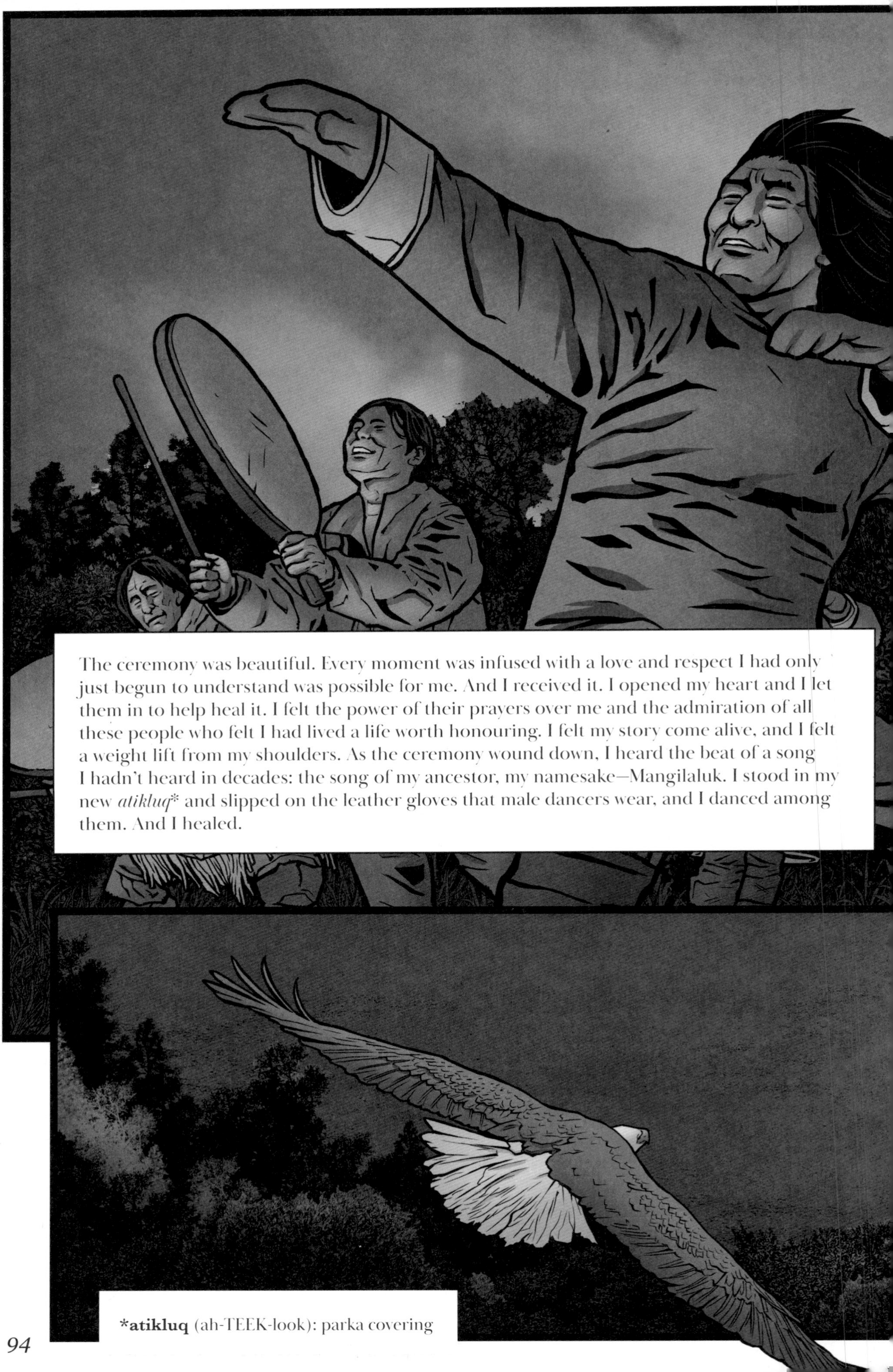
The ceremony was beautiful. Every moment was infused with a love and respect I had only just begun to understand was possible for me. And I received it. I opened my heart and I let them in to help heal it. I felt the power of their prayers over me and the admiration of all these people who felt I had lived a life worth honouring. I felt my story come alive, and I felt a weight lift from my shoulders. As the ceremony wound down, I heard the beat of a song I hadn't heard in decades: the song of my ancestor, my namesake—Mangilaluk. I stood in my new *atikluq** and slipped on the leather gloves that male dancers wear, and I danced among them. And I healed.
***atikluq** (ah-TEEK-look): parka covering

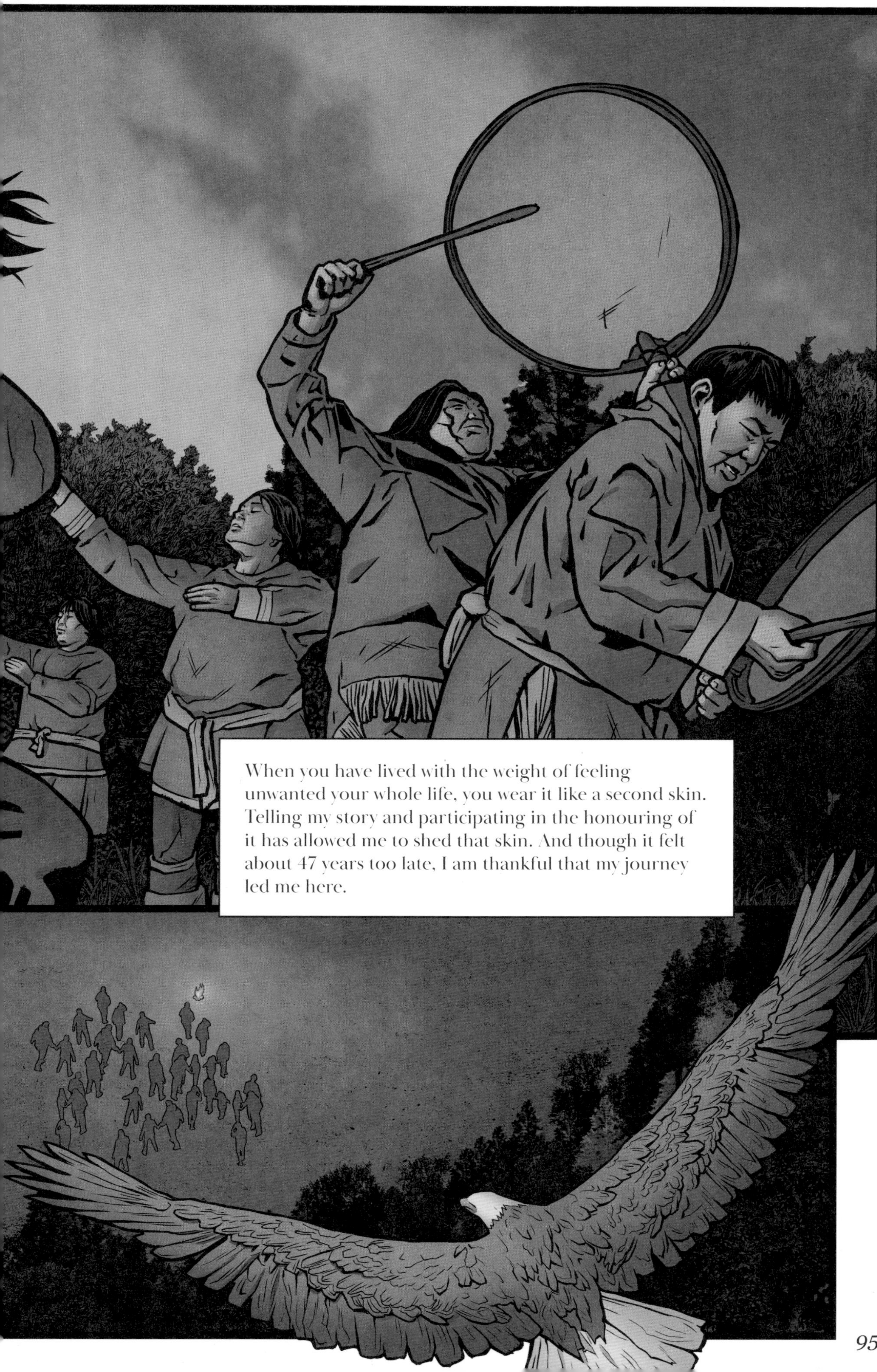
When you have lived with the weight of feeling unwanted your whole life, you wear it like a second skin. Telling my story and participating in the honouring of it has allowed me to shed that skin. And though it felt about 47 years too late, I am thankful that my journey led me here.

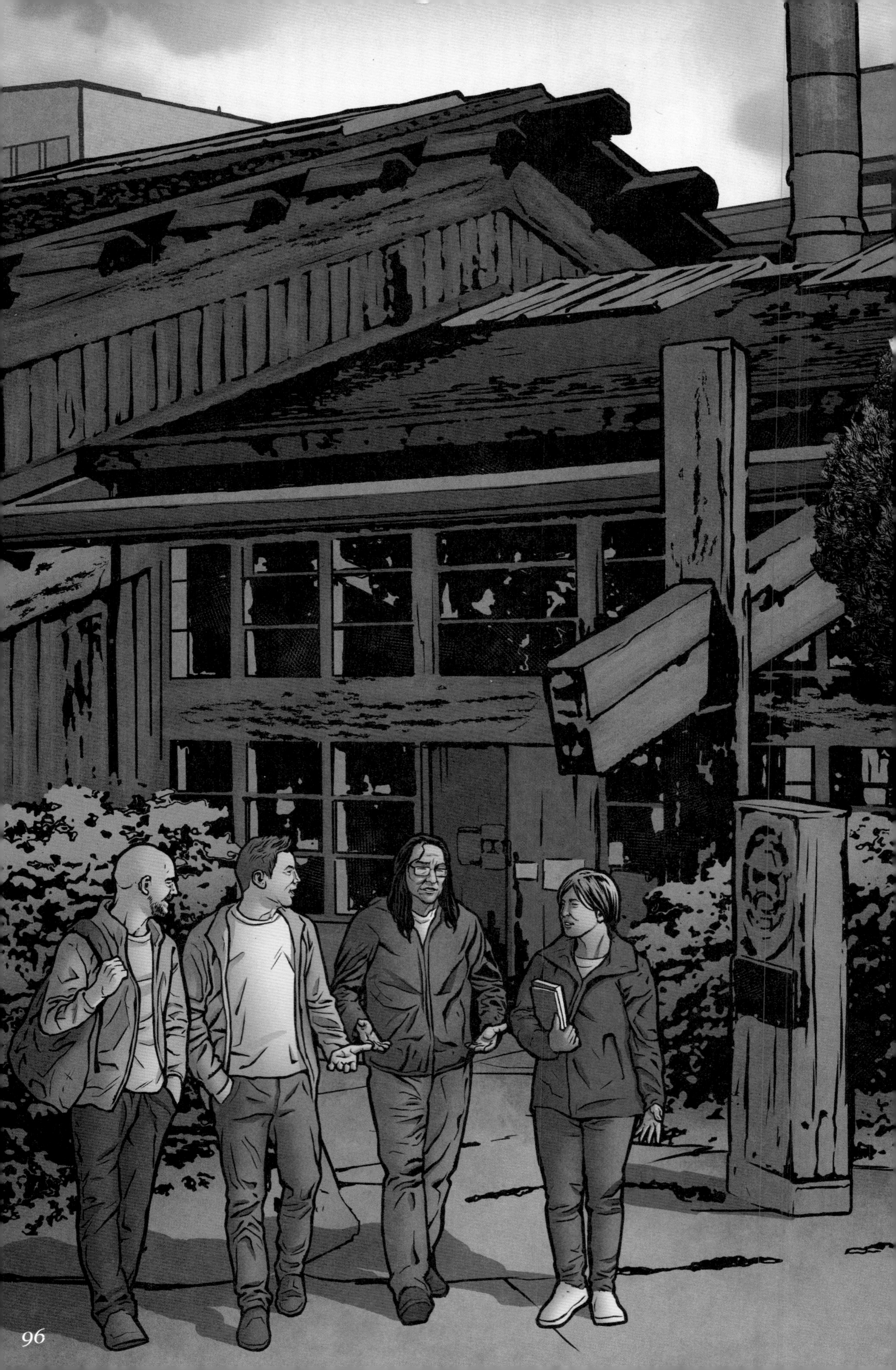